Translated Texts for Historians

This series is designed to meet the needs of students of medieval history and others who wish to broaden their study by reading source material, but whose knowledge of Latin or Greek is not sufficient to allow them to do so in the original language. Many important Late Imperial and Dark Age texts are currently unavailable in translation and it is hoped that TTH will help to fill this gap and to complement the secondary literature in English which already exists. The series relates principally to the period 300–800 A.D. and includes Late Imperial, Greek, Byzantine and Syriac texts as well as source books illustrating a particular period or theme. Each volume is a self-contained scholarly translation with an introductory essay on the text and its author and notes on the text indicating major problems of interpretation, including textual difficulties.

Editorial Committee
Sebastian Brock, Oriental Institute, University of Oxford
Averil Cameron, Keble College, Oxford
Henry Chadwick, Oxford
John Davies, University of Liverpool
Carlotta Dionisotti, King's College, London
Peter Heather, University College, London
William E. Klingshirn, The Catholic University of America
Michael Lapidge, Clare College, Cambridge
Robert Markus, University of Nottingham
John Matthews, Yale University
Claudia Rapp, University of California, Los Angeles
Raymond Van Dam, University of Michigan
Michael Whitby, University of Warwick
Ian Wood, University of Leeds

General Editors
Gillian Clark, University of Liverpool
Mary Whitby, Oxford

Front cover: Head of Plato in the Staatliche Museen, Berlin (from G. M. A. Richter, *Portraits of the Greeks*, Phaidon, 1965).

A full list of published titles in the Translated Texts for Historians series is available on request. The most recently published are shown below.

Venantius Fortunatus: Personal and Political Poems
Translated with notes and introduction by JUDITH GEORGE
Volume 23: 192 pp., 1995, ISBN 0–85323–179–6

Donatist Martyr Stories: The Church in Conflict in Roman North Africa
Translated with notes and introduction by MAUREEN A. TILLEY
Volume 24: 144 pp., 1996, ISBN 0–85323–931–2

Hilary of Poitiers: Conflicts of Conscience and Law in the Fourth-Century Church
Translated with introduction and notes by LIONEL R. WICKHAM
Volume 25: 176 pp., 1997, ISBN 0–85323–572–4

Lives of the Visigothic Fathers
Translated and edited by A. T. FEAR
Volume 26: 208 pp., 1997, ISBN 0–85323–582–1

Optatus: Against the Donatists
Translated and edited by MARK EDWARDS
Volume 27: 220 pp., 1997, ISBN 0–85323–752–2

Bede: A Biblical Miscellany
Translated with notes and introduction by W. TRENT FOLEY and ARTHUR G. HOLDER
Volume 28: 240 pp., 1998, ISBN 0–85323–683–6

Bede: The Reckoning of Time
Translated with introduction, notes and commentary by FAITH WALLIS
Volume 29: 582 pp., 1999, ISBN 0–85323–693–3

Ruricius of Limoges and Friends: A Collection of Letters from Visigothic Gaul
Translated with notes and introduction by RALPH W. MATHISEN
Volume 30: 272 pp., 1998, ISBN 0–85323–703–4

The Armenian History attributed to Sebeos
Translated with notes by R. W. THOMSON, Historical commentary by JAMES HOWARD-JOHNSTON. Assistance from TIM GREENWOOD
Volume 31 (in two parts): 240 pp., 224 pp., 1999, ISBN 0–85323–564–3

For full details of Translated Texts for Historians, including prices and ordering information, please write to the following:
All countries, except the USA and Canada: Liverpool University Press, 4 Cambridge Street, Liverpool, L69 7ZU, UK (*Tel* +44-[0]151-794 2233, *Fax* +44-[0]151-794 2235, *Email* J.M.Smith@liv.ac.uk, http://www.liverpool-unipress.co.uk). **USA and Canada:** University of Pennsylvania Press, 4200 Pine Street, Philadelphia, PA 19104-6097, USA (*Tel* +1-215-898-6264, *Fax* +1-215-898-0404).

Translated Texts for Historians
Volume 35

Neoplatonic Saints
The Lives of Plotinus and Proclus by their Students

translated with an introduction by
MARK EDWARDS

Liverpool
University
Press

First published 2000
LIVERPOOL UNIVERSITY PRESS
4 Cambridge Street
Liverpool, L69 7ZU

Copyright © 2000 Mark Edwards

All rights reserved. No part of this book may be reproduced
in any form without permission in writing from the publishers,
except by a reviewer in connection with a review for inclusion
in a magazine or newspaper.

British Library Cataloguing-in-Publication Data
A British Library CIP Record is available
ISBN 0-85323-615-1

Set in Monotype Times by
Wilmaset Ltd, Birkenhead, Wirral
Printed in the European Union by
Bell and Bain Limited, Glasgow

TABLE OF CONTENTS

INTRODUCTION	vii
PORPHYRY: *ON THE LIFE OF PLOTINUS AND THE ARRANGEMENT OF HIS WORKS*	1
THE *SUDA* ON MARINUS	55
MARINUS OF NEAPOLIS: *PROCLUS, OR ON HAPPINESS*	58
APPENDIX: THE CHRONOLOGY OF PORPHYRY'S *LIFE OF PLOTINUS*	117
BIBLIOGRAPHY	121
INDEX TO PORPHYRY	143
INDEX TO MARINUS	148
MAP 1: THE WORLD OF THE NEOPLATONISTS	152
MAP 2: ATHENS IN THE TIME OF PROCLUS	153

INTRODUCTION

Quae quibus anteferam? – what shall I put before what? – is the inevitable question for an editor who assumes the task of writing an introduction to the two works that are translated in this volume. Porphyry's notice *On the Life of Plotinus and the Arrangement of his Works* and the *Proclus, or on Happiness* by Marinus are both, for want of a better term, biographies; but biography in the ancient world was seldom a branch of history, and a narrative of the life and times of Proclus and Plotinus would add little to the reader's understanding of either text. For one thing, as philosophers are private men, there are scarcely any materials for such an account outside the works of Porphyry and Marinus; for another, both biographies were conceived within a literary tradition, and presuppose knowledge of their antecedents, even or especially when these were written centuries before. Both Porphyry and Marinus belonged to an intellectual fraternity, and appear to have addressed their books to members of the same circle whose chief interest was philosophy. I have therefore mixed philosophy with history in this lengthy introduction; but I must ask philosophers to recognise that the doctrines that I have sketched here – summarily, superficially and all too magisterially – are the ones that it seemed most necessary to cite in preparation for the reading of these memoirs. They may not be the ones that a modern commentator on Plato, Aristotle, Plotinus or Proclus would identify as the most essential or enduring elements in their thought.

FROM PLATO TO NEOPLATONISM

If a person styled himself a Platonist in antiquity, he was sure at least to mean that he did not regard the senses as a reliable criterion of knowledge. The things that we encounter in the physical world (he would say) are not pure entities but transient phenomena, whose surface tells us little of the essence that defines, the laws that govern or the causes that produce them. The mind that tries to rest on them is beguiled by multiplicity and change: one man may be mistaken for another even if he is not much like him, what is beautiful to one eye or at one time is not always or ubiquitously beautiful, and one line which is equal to a second may be unequal to a third.[1] Yet, fallible and contingent as perceptions are, and infinite as their objects are in number and permutation, we continue to use a fixed vocabulary which presumes the rigid identity and permanence of the things that it denotes. Does this imply that language, or the logic that informs it, is acquainted with a higher world where nothing is vague, unstable or deceptive?[2] Or does it simply mean that our inquiries cannot hope to do more than banish the impossible and identify the most probable conjectures? The second is the sceptical position, while the first is the one that is widely known today as Platonism. Both can be traced to Plato's Socrates (c. 469–399 B.C.), the principal speaker in his dialogues, for though he treats the Beautiful and the Good as the ultimate objects of inquiry, he offers no definition of either term. Even if the theory of Forms is true, and even if we are logically persuaded that they are unitary objects in a higher realm, we do not yet have a theory (the sceptic argues) that enables us to identify what is good or beautiful in the present world.

The sceptical wing of Platonism seems to have been the dominant one in the Hellenistic era (323–30 B.C.). The more dogmatic alternative, which postulates a world of intellectual Forms transcending that of sensible particulars, was too easily disparaged. If the Large (let us say) is a single entity, characterised by nothing but the property of largeness, it could not be parcelled out to an indefinite number of discrete particulars, for how could its largeness be preserved in all the magnitudes that would result from this division?[3] If, on the other hand, the one is not divided, how can it become present to the many? The answer that they are copies, and the Form is the original, is if anything still less plausible, for how can they all resemble one thing equally, and why is their likeness to it more significant than their likeness to each other? If we deduce the

---

1 See Plato, *Theaetetus* 193c–e on errors of perception; *Phaedo* 100d and *Symposium* 211d on beauty; *Phaedo* 74a on equality.

2 See Plato, *Republic* 476–80, with Vlastos (1965) on degrees of reality; Barnes (1989) on the revival of dogmatism under Antiochus of Ascalon.

3 For Plato's discussion at *Parmenides* 131d see Fine (1996), 82–7. These and other objections are recorded here because they were made, not because I wish to endorse them. They rely upon a literal, not to say pedestrian, reading of an author whose protean style continues to attract a variety of interpretations. The discussions by Crombie, Fine and Meinwold cited here reveal that it is possible to translate the hints of Plato into theses that remain tenable today.

existence of the Form from a single postulate, the resemblance between particulars, and then suggest that the Form itself resembles the particulars, our original postulate will now compel us to deduce the existence of another Form, which both the first Form and the particulars resemble. If this Form in turn bears a resemblance to the first Form and the particulars – the continuation is obvious, and famous enough in antiquity to have its own name, the "third man" argument.[4] In any case, is it logical to suppose that the Form itself contains the property to which its name is given? It would be scarcely intelligible to say that the Form of Equality is "equal", since it cannot be equal to everything at once.[5] And if everything that has a definition has a Form, are we to postulate forms of artefacts? In that case, shall we say that the Form comes into being only when the first object is created, or that Forms of possible artefacts exist (and will perhaps exist for ever) without any instantiation in the world?[6]

These objections are already aired in a number of dialogues by Plato (c. 429–347 B.C.), who was frequently believed to have concealed his own solutions.[7] Aristotle (384–322 B.C.), the ablest of his pupils and the founder of the Peripatetic school, accepted (a) that the contents of the understanding are not material entities but the essences or forms that circumscribe them. If we conflate his *Categories* and his *Metaphysics*,[8] it appears that *eidos* (form) denotes the character that an individual has as a representative of its species, while *ousia* (essence), functioning on occasions as a synonym for *eidos*, is more strictly applied to the concrete

---

4 *Metaphysics* 990b etc. For discussion and bibliography see Fine (1993), 202–24 and 255. A different chain of reasoning (Plato, *Parmenides* 132a–b) attempts to derive the "third man" from the premiss that the particulars possess their common predicate by virtue of the Form; Vlastos (1969) gives a logical form to this argument at the cost of introducing an avowed fallacy. Fine (1993), 204–11 propounds a weaker version, which is not decisive against every formulation of Plato's theory.

5 Fine (1993), 151–9, again with reservations on the validity of the argument.

6 Fine (1993), 81–8. Plato seems to allow such Forms at *Cratylus* 389a, *Gorgias* 503e and *Republic* 596b; the last passage also implies that the Form is in the mind of God.

7 See especially *Parmenides* 130–2, with Meinwold (1992). Crombie (1963), 319–25 proposes that Plato already held an Aristotelian view of the Forms. Fine (1993), 36–41 suggests that Aristotle's early criticisms of Plato in *On Ideas* stimulated the writing of the *Parmenides*, in which there is a minor character named Aristotle. Her argument is consistent with the thesis of Jaeger (1948) that Aristotle began his philosophical career as a critic of Platonism from within.

8 Graham (1987) argues that the two are incompatible, but not all modern scholars agree and the ancients plainly did not.

amalgam of form and matter. He also (b) agreed with Plato's Socrates that a causal explanation of an action or a happening tells us nothing without some notion of a lawlike end to which it is directed. The equation of knowledge with certainty, and of the question "what?" with the question "why?", are as typical of the pupil as of his master; yet he held both tenets without subscribing to a bicameral universe of mundane particulars and transcendent Forms. As to (a), the species – man or horse or ox – is not an eternal and self-subsistent archetype, as in Plato, but a "quiddity" which exists only insofar as it can be predicated of the individual. As to (b), the exemplars of the species in his *Categories* are (as we can see from the previous sentence) natural kinds, not archetypal predicates like the Good, the Just and the Beautiful, which were rigorously, if not quite fairly, handled in the *Nicomachean Ethics* and the treatise *On Ideas*. The good, for Aristotle, is not one thing, but is relative to the agent or the action, and identical with the final cause, or end, to which it is naturally disposed.[9]

Without a realm of Forms there is no place – and, more importantly, no object of cognition – for the disembodied soul. Plato taught that the purpose of philosophy is to reconcile the soul with the god, and hence with the Form, that it once pursued in heaven before its fall into the wheel of transmigration. Since then it has passed from one corporeal vehicle to another, exhibiting in each life the fruits of merit or demerit in the last. This account, according to which the soul and the self are one, is contradicted by the Aristotelian notion of the soul as the form or *eidos* of the body.[10] While its functions may not coincide exactly with those of physical organs, its perceptions are dependent on, and leave traces in, the bodily sensorium. Soul being indissolubly united to the body, there can be no rewards and punishments in the afterlife, and nothing to reimburse us for the loss of health, prosperity and honour; thus Aristotle, unlike Plato, holds that even the virtuous are unlikely to be happy[11] without these goods. This conclusion leaves to providence

---

9 See Flashar (1977) on the modified retention of Plato's "connection between being and value" in Aristotle.

10 Robinson (1991) argues that the mind is not reducible to its functions in Aristotle, and that his chief concern is to find a ground for individuation, not to solve the "mind–body problem" bequeathed to modern philosophy by Descartes.

11 "Happy" is a notoriously inadequate rendering of the word *eudaimôn*, which denotes a state of well-being approved by others as well as by the agent. For notable treatments see Kenny (1966) and Austin (1967).

little but the regular interplay of final causes. Aristotle had no use for the myth of the *Timaeus*, which attributed the origin of the cosmos to a god's benign desire to impress the Forms upon the anarchy of pre-existent forces. Natural or logical necessity displaces the lesser gods whose task in Plato is to superintend the revolutions of both souls and stars.

None the less Aristotle is both a theist and a Platonist.[12] Among the most famous passages in his popular or "exoteric" treatises was an argument that the ordered beauty and motion of the world bear witness to a presiding intellect.[13] In the *Metaphysics* he postulates God as the final cause to which all motion tends, and declares that he enjoys the state of perfect actuality in which all the essential properties of a subject have been realised. Such properties are actualised in the subject by the presence of its natural form, but are only potentialities of the matter with which the form has been compounded. Every embodied individual thus contains a residue that does not share in the attributes which define that individual. The consequence, that no material object is identical with its essence, explains how there can be different representatives of a common species; from the actuality of God it follows both that he is immaterial and that he is one. As an unmixed intellect, he thinks of course, but since the mind, on Aristotle's theory, assumes the form of every entity that it contemplates, his God could not remain immutable if he thought of anything but himself. Therefore he does not create the world, he does not design it, and he moves it not as an efficient cause, but as an object of desire. The premiss of this cosmology, that love is the unreciprocated yearning of the lower for the higher, is derived once more from Plato, who always puts it into the mouth of Socrates, but only in the dialogues on beauty and human friendship.[14] The Aristotelian God resembles Plato's Form of the Good, which merely waits for the approach of the philosopher, rather than his Demiurge, whose overflowing goodness begets the impulse to create.[15]

---

12 See Norman (1969) on his God as a paradigm for the philosopher who actualises his intellect; Owen (1966) for a seminal discussion of Aristotle's dependence on Plato.
13 See Chroust (1973), 159–93 for a reconstruction of the tract *On Philosophy*.
14 *Lysis* 216c–222b; *Symposium* 202c–204a. See Robin (1964), 102–8 on cosmological interpretations of the latter in later Platonists.
15 *Metaphysics* 1074b–1075a. Gerson (1994), 235 n. 30 stresses that Aristotle's God is only a final cause, and therefore not the sole ancestor of the One. Kahn (1992), 374 opines that the thought of God must have some content even in Aristotle, adducing *Metaphysics* 1075b2–5.

By the Roman period some Platonists had conceded to Aristotle that the doctrine of a temporal creation was untenable, as an omnicompetent deity would not have had a reason to effect it at one time rather than another. Aristotle's theology appeared to supply the clue to an enigma that had puzzled every reader of the *Timaeus*: what is the relation between the Demiurge who creates the world and the realm of Forms which furnishes him with a model (*paradeigma*)? One answer might be that each is a different actuality of the Aristotelian God. The first would be the fulfilment of his capacity for being, the second of his capacity for action. By equating the first with the paradigm and the second with the Demiurge, one could avoid the uncomfortable inference that the god who made the world was not responsible for the pattern that informs it. At the same time Aristotle's objection to the existence of the Forms without a substrate was disarmed, for, if the Forms were the contents of the paradigm, they had now become the thoughts in the mind of God.[16] Aristotle had argued in his treatise *On the Soul* that all our cognitive and reflective powers require a "maker mind" (the *nous poietikos*), which does not so much think as render other objects thinkable. Aristotle left it to his followers to deduce that the maker mind was God, but he himself admitted that there was something divine about it, and Platonists could not fail to catch an echo of a celebrated parable in the *Republic* when his commentators likened it to the fecund and illuminating sun.[17]

A PHILOSOPHIC RELIGION

So far the subject of this introduction has been philosophy, but in the Roman Empire Platonism was also a religion. To live without some form of worship had indeed been barely possible in the classical period, but the faiths of late antiquity were practised with much greater

---

16 See *Physics* 202a on double actuality, with Lloyd (1987), 167–9 on the Neoplatonic use of this notion. Rich (1954) follows the evolution of the theory of Forms as thoughts in the mind of God; Armstrong (1960) stresses the role of Alexander of Aphrodisias (second century A.D.), while Barnes (1989) doubts that of Antiochus of Ascalon (first century B.C.).

17 See *Republic* 509b, where the sun represents the Good, the last object in a process of training the eyes that begins with shadows. For the image applied to the active intellect (*De Anima* 429b–430a) see Schroeder and Todd (1990). On the active intellect after Aristotle, see Blumenthal (1991); for a modern analogy between the active intellect and God see Norman (1969). Kosman (1992) argues that the active intellect must actualise both mind and objects at the same time.

ostentation, sometimes governing the whole of a person's life and giving rise to new forms of literature that ranged from the solemn to the picaresque. The representative Platonists of this epoch were not the strict philosophers like Atticus, who, with a cry of "back to Plato", took Aristotle to task for his erroneous belief in the eternity of the world, the inseparability of soul and body and the necessity of external goods for happiness.[18] More typical was the African Apuleius, and not only because his minor works included both an exposition of Peripatetic logic and a digest of the whole Platonic system. He owed his reputation not to these but to an essay *On the Genius of Socrates*, which is a classic text on the nature of intermediate beings, or daemons; an *Apology* in which he flaunts his knowledge of exotic mysteries even as he denies a charge of magic; and a novel, *The Golden Ass* or *Metamorphoses*, which, though it seems to pose as an autobiography, abounds in tales of magical illusion, contains the most voluptuous of Platonic myths and ends with the miraculous conversion of the hero to the cult of the Egyptian goddess Isis.[19] He almost deserves his false renown as the author of the *Asclepius*, the eighteenth and final treatise in a popular collection called the *Hermetica*, which must have originated among the Greeks of Alexandria.[20] The fundamental doctrine of the *Hermetica* is that the human soul is a prisoner in matter, and can be delivered only by the collaboration of intellectual virtue with astrology, alchemy and the love of God.

Authors of the early twentieth century, to whom it was an axiom that the healthiest condition of society is one without religion, saw in such

---

18 For the major excerpts (in Eusebius' *Preparation of the Gospel*) see the edition of Baudry (1931). Alcinous, author of the *Didascalicus*, is often regarded as the one Platonist who survives *in toto* from the second century, but since Whittaker (1987) convinced most scholars that he is not the same man as Albinus, neither his date nor his affiliation can be deemed secure. He is, however, the source of the *On Plato* attributed to Apuleius (see next note).

19 See Walsh (1981) on Apuleius' relation to Plutarch and second-century Platonism; Hijmans (1987) on the authenticity of the Platonic writings ascribed to him; Mortley (1972) on his allusions to the unknown god. On the Platonic allegory of the tale of *Cupid and Psyche* (books 4–6 of *The Golden Ass*) see Merkelbach (1958). The end of *The Golden Ass* is treated as a personal document by Nock (1933), 138–55, as well as by Gwyn Griffiths (1975).

20 Now translated by Copenhaver (1992). The most reliable edition is that of Nock and Festugière, but Scott (1925–36) remains a mine of otherwise recondite information, especially (in vol. 4) on Zosimus the alchemist of Panopolis. See Festugière (1948–54), especially vol. 1, on the occult literature of the Roman Empire.

works a proof of the enervation of the Greek spirit, or at least of the diffusion of Greek culture to the unworthy. "Failure of nerve" and "age of anxiety" are two celebrated formulae embraced by holders of the Greek Chair in Oxford. Even those who argued, like Festugière, that the world was being prepared for a better faith, found natural causes for the efflorescence of "personal religion". Now that every Greek had a Roman master and the Empire had engulfed the city, was it not inevitable that the progeny of Pericles and Solon would appeal to other gods?[21] There is, however, little sign of anxiety in the elegant Greek literature of this epoch: writers such as Dio, Lucian, Aelius Aristides and Philostratus do not appear to doubt that they can match the ancient figures whom they emulate and occasionally disparage. Moreover, since they all at some time made their living as sophists or itinerant rhetoricians, there must have been many cities that were affluent enough to repay their eloquence and proud enough to accept their specious praise. Perhaps it will be suggested that the populace, if not the intellectuals, were driven to superstition by a sense of loss and impotence; but we have no reason to think that they experienced this under Roman occupation more than under previous governments. It is true that the number of magical papyri in Greek is very much greater in imperial times than in the classical or Hellenistic periods; but since the whole of this plethora comes from Egypt, what does this show except that Greek was now the language of a large community in that region? It is true that in these times a "holy man" could enjoy the global, rather than merely civic, eminence that was necessary to make a true celebrity; nevertheless the "Hellenistic divine man (*theios anêr*)", who scatters healings, exorcisms and miracles as he passes, is a fabrication of New Testament scholarship.[22] Now, as ever, the true divine man was one who had inured himself so perfectly to

---

21 See Murray (1935), xiii, quoting J.B. Bury, for the failure of nerve; Dodds (1965) for the anxiety; Festugière (1954) on personal religion. Both Dodds and Festugière give excessive prominence to the *Sacred Tales* of Aelius Aristides, a small part of the *oeuvre* of this sickly eccentric. The vitality of Greek culture in this period is demonstrated by Bowersock (1969) and Swain (1996).

22 See now Flinterman (1996). For the term *theios anêr* in Plato, meaning a man of spontaneous virtue, see *Meno* 99d–e. In Philostratus, *Apollonius* 1.1–2 the criteria are wisdom and divine virtue, as also at *Prolegomena to Plato* 5. On the adulation of great men as a feature of late antiquity see Brown (1978); on the social and cultural factors which led to the proliferation of biographical literature see Swain (1997).

the ways of truth and virtue that he appeared to derive his insight from the gods.

Perhaps it is only since the late eighteenth century that societies have endured without belief in the supernatural, and that a permanent state of warfare has prevailed between religion and philosophy. So far as we know, the second century was anomalous only in its material prosperity and its intellectual vigour. The expansion of the Greek mind is attested by Numenius of Apamea in Syria, the most eminent precursor of Plotinus. Numenius was a passionate opponent of the sceptics,[23] as he had to be, for many of his doctrines were supported by a fragile coalition of authorities, not all of whom passed muster in the philosophic schools. In spite of Aristotle, he taught that the soul could live without the body, and blended the thought of Plato with an allegorical reading of the *Odyssey* as he mapped its peregrinations after death.[24] For light on other questions he was willing to consult the Indian Brahmins, the astrologers of Persia and the sorcerers of Egypt; he even knew enough of Judaism to be credited with the dictum "What is Plato but an Atticizing Moses?"[25] His thought was either nourished by or (more probably) helped to father the so-called *Chaldaean Oracles*, traditionally supposed to be the work of two theosophists in the second century.[26] The *Oracles* claimed the gods, not Plato, as their inspiration, but they expressed in a purple style the Aristotelian distinction between the active and the potential intellects. The first, paternal intellect is a monad of which nothing is predicated but *hyparxis* or existence; its logical successor is a dyad, the precondition of all plurality in number and hence of multiplicity in the world. This dyad is the matter, or potential being, of the second intellect, which objectifies the contents of the first.[27] Numenius, for his part, wrote a new Platonic myth in which the mind that contained the Forms suffered bifurcation and became two minds,

---

23 See especially Frs 25–8 Des Places, *On the Defection of the Academy*, where, as Lamberton (1986), 54ff notes, Numenius makes comic use of Homeric allegory.

24 See Frs 30–35 Des Places, with Lamberton (1986), 54–77.

25 See Fr. 1 Des Places (on Brahmins), 60 (on Mithras), 8 (on Moses).

26 For discussion of the traditional date, which some reject in favour of the third century, see Saffrey (1981). Dodds (1960) argued for the dependence of Numenius, Fr. 58 on the *Chaldaean Oracles*.

27 See especially Fr. 3 Des Places (on the remoteness of the Father), Fr. 4 (on power as an intermediary between Father and Nous), and Des Places, *OC* (1971), for the recapitulations of the doctrine in Psellus.

one still looking inward like the God of Aristotle, while the other looked down toward the realm of matter. Even two was not enough, for the hegemonic role belongs in Platonism not to all the Forms in combination, but to that of the Good alone. This Form became the First God and First Mind in the cosmology of Numenius. Thus there were three: the First, or the Good, the Second, or the realm of Forms, and a third which arose from a schism in the Second.[28]

The Chaldaeans, like the Persians, lived on the borders of the Roman world, which occasionally received conspicuous visitors from India;[29] Jews and Egyptians were provincial subjects, like the Greeks. As records were almost always in the hands of priests, most peoples were defined (at least for others) by their religion, and the success of Platonism in late antiquity is largely a result of its ability to appropriate almost everything that was of religious value in the Empire. This would have been more difficult to accomplish without the expedient of theurgy,[30] a pot-pourri of rituals for the union of the soul with the divine realm, which, according to its practitioners, was the common heritage of the eastern nations. Although the first Greek specimens purport to be Chaldaean, we find much of the same vocabulary among Christian heretics whom some call Gnostic, and also in the Delphic and Hebraic texts collected in the third century by Porphyry of Tyre.[31] Once this had become the handmaid of philosophy, one could be a Syrian Platonist, a Phoenician Platonist, an Egyptian Platonist, and above all a religious Platonist, without waiving the conventional antithesis between myth and dialectic and without falling on the wrong side of the line that still divided the barbarian from the Greek.

---

28 See especially Fr. 11 Des Places (on the schism) and 16 (on the First as the true Good, while the Second appears to be the Beautiful). On Numenius as a forerunner of Plotinus see Dodds (1960). Dillon (1977), 361–2 argues for a *floruit* before 165. Frede (1987), 1059 points out that Numenius needed a deity higher than the Forms.

29 On relations (both real and imaginary) between the Empire and India see André and Filliozat (1986).

30 For an illuminating and extensive treatment see Shaw (1995).

31 On the Being–Life–Mind triad in the oracles and the Gnostic *Zostrianus* and *Allogenes* see Majercik (1992). Hadot (1967) argues that Porphyry built his own metaphysics on this triad, though his reconstruction is criticised by Edwards (1990a). On Porphyry's knowledge of the *Oracles* see Lewy (1956), 1–61.

PYTHAGOREAN TRADITION IN PHILOSOPHY AND BIOGRAPHY

Tradition states that Plato set up a school, called the Academy, in Athens, and that after his death in 353 B.C. his relative Speusippus received the post of head, or scholarch, to be followed in 339 B.C. by Xenocrates.[32] Many historians doubt that the school existed before the Emperor Marcus Aurelius established chairs in the city for the teaching of philosophy around 176 A.D. Be that as it may, it is certain that Speusippus and Xenocrates taught in Athens, and refined what Aristotle had rejected in the ore of Plato's teaching. They too disowned the theory of transcendent Forms, but they also denied the primacy of the composite particular. Instead they found the elements of reality in mathematics, a science that Aristotle merely glanced at, while Plato praised it only as an adumbration of the highest knowledge. Xenocrates, defining soul as a number that moves itself, implied that its salient qualities belong to it independently of the matter that it animates. Speusippus, in his study of the foundations of arithmetic, concluded that the first number is the first principle of being.[33] Perhaps he was interpreting the *Parmenides* of Plato, where a series of antithetical propositions on the One and the Many supervenes on a rigorous critique of the theory of Forms. Or he may have been one of the few who kept his seat at Plato's celebrated lecture *On the Good,* which quickly emptied the auditorium when it proved to be a sermon on the hierarchy of numbers.[34] For Greeks of the Roman period, however, both Parmenides and Plato were disciples of Pythagoras, the man with the golden thigh.

Born in Samothrace, an Aegean island, in the sixth century B.C.,

---

32 See Glucker (1978) on the poverty of evidence for the existence of a physical Academy, or even a line of succession, before the second century A.D. For the doctrines of Speusippus (d. 339) and Xenocrates (d. 314) see Dillon (1977), 11–39. Xenocrates is generally held to have been the first to say that the temporal creation of the world in the *Timaeus* was mythical: in defence of this position see Cherniss (1944), 426–31.

33 Merlan (1960) and Halfwassen (1992) have both made out a strong case for Speusippus as the father of Neoplatonism.

34 On the *Parmenides* in Neoplatonism see Rist (1962b). Cherniss (1944) denies that Aristotle had access to any unwritten doctrines, as the tenets that he ascribes to Plato could all be collected from his written dialogues. This, as De Vogel (1953) contends, is what we should expect in any case. *Epistle 7,* which asserts that the doctrine of Plato is not written, does not imply that if written it would contradict his extant compositions. For the unpopular lecture *On the Good* see Riginos (1976), 123–6.

Pythagoras made his home among the Greeks of southern Italy, establishing communities which fermented intellectual, political and religious innovation for 150 years. Although he left no writings, he bequeathed to his sect such durable, if enigmatic, utterances as "do not eat the heart" and "do not poke the fire with a stick". Within a generation of his death he was both a legend and a laughing-stock, remembered less for his geometrical theorem and his study of harmonics than for his doctrine of transmigration and the vegetarian diet that it entailed. Aristotle's treatise *On the Pythagoreans* contains the earliest specimen of research into the life of a dead philosopher, undertaken not for its own sake but because the personality of the founder was believed to stamp his teaching with divine authority. Thus Aristotle records, without conviction, that Pythagoras exhibited clairvoyance on a number of occasions, that he was present simultaneously in two cities, and that he showed his golden thigh to reveal himself as the Hyperborean Apollo.[35] According to this witness, his disciples were of two sorts. Simple "listeners", the *akousmatici*, were content to obey his precepts with a literal fidelity and no other gloss than "he himself has said it"; the more systematic thinkers (the *mathêmatici*) declared that the bodily acts were enjoined as symbols of internal dispositions, and devised an allegorical construction for every saying.[36] They seem also to have maintained the ontological priority of numbers, correlating the integers from 1 to 4 with point, line, plane and solid. Numbers were for them the material constants of the universe, from which one could deduce the cardinal virtues, the four elements and the music of the spheres.[37]

The political and cosmological texts that style themselves Pythagorean in the epoch after Plato are often simple plagiarisms from him, and problems of attribution are compounded by the use of pseudonyms. The revival of the metaphysical, mystical and psychological doctrines in the first century B.C. was partly the work of Platonists, and partly of Roman amateurs with a taste for the occult. To the second class belong

---

35 See summary in Lévy (1926), 10–19.
36 On the state of the evidence see Burkert (1972), 166–91 (*akousmatici*) and 192–217 (*mathêmatici*).
37 See Hippolytus, *Ref.* 6.23 on the evolution of solids; Heath (1913), 105–15 on the harmony of the spheres. Whittaker (1969) discusses the principle of *aphairesis* or abstraction in the mathematical literature of the Neopythagoreans, which may have made a contribution to "negative theology" (the doctrine that God can be spoken of only by reference to what he is not).

Nigidius Figulus, whose consular rank did not preclude experiments in necromancy, and Varro the antiquarian, who credited a Pythagorean king with the discovery of the primitive modes of sacrifice, and celebrated the sacred properties of the number seven.[38] The earliest representative of the first class is Eudorus of Alexandria. Recalling that in Aristotle's time the Pythagoreans had constructed parallel columns of antithetical goods and evils, he suggested (with a little help from Plato's unwritten doctrines and *Philebus*) that it was possible to derive the whole of nature from the polar opposition of the one and the illimitable Dyad.[39] Since Pythagoreans were great believers in authority, it is no surprise that one of them, Thrasyllus, was the first to draw up a canon of Plato's writings, with an order that was intended to conduct the mind from sensible phenomena to the regions of the intellect and beyond.[40] Thrasyllus, better known as the astrologer of the Emperor Tiberius (14–37 A.D.), was not in the modern sense a strict philosopher; no more was Nicomachus of Gerasa (fl. 150[41]), whose essay on the derivation of numbers from the Monad and the Dyad was entitled the *Theology of Arithmetic*. There are many modern scholars who would gladly barter this for a longer specimen of Moderatus of Gades, an earlier, less devout and more analytical philosopher, who seems to have anticipated the Neoplatonic doctrine of the One.[42]

Nicomachus was in one sense the more complete philosopher: to his digest of Pythagorean teachings, he added a manifesto for the Pythagorean life. His vehicle was a biography of Pythagoras, in accordance with a precedent set by Aristotle and recently confirmed by Apollonius of Tyana, an itinerant sage and mystic of the first century A.D.[43] In paying this debt of honour to the past, Nicomachus had also caught the fashion of his day, for there was perhaps no form of literature that enjoyed such an efflorescence as biography among Greeks of the

---

38 The main source for Varro as Pythagorean is Aulus Gellius, on whom see Holford-Strevens (1988), 193–5. On Nigidius see *ibid.*, 116 with Rawson (1990), 239–40 and Apuleius, *Apology* 42.7.
39 See Dillon (1977), 115–6 on Eudorus, whom he dates to the first century B.C.
40 See Tarrant (1993) and my notes to Plotinus, chapter 24.
41 Or later, if we follow Dillon (1969) in calculating the date of 196 from Marinus, *Proclus* 28. On his mathematics see O'Meara (1989), 14–23.
42 According to the classic thesis of Dodds (1928). On the doctrine of Moderatus see Dillon (1977), 344–50.
43 See Rohde (1871–2) on these precursors of Iamblichus.

Roman Empire. It grew from a slender stalk, for nothing remains from the classical age that we would call biography, if by that we mean a scholarly, chronological and dispassionate account of a person's life from the beginning to his death. What we can glean – a handful of panegyrics by Isocrates and Xenophon, the latter's reminiscences of Socrates, the *Contest of Homer and Hesiod* (mere fantasy) and a few laconic notices affixed to the works of poets – does not begin to match the harvest of the imperial epoch, which includes the *Lives of the Sophists* by Philostratus, the *Lives of the Philosophers* by Eunapius, the *Lives and Opinions of the Great Philosophers* by Diogenes Laertius and a number of works devoted to a single life, not all of them as short as the ones translated in this volume.

To Greeks of the time biography was a keepsake from the wreck of history. Their cities had survived the Roman conquest, sometimes with their nominal rights intact, but they had lost the power to pass their own laws, to fund their own enterprises or to meddle with the governments of others. Henceforth there could be no political narratives involving Athens, Sparta, Pergamon or Alexandria, and even the grandiose triumphs of the past now seemed to have ended in futility. The wealthiest citizens bought themselves parochial fame through public works and monuments, but the greatest benefactor was the Emperor, and it was not the weathered glories of the city but its sophists, or professional declaimers, who could move him to legislation or largesse. Whereas Latin writers of biography took the emperors as their subject, Greeks extolled the masters of the intellectual disciplines in which their own supremacy was admitted. Diogenes Laertius wrote a preface to his compilation, urging that the Greeks were the true inventors of philosophy; the purpose of Philostratus was to demonstrate that the sophists of the last century lacked nothing by comparison with their namesakes in the time of Socrates.[44] Plutarch's *Parallel Lives* of Greeks and Romans were exceptional in their choice of subject, not in their estimate of Hellenism. His noble Greeks are statesmen and commanders of the time before Rome established her hegemony; the last of his noble Romans is Mark Antony, as though to say that the Empire had impoverished the virtues of the conquerors and not only of the Greeks.

Plutarch's philosophical writings, the *Moralia*, include robust defences of the meatless diet, as well as a dialogue *On the Sign* [or

---

44 On the defence of Hellenism in Philostratus see Swain (1999) and Flinterman (1995).

Daimonion] of Socrates, in which the chief speakers are Pythagoreans. The work is not without biographical interest, for its setting is the occasion when a band of Thebans won their citadel back from a Spartan garrison in 372 B.C.[45] For those who held, like Plutarch and his characters, that the man outlives his city and that inward probity is more remunerative than public reputation, such great events could not but prompt reflection on the nature of the soul and the identity of its supernatural helpers. In fact this is only one of a number of dialogues by Plutarch that populate the air between the earth and the moon with demigods called "daemons". Eros in the *Symposium* of Plato is the most famous representative of the class, though in the works of this disciple it is widened to include the souls of the just, the divine ambassadors at oracles and tutelary spirits of the kind that were alleged to have befriended Socrates. This last is not so much the mind's companion as the mind itself, which in wise men will have no need of oracles, because it is already a plectrum for the divine intelligence. Reviving myth and dialogue as vehicles of theology, Plutarch overlooks the Platonic theory of transmigration, but allots the moon and sun as destinations to the ascending soul and mind.[46] From Plato he inherits a distaste for hermetic readings of Greek poetry, but like many of his contemporaries he draws eclectically on Greek philosophy in expounding the ancient mysteries and the cults of other peoples.[47] A precedent had been set by Plato's *Phaedo* and *Symposium*, though the mysteries in these dialogues are Greek and the epiphanies are always metaphorical. Aristotle seldom borrows the language of initiates, and if Plutarch sometimes gives the name of God to his highest principle, it is not because he has read the *Metaphysics*, but because he is a Delphic priest who shares the religiosity of many intellectuals in his time.

There is no life of Pythagoras by Plutarch. Born in Chaeronea, he was almost an Athenian, and so all the less disposed to admire the Samothracian polymath whose wisdom was alleged to have been the fruit of peregrinations in Chaldaea, Assyria, Egypt and the Levant. All the main biographers of Pythagoras – Apollonius, Nicomachus, Porphyry, Iamblichus – were easterners; the first, a brilliant sophist and ascetic in

---

45 See Brenk (1996) on the daemonic role of the human characters.

46 See Brenk (1977) on demonology in Plutarch, and (1998) on his desire for the complete emancipation of the soul, which, as Alt (1993), 227–8 observes, is not matched even in Plotinus.

47 See *On Listening to the Poets* and *On Isis and Osiris*. On his knowledge of Egyptian mysteries and interpretations see Gwyn Griffiths (1965).

his own right, was posthumously regarded as a charlatan, a thaumaturge, a sorcerer and a new Pythagoras. The great surviving *Life of Apollonius* (more properly *Things concerning*, or *in Honour of Apollonius*), the most ambitious and the most favourable portrait, is the work of the same Philostratus who immortalised a gallery of sophists. There is no doubt that in his third-century masterpiece Apollonius has become a Greek again. First, he does not profess to enchant the elements and seldom even works a healing miracle; his power resides in his tongue and in an intellect so pervaded by the gods that it detects the invisible presence of a daemon and perceives events far off in space or time. Secondly, although he visits India and is amazed by what he sees there, he learns none of his philosophy from barbarians, and in Egypt he finds the Naked Sophists far inferior to their reputation. Thirdly, he shows no fear of Nero or Domitian, who, like all tyrannical emperors, hate philosophers and especially the Greek ones; instead he is prepared to beard Domitian in his den, and even in his dungeon has a long oration ready, which he fails to deliver only because he spirits himself away to another city.[48] His doctrines also have an excellent pedigree: his strictures on the use of cultic images are sophistic commonplaces of the period, and his undelivered speech before Domitian, with its premiss of a natural affinity between wise men and gods, would have been at home in Plutarch or the Stoics.[49]

The *Life of Apollonius*, while it may have added little to the history of ideas, cements the ancient bond between philosophy and life. In its wake the number of long biographies devoted to a single man increases, and for pagan Greeks the subject is almost always a philosopher. By this means they were able, without suspicion of vainglory, to add more

---

48 See *Apollonius* 4.10 for the daemon at Ephesus; at 8.26 Apollonius witnesses the murder of Domitian at a great distance. See *Apollonius* 6 *passim* on the Naked Sophists; 4.42–4 on Apollonius' indifference to Nero. The oration at 8.7 is undelivered and at 8.8 Apollonius effects the miraculous escape of which he had already proved himself capable at 7.38.

49 See especially *Apollonius* 8.7.22 on the natural affinity with the gods; 6.19 on the mendacity of images, a passage now also famous as the first instance in Greek literature of a contrast between *phantasia* (a form of imagination) and *mimesis* (reproductive imitation). See further Sheppard (1991). Apologies for images include Dio Chrysostom, *Oration* 12, Maximus of Tyre, *Philosophumena* 2 and Porphyry, *Statues*. The iconoclastic literature which they seem to presuppose has perished, except perhaps for the Fragments ascribed to the ancient philosopher Xenophanes. Gillian Clark suggests to me that the Platonists may have felt the need to temper the disparagement of the plastic arts at *Republic* 596–7.

recent names to the national roll of honour; since many of the biographers, Philostratus included, were friends of the governing class,[50] they will also have been aware that busy Romans had more time for ethics than for metaphysics, and would learn more readily from a human paradigm than an abstract dissertation. Nothing survived unchanged in this new climate, and biography, constrained as it was by few generic precedents, was a perfect medium for the transformation of Greek culture. When (as often happened) an author elected to write the life of a contemporary, he had no excuse if he failed to take account of novel tastes and changing circumstances. Philostratus meets the thirst for innovation in his fourth book by exposing certain false or ingenuous passages in Homer; in his third he introduces an unusual series of miracles, which seem to be based on those ascribed to Jesus.[51] Homer was in the blood of every Greek, while Christianity had lately become a fashionable target of polcmic; as the sophist's art dictated, nothing in the *Life of Apollonius* is unfamiliar, yet everything is new.

THE PHILOSOPHY OF PLOTINUS

Neoplatonism, as it is now defined by scholars, was born into this second spring of Greece. It was, however, a late child and the third century has often been described as a time of crisis for the Empire.[52] That verdict is now contested by historians, but it cannot be denied that this was an age when it was dangerous to be wielding power and fatal to have lost it. Most reigns were short and terminated by assassination; armies were embattled simultaneously on more than one frontier and it was common for a general to purge defeat or build on victory by aspiring to the throne. A ruler who failed to pay his troops would not survive; the consequent depletion of the exchequer was not repaired by the debasement of the currency or even by the *constitutio Antoniniana* of 212, which extended citizenship (and hence new fiscal liabilities) to all free

---

50 See Swain (1999), 174–6 on the association of Philostratus and other sophists with the Empress Julia Domna (*Apollonius* 1.3 etc.).

51 See *Apollonius* 4.15–16 for Apollonius' interrogation of Homeric heroes, together with the *Heroicus*, where he contradicts the whole of Homer's narrative (cf. Dio Chrysostom, *Oration* 11 (*Trojan*) for another sophistic exercise of this kind). For the few parallels to Gospel miracles see *Apollonius* 3.38, with the judicious remarks of Francis (1995), 118–126.

52 See Rostovtzeff (1957), vol. 1, 433–501. On the Emperor as benefactor see Veyne (1990), 347–77.

men and women. The smallholders of republican times had now become the tributaries, and were soon to become the serfs, of the great landowners; the latter, as they saw their prerogatives passing to imperial officials whom they regarded as barbarians, allowed the Emperor to supplant them also in the role of benefactor to the cities. Municipal duties fell instead on those who were not rich enough to evade them; since the people had to be fed, the peasantry was fleeced by the exactions of the town. In short, this was a time when if one had a private income it was good to be a private citizen.

It was not a good time for literature, for, if we make an exception for the histories of Herodian, almost all that survives from between the years 250 and 290 is philosophy. It may not be an accident that the majority of the works which can be dated belong to the reign of Gallienus (253–68).[53] Although his realm was torn apart by constant insurrection, he ruled for a continuous span of fifteen years, if we count ten years as a colleague of his father Valerian (253–63). The conditions for stable patronage were present, and Gallienus is generally acknowledged to have fostered, or at least to have tolerated, a renaissance in the arts. It was fortunate for philosophy that he also tolerated the rebel kingdom of Palmyra, which played host to the great Longinus, and suspended the persecution of Christianity which had been initiated in 250 by the Emperor Decius' ordinance of universal sacrifice.[54] While this measure was not aimed at philosophers, it was one with which the proud and conscientious founder of Neoplatonism might have scrupled to comply.

Plotinus, the founder of Neoplatonism, was born in 204 A.D. and spent his youth in Egypt, though his place of birth is uncertain. We cannot hope to determine now how much of his philosophy was his own, and how much he derived from his tutor Ammonius;[55] we know at least that none of it was written down until his fortieth year, when, after a brief and unsuccessful term of service in the army, he became the master of a school in Rome. His students were of many nationalities,

---

53 See chapter 3 on the pagan Origen. On Gallienus' policies see De Blois (1976), though I believe that he greatly exaggerates the intimacy between Plotinus and the Emperor.

54 Rives (1999) assembles the evidence on the content of the decree and suggests that Christians were casualties rather than the intended targets. Clarke (1973) rebuts the theory that the first edict was aimed directly at leaders of the Church.

55 On our knowledge of him see Schroeder (1987). Langerbeck (1957) attempts to reconstruct some of his doctrines from comparison of the Christian Origen with Plotinus, but Edwards (1993a) doubts whether Ammonius Saccas was the teacher of the former.

though all Greeks by education. Along with a high proportion of Egyptians, his circle included a number who, like himself, bore Roman names: most prominent were the senator Rogatianus, the philosopher Amelius and the high-born woman Gemina. Numenius, Moderatus and Nicomachus, together with Aristotle and his commentators, were studied in his lessons, though the infallible authority was Plato.[56] Plotinus abstained from meat, and some of his pupils counted vegetarianism as a mark of true discipleship. He nursed the Pythagorean dream of founding his own community, but though he is alleged to have been a friend of the Empress Salonina, he failed to secure a patron for this costly anachronism. His following melted away before his death, but the publication of his teachings, whether authorised or unauthorised, had already proved him, even in the judgment of his rivals, the most acute philosopher of recent times.[57]

It was Longinus, an eminent critic and once a teacher of Platonism in Athens, who defined most clearly what was new and unpalatable to him in the system of Plotinus. A perusal of the *Timaeus* – philological, rather than philosophical, as his adversaries called it[58] – convinced Longinus that the transcendent Forms are not contained in but are external to the demiurgic intellect. Plotinus, for his part, urged that the intellect which fails to possess its objects cannot be said to know them, and concluded that if the Demiurge is to have a perfect knowledge of the Forms he has to be united with them. Ordinary minds are not identical in the fullest sense with any of their objects: that would be possible only through a union with the Naked Form, whereas in the usual case we apprehend the Form through its sensuous or phantastic envelope. Unable to embrace all possible objects in a single intuition, the common mind is ceaselessly exchanging one for another, and is only temporarily and partially at one with any of them. The demiurgic mind is like all others in that its actuality consists in thinking; it differs from them in that it has no residue which awaits conversion into actuality. Its objects never change, because a knowledge of the Forms, which are eternal, necessary and simple entities, cannot be transitory or contingent. Perceiving them eternally, it is fully

---

56 See chapters 7–9 and 14 with my notes thereto.
57 See chapters 2 (refusal of animal remedies), 12 (Platonopolis project), 3 and 19 (publication).
58 See 14 for this comment, with my notes on Longinus. See chapter 20 for Longinus' allusion to his own controversy with Plotinus.

united with them, and for such a mind its objects are its contents. Moreover, as every Form implies the rest, the demiurgic intellect must be able to contain them all in a single, timeless act.[59]

What the Forms are objectively the intellect is subjectively. To say this is not to annihilate all distinction between the thinker and his thought, and indeed there is a sense in which the intellect remains prior to its contents. But what is it that guarantees the unity of intellect as it contemplates the multitude of Forms? Not its enigmatic substrate "intelligible matter", which appears to act as a genus to the Forms and thus supplies the precondition of their diversity even while it unifies them.[60] The source of unity cannot admit plurality; it cannot even have a form, an essence or a characteristic predicate if these are distinguished from the thing itself. A "thing" indeed it cannot be, nor a substance nor an entity; for the paradigmatic instances of all these are the immaterial Forms. The principle of all principles is called the One, but only as the *cause* of unity; it is called the Good, but only because whatever is estranged from unity is estranged from being, and hence defective in its kind. Sometimes it receives the honorific title *theos,* even *ho theos*, which is the nearest that Greek comes to using "God" as a proper name; for all that, it is not to be endowed with the personal qualities, such as wisdom or benevolence, that we normally regard as the prerogatives of divinity. Unlike the God of Christians, it neither thinks nor loves. Whatever has unity – be it an individual, an army or the cosmos – it is by virtue of the One, and yet the latter neither inhabits nor creates the world and does not share in the properties of any of its creatures. Its logical ubiquity is not "immanence", let alone the pantheism that is all too often fathered on Plotinus. It would also be misleading (though Plotinus sometimes condescends to the metaphor) to say that all things flow from the One by a process of emanation. On the other hand it would be equally erroneous to conflate it or contrast it with the Christian God by specious talk of "infinite transcendence"; since we know it not through revelation but by inference, not in itself but only from its

---

59 See especially *Enn.* 5.5. On the Aristotelian premisses of this argument see Rist (1989), O'Meara (1993), 35–7 and Gerson (1994), 51–5.

60 Following Rist (1962a). Plotinus' contemporary Aculinus defined intelligible matter as the ordering principle in generation (Lydus, *Mens.* 128.11–15 Wünsch). As Lloyd (1987) shows, the notion that Nous or Intellect "emanates" from the One must be divested of material and temporal connotations, and even then must be stated cautiously, as there is something after the One and prior to Nous.

signature in the unity of other things, the One without the world is as inconceivable as the world without the One.[61]

The notion that the first principle is ineffable was already a commonplace in Alexandria. Philo, the Jewish philosopher and exegete of the first century A.D., maintained that we can only speak of god as "the one who is".[62] Speculative Christians – Basilides, Valentinus and the Gnostics – had showered the eternal Father with such epithets as "invisible", "incomprehensible", "incorporeal" and even such apparently senseless paradoxes as "neither incorporeal nor corporeal".[63] The bishops declared them heretics, but it was possible to meet a more sober version of such doctrines, around the time of Plotinus' birth, in Clement of Alexandria. No wonder that when Plotinus came to Rome he bewailed "lost friends" among the Gnostics whom he attacked in one of his bitterest polemics. The teaching of the sect was much the same here as elsewhere: since evil cannot abide in God, our own benighted world must be the product of a lamentable accident, a fall or deviation in the lower intellect. Personified mythologically as Wisdom and metaphysically as Soul, it either irradiates the underlying darkness or falls into it, leaving as its offspring a mere "shadow of a shadow", which can do no more than create a penumbral representation of the eternal realm.[64] This inferior, demiurgic aspect of the Godhead would be at home in the cosmogony of Numenius, who appears to have known something of the Gnostics. His doctrine of two intellects, one simple and one divided, was thought by some to have been the hidden template for the system of Plotinus;

---

61 See *Enn.* 6.9 on the necessity and unknowability of the One; 6.8 on its self-creating will, which is not, however, providential. Rist (1962a), while noting that the term *theos* is applied to Intellect as well as the One, argues that the beginnings of a distinction appear in Plotinus' tendency to reserve the term *ho theos* ("God") for the One. Rist (1989) argues that the distinction between the Christian Creator and the One, though real, must not be made too stark.

62 On Philo's use of the formula "he who is" (from Exodus 3.14), and on possible traces of it in Greek philosophy, see Whittaker (1967).

63 See Hippolytus, *Ref.* 7.21–2 on Basilides, with Wolfson (1957), and Clement, *Stromateis* 5.83. Had they been writing in the twentieth century, the Gnostics would have said that it is a category mistake to ask whether God is incorporeal or corporeal, just as it is a category mistake to ask whether virtue is long or short. On affinities between them and the Neoplatonists see Dillon (1999).

64 Plotinus, *Enn.* 2.9.10 (on Sophia), with Edwards (1989) on the severed friendship of Plotinus and the Gnostics. On the philosophy of the Gnostics see my notes to *Plotinus* 16, and for more detailed comparisons Elsas (1975) and O'Brien (1993).

this, as is now agreed, cannot be true, for the higher intellect in Numenius is not characterised exclusively by privative terms and hence is not the One. Furthermore Plotinus is neither Gnostic nor Numenian in his account of the procession of the universe from Intellect. The mediating agent is the Soul, which, like the World-Soul in the *Timaeus* of Plato, is not the Demiurge but the instrument of his superabounding goodness. While there is only one soul at the origin, it is identical (in a certain sense) with every soul, and thus is at the same time one and many. As all plurality requires a substrate, there is a natural propensity in soul to generate matter, or at least to associate with it; its function is then to cover it and imbue it with a unitary form.[65]

Unlike that of the world, our souls are fallen, but, for all that, they are more than its parts or copies. Each soul is a *logos* of the upper Soul, which is to say that it stands in the same relation to it as the utterance of a word to the word itself. The circumstantial factors which commute, disguise or falsify our utterances take nothing from the word; in the same way the higher Soul is present in each of us without defect, although we suffer as individuals from the blemishes engendered by our perilous communion with the body.[66] Our soul is not, as in Aristotle, the form or actuality of the body, and the latter is more a vehicle than an element of the self. Even soul and self are not quite synonymous, for as it roves from one corporeal tenement to another, the soul is always at a distance from the unfallen intellect and from the enduring Form that constitutes the person.[67] Though matter is the prime evil, we are not to regard the soul as a blameless prisoner, for it is not its mere conjunction with the body, but its decision to love the body more than itself and more than intellect, that draws it into error.[68] Ordinary or practical virtues can restrain the passions, but the purpose of philosophy is to purify the soul

---

65 O'Brien (1981), (1993), etc. has strongly defended his view that soul generates matter against the reservations of e.g. Corrigan (1986). The key text is *Enn.* 4.8.6.18–23, on which see Gerson (1994), 263–4 n. 23, supporting O'Brien.

66 See *Enn.* 4.3.5 on souls as *logoi* and 4.8 on the fall of souls. See Helleman-Elgersma (1980), 57–63, on the differentiation of individual souls from the all-soul, which Gerson (1994), 63 takes to be the soul of the Demiurge. Soul itself is a *logos* of intellect (*Enn.* 5.1.3); this usage should not be confused with the Christian application of Logos as a proper name to Christ.

67 See Gerson (1994), 139–51. On Forms of individuals see *Enn.* 5.7, though there seems to be a conflict with other statements in the *Enneads*, as Blumenthal (1966) points out.

68 See *Enn.* 1.8 and 2.4 on matter as source of evil, with Rist (1961). See Corrigan (1985) on the mutual influence of soul and body.

and thus release it from the turbulence of the body. Once this has been effected it will be possible for the sage to live entirely in his intellect. Though beauty will be his lodestar at the outset of his voyage, he must not be dazzled by it if he is to rise above "whatever in the intellect is lower than the highest".[69] In this ascent the Forms, which remained so empty as mere postulates of reason, become the objects of immediate intuition. The self becomes a god, indeed the womb of gods, as it climbs beyond sense, beyond intellect, beyond memory of its past. It does not, however, climb beyond identity: as the Good is always good for someone, so the One is always unifying something, and the final state is therefore one of absolute integrity, "alone with the alone".[70]

We know Plotinus' doctrines from his *Enneads*, a collection of 54 treatises arranged, not chronologically, but according to their subjects, in six unequal dossiers of nine. Ethics is the subject of the first series, physics of the second and third, while the last three are successively devoted to the Soul, the Intellect and the higher principles of being. This syllabus, prefigured more than once by the ingenuities of Plato's commentators, is designed to lead the student through the grades of virtue and knowledge to the point where he transcends both in the presence of the One.[71] We are fortunate in Plotinus' case to be able to compare this pedagogic architecture with the chronological order of his writings. All our information comes from Porphyry, the editor of the *Enneads*, who came to Rome in 263 and tarried with Plotinus for the five years that he held to be the most productive of his master's life. He had formerly studied in Athens with Longinus, who regretted his migration, because when the young man changed tutors he also changed his opinion on the relation of the intelligibles to the demiurgic intellect.[72] We cannot say what Plotinus would have felt had he foreseen that his reputation would be confided to one whose temperament was so much more religious, more dogmatic and more credulous than his own.

---

69 The famous rapture at *Enn.* 4.8.1. See Gerson (1994), 292 nn. 46–7 on different interpretations of the notion of "union with the One"; O'Meara (1993), 45 doubts whether Plotinus rises any higher than the intellect in this passage.

70 *Enn.* 6.9.11. On the virtues see *Enn.* 1.2 and on the pursuit of beauty *Enn.* 1.6 (the earliest treatise). On the generation of gods see *Enn.* 6.9.9.

71 See my notes to chapters 24 and 25.

72 See *Plotinus* 20 (on Porphyry's defection) and 4–5 (on his sojourn with Plotinus).

THE PHILOSOPHY OF PORPHYRY

Porphyry was born in Tyre in 232 or 234 A.D. and lived to be at least 67.[73] His Greek name is a sobriquet meaning "purple", as his Phoenician birthname Malkus signifies royalty. The catalogue of his works includes a treatise of wide learning *On the Philosophy to be Derived from Oracles*, and another (or perhaps a part of the same one) *On the Reversion of the Soul*, which seems to take the *Chaldaean Oracles* as its guide.[74] Sometimes he attached the same authority to writings that had not received divine accreditation: thus he allegorised a topographical detail from the *Odyssey* in his essay *On the Cave of the Nymphs*, with the plea that nothing written by the ancients could be false or nugatory.[75] A long fragment on Pythagoras from his *History of Philosophy* gives equal weight to the miracles and to the teachings of its hero. The antiquity of Plato's dialogues rendered them immune to contradiction, though the thought could still be interpreted, defended and compressed in a neat antithesis: beasts have memory, humans recollection; what is greater in power is less in volume; the body of a text is its verbal meaning and its soul the author's meaning.[76] The chronology and number of his writings are disputed, but it is fair to say that system rather than rigour was his goal throughout his life, and that he never displays the tentative, self-critical and endlessly inquiring sensibility of Plotinus, either before or after his residence in Rome.

It would not have occurred to Porphyry, after his studies with Plotinus, to doubt that the One, the Intellect and the Soul were the ultimate principles of being. Nevertheless there are works of his, undoubtedly written after his master's death, in which the One is never mentioned and its place is taken by the less inscrutable "God over all".[77] Admittedly this

---

73 See *Plotinus* 23 for his age, and 17 for his name.

74 O'Meara (1959) contends that these were the same work. Others, following Bidez (1913), have seen in the first a product of youth and in the second an exhibition of maturity.

75 See Lamberton (1986), 124–6 on Porphyry's rejection of Cronius' view that the cave is mere allegory. Porphyry argues for an intentional plurality of meanings, as Pépin (1967), 243–8 explains.

76 See Fr. 255 Smith on men and beasts; *Sent.* 35 (39.13 Lamberz) on volume and power; Fr. 416 Smith on hermeneutics. The first supports the view that the souls of men and beasts have different histories; the second is fundamental to all speculation on the One; the third is a charter for allegory, hitherto regarded with misgiving or contempt by Platonists.

77 On the transformation of Plotinus' doctrine see Dillon (1992b), with my notes to *Plotinus* 23. On the neologisms and shifts of meaning which enabled later Neoplatonists to assign some mode of "being" to the Supreme principle see Rist (1964a).

deity receives only the most exiguous of devotions – the vegetarian diet excludes all carnal sacrifices and prayer is offered more for the votary's sake than for the god's[78] – but cult of a kind is presupposed, and Porphyry was nonplussed by the refusal of his master to engage in any kind of public worship. To Porphyry it was just as much an axiom that the gods assist the just as that the ancients cannot lie. Both these pious assumptions were inherited from the religious Platonism of the second century; indeed it was a byword among the later Neoplatonists that if we meet one opinion in Numenius we do not expect another from Porphyry.[79] He was naturally suspected of reducing the highest principle to an intellect in the anthropomorphic fashion of his mentors; the truth is hard to ascertain because – and this is another second-century trait – the subjects that predominate in his writings, lost or extant, are theology and ethics. Of his didactic works the best preserved is a treatise in four books *On Abstinence*, an invaluable thesaurus of the arguments, both moral and religious, that had been adduced by vegetarians or their adversaries. Although it honours the memory of Plotinus, it could hardly have been written in a less Plotinian spirit, with its antiquarian pedantry, its word-for-word excerpting of authorities and its indiscriminate muster of foreign analogues to Pythagoreanism, from the Brahmins to the Jews.[80]

Porphyry could assimilate philosophies as easily as religions. He saw that it was impossible to reconcile the logic of Aristotle with the ontology of Plato, since the ideal entities posited by the latter are regarded by the former as mere predicates of the true entities, namely concrete individuals. He did not, however, simply decide the issue in Plato's favour, as Plotinus had in a series of polemics. Where his master had protested that the Aristotelian categories cannot govern incorporeals, Porphyry avers that they were never intended to: Aristotle's reasoning pertains to the physical, Plato's to the intellectual order of existence. We need the semantic clarity of one to bring intelligence and order to our perceptions of phenomena; we need the dialectic of the other to raise the mind above its physical environment to the essences that determine the very

---

78 See e.g. *Marc.* 281–2 Nauck. Marcella, the recipient of this letter, was a widow with five children, reputedly a Jewess, whom Porphyry married late in life not, as he frankly tells her, for her wealth, her reputation or her beauty, but to appease his natal daemon: 273–4 Nauck.

79 Proclus, *Tim.* i, 77.22–3 Diehl, cited as Numenius Fr. 37.25–6 Des Places.

80 See 245–51 on the Jewish ascetics called Essenes (following Josephus) and 265–6 on the Brahmins.

character of being. A similar expedient will accommodate both the Aristotelian and the Platonic theories of the soul, which occupies a level of being between the intellectual and the physical. So long as it is embodied, it is properly described as the form or entelechy of its material substrate; in itself, however, it has no natural connexion with the body and is free to survive without it.[81] Porphyry wrote a *Harmony of Plato and Aristotle* which has not survived, but his *Isagoge,* or introduction to Aristotle's *Categories,* is still extant, having become a standard textbook within a century of his death.[82] He did not attempt a *rapprochement* between Platonism and any other school, but he is happy to record that there are elements of Stoic thought in the teaching of Plotinus, and we have seen that all his writing on the Pythagoreans bespeaks his admiration for the sect.

On one great point, however, he departed from authority: he believed in transmigration but did not admit that the soul can pass from one frame to another as peremptorily as a rider changes mounts.[83] The human soul, he taught, inhabits only human bodies, and when it quits one it takes with it a carapace of memories that serves it as a medium of sensuous perception (or more properly of *phantasia*) in the interval between embodiments. All Platonists confessed that some residuum of the previous life contributes to the soul's choice of the next, but it was Porphyry who personified this as the natal daemon, a "marine and material deity", whom the soul is bound to appease before it consummates any progress

---

81 Smith (1974), 10–19 suggests that the notion of power or *dunamis* allows Porphyry to refine Plotinus' distinction between the transcendent soul and the lower one which acts as the immanent form of the body.

82 See Ebbesen (1990a), 141–71 on the logic, which he believes to have been misinterpreted even by Dexippus in the fourth century. At 152–4 Ebbesen argues that Porphyry either stated or presupposed an important distinction between universals *ante rem* (Platonic Forms), *in re* (enmattered forms) and *post rem* (mental abstractions). For Porphyry's contention that the strictures of Plotinus (*Enn*. 6.1–3) have no bearing on the true doctrine of Aristotle see Hadot (1990), 126–7.

83 See especially Fr. 300 Smith, drawing on Augustine, *City of God* 10.30, 12.27 and 13.19. Although Augustine is our only witness, I see no reason not to accept his testimony; it implies that Porphyry took the *Phaedrus* of Plato literally, the *Republic* and *Timaeus* metaphorically. Smith (1984) remarks that Porphyry allowed a change of body but not of nature in transmigration, and spoke of transmigration into animals as "no myth, but true and a physical logos". I take the former to mean that souls can pass into a different human body but not into one of another nature, and the second to mean that Plato's myths, though literally false, remain as true as (say) a pictorial representation of the gods. For further discussion see Deuse (1983), 6–7 and Carlier (1998).

in the virtues.[84] Plotinus had suggested that at birth we are allocated to a custodian, which Plato called a daemon and astrologers our star: for him this is the best state that the self can aspire to in its present sojourn, but Porphyry, in his life of his master, adopts a more superstitious notion of it as a resident companion, a daemon or occasionally a god, who could be evoked by incantations. The discipline of the soul, as he conceives it, has two elements: priestly or theurgic acts which banish the ills arising from collusion with the body, and philosophy which implants the seeds of virtue. His *Sententiae,* or *Introductory Maxims to Philosophy,* derive a fourfold scheme from intimations in Plotinus: first the practical virtues, then the political, then the purificatory or cathartic, and at last the paradigmatic. To borrow more religious terms, the aspirant is first a man, then a daemon, then a god and at the best a father of gods.[85]

Even the most receptive brain is not an Aeolian harp to every wind. Porphyry held that higher gods were more worthy of veneration than their inferiors, and in his *Letter to Anebo* he put a number of difficult questions – maybe in a spirit more provocative than polemical – to the ritualists of Egypt.[86] He admired the invisible deity of the Jews, but he detested Christianity, as it advanced its claim to revealed and perfect truth. It was he, and not Plotinus, who identified the Gnostics as Christian heretics; it is characteristic of him that he answered them by showing that their book of Zoroaster was a forgery, and not the authentic work of the Persian prophet, just as he devoted part of his tract in fifteen books *Against the Christians* to denying the authenticity of the book ascribed to Daniel in the Old Testament. It is plausibly suggested that he wrote this polemic under Diocletian, who initiated the last and harshest persecution of Christians at the beginning of the fourth century.[87] If

---

84 See Bregman (1982), 145–51 on the teaching of Porphyry and his plagiarist Synesius on the survival of *phantasia*. On "marine and material deities" see *Nymphs* 80.14 Nauck. Smith (1974), 48–54 argues that the soul at last ascends to a condition without *phantasia*, though he doubts that Porphyry is guilty of the conflation of soul with *nous* that is frequently imputed to him.

85 See *Plotinus* 10 and *Regr.* on the uses and limitations theurgy; on the scale of virtues see my notes to *Plotinus* 10 and *Proclus* 3 with reference to *Sententiae* 32.

86 On different types of sacrifice see *Abst.* 163 Nauck etc., with Smith (1974), 97 on *Oracles*; *Anebo* is reconstructed from excerpts in Eusebius and polemical citations in Iamblichus by the edition of Sodano (1958).

87 *Oracles* cites a number of oracles concerning the God of the Jews. The case for dating *Against the Christians* to the reign of Diocletian is made by Barnes (1973), overthrowing

so, it coincided with the appearance of a monograph by Sossianus Hierocles, which unfavourably contrasted the works of Christ with those of Apollonius of Tyana.[88] When we reflect that Hierocles was answered by Eusebius, a Christian writer of the next generation, and that the history of the early Pythagoreans by Iamblichus must already have been current before the end of Diocletian's reign, we can see that it had never been more fashionable to treat the lives of intellectual figures as apologetic or controversial weapons. Porphyry did not lack either motive when he came to write his memoir of Plotinus as a preface to the *Enneads*, shortly after 300 A.D.

THE HISTORICAL AND LITERARY VALUE OF PORPHYRY'S BIOGRAPHY OF PLOTINUS

First the life and teaching of Plotinus were in need of vindication. His most outspoken foes were the astrologers, who denied that it was possible to be so much the pilot of our own fortune as the Platònists contended. Plotinus in particular had offended them by writing that the stars are more a testament than a cause of things to come, and that the soul of a philosopher cannot be stripped of real goods by the cosmic forces that enthrall the body. The body of Plotinus had suffered painful deterioration before his death, and in his handbook of astrology, the *Mathesis*, Firmicus Maternus killed the corpse a second time with aggravated symptoms, sneering that the philosopher had no more power than any man to countermand his fate.[89] Porphyry's retort is not to hide, postpone or attenuate the illness, but to make the earliest datable occurrence in a carefully-charted narrative. It was an old Platonic maxim that philosophy is a preparation for death, and that his master died so tranquilly in the midst of great afflictions was for Porphyry a condign proof of his merits. As the dissolution of the flesh is the deliverance of the soul, it is at this point (near the end of the second chapter) that Plotinus reveals

---

previous assumptions that it was written about 270. None the less the date and title continue to be disputed: on the evidence, certain and conjectural, see Meredith (1980) and Beatrice (1991). The latter notes that the phrase "against the Christians" may not have been intended as a title in Augustine, *Letter* 102. On the book of Daniel see Casey (1976), who argues that Porphyry owed something to Christian exegetes.

88 See Frede (1999), 231–5.
89 See my notes to *Plotinus* 2.

the deity within him.[90] The rest of the biography is designed to show that even in his mortal life he had been divinely guided, and indeed had been (in Porphyry's terms) a god. Nowhere is this purpose more apparent than in chapter 10, where the sage allows his god to be evoked and bests a rival who was trying to injure him through astral magic. The outcome shows that Plotinus, in the tradition of Pythagoras, "had something more in him by birth than most men". Porphyry goes on to say that his master, having studied the science of horoscopes, found it lacking in precision; he does not say why he elected to conceal his own date of birth.[91]

The posthumous reputation of Plotinus was in less danger from magicians than from philosophical critics. We have seen how modern scholarship would temper the charge of wholesale plagiarism from Numenius; Porphyry, leaving abstract disputation to the *Enneads,* is content with a long quotation from Longinus, who, as an eminent opponent of the Roman school, would not have given it better than its due. As for the other Athenians who put controverted questions to Plotinus, his disciple thinks it enough to say that he was always a match for them.[92] Other misconceptions are addressed in the fifteenth chapter, where the teaching of Plotinus is discovered to be compatible with poetry (at least of a turgid and ecstatic kind) but not with homosexual intercourse. Plotinus had been too austere to invoke a revelation against the Gnostics when they pretended that their own oracles had enabled them to fathom depths of the intellect that Plato and his admirers failed to penetrate; Porphyry, on the other hand, does not scruple to cite Apollo as his witness to the profundity of Plotinus' understanding and his ascent to a higher plane. His own commentary on the Delphic poem does something to correct its crude mythology, but he may have hoped that Christians, whether orthodox or heretical, would take notice when he testified that Plotinus had enjoyed communion, not with "the One", but with the "God over all". It has even been found possible to argue that his *Plotinus* was intended as a pagan gospel, whose hero, like the Christ of the Fourth Evangelist, is inhabited by a deity, vexed by priests,

---

90 See my notes to chapter 2.

91 See my notes to chapter 10 (Olympius and the priest) and 14 (astrology). The notion of Plotinus as magician, deriving from Merlan (1944), is endemic in De Blois (1976).

92 See my notes to chapters 15 and 17.

indifferent to local cults and sacrifices and the master of his own spirit at the chosen hour of death.[93]

But Porphyry had at least as much to say on his own behalf as on his master's. Compared with other pupils, he had joined the circle late and left it early; it was not he but Amelius who was generally regarded as the vicegerent of Plotinus,[94] not he but Eustochius, the doctor from Alexandria, who attended the philosopher at his death. These are the disciples who appear first and recur most frequently in Porphyry's memoir. Amelius is convicted in the first chapter of a foolish and idolatrous attempt to steal the features of his master for a portrait; in the third he makes notes of the seminars, which are subsequently revealed to be defective; and in the tenth his superstitious visiting of festivals is derided by Plotinus. Eustochius, who may have produced an edition of Plotinus' works before the *Enneads*, fails as a physician in that he comes too late to relieve Plotinus' symptoms on his deathbed and appears to have been pre-empted by the god Asclepius. No pupil's name occurs in the *Plotinus* more often than that of Porphyry, which is almost always coupled with the emphatic pronoun *ego*.[95] It is he who either refutes or is refuted in the most solemn disputations; he whose questions prompt the subtlest reasoning from Plotinus; and he who, in the verdict of the latter, is declared to be at the same time prophet, priest and revealer of sacred truth. His absence at the end he almost turns to his own advantage by explaining that, in contrast to Amelius, he left at the master's bidding; as my notes to chapter 11 indicate, Eunapius preserves a more discreditable account in which he leaves for Sicily of his own accord.

So much for the motives; what of the literary form? This preface to the *Enneads* does not adopt the plan that we and many of the ancients would regard as the conventional pattern of a "life" or *bios*. The life of a philosopher in Diogenes Laertius will commence with his birth and parentage and conclude with his death and burial, or sometimes with his will. The promise of the title – *Lives and Opinions of the Most Eminent Philosophers* – is fulfilled by the ample summaries of doctrine which are appended to the longest narratives. But Diogenes would appear to have

---

93 See Edwards (2000) for developments of the points made in this paragraph.

94 See Longinus in *Plotinus* 20. Most of our information about Amelius comes either from Porphyry or from Proclus. On the evidence see Brisson (1987a), and for comparison of his primordial triad with those of Porphyry and Plotinus see Corrigan (1987).

95 See Brisson (1987a), 806 on Eustochius, and Schroeder (1987) on the frequency with which Porphyry speaks of himself in the *Plotinus*.

INTRODUCTION   xxxvii

been writing before the middle of the third century, and since then a more ambitious generation had arisen. Even the titles given to works of biographical literature in this period reflect the mixed intentions of their authors.[96] Iamblichus attempted, not the customary *bios* of Pythagoras, but a treatise *On the Pythagorean Life*, which served as the preface to a grand encyclopaedia. Eusebius' lucubration *On the Life of Constantine* may pass with us as the first biography of an Emperor to be written by his own subject, but Greeks with a care for words said plainly enough that it was not so much a "life" as an "encomium in four books".[97] Porphyry's monograph *On the Life of Plotinus and the Arrangement of his Works* is shorter than either, but at least equally tendentious in construction, as will be evident from the following synopsis:

1. Proem against pictorial representation, with implied disparagement of Amelius.
2. Plotinus' divinity proved by the manner of his death.
3. Early life of Plotinus.
4–6. Chronology of the *Enneads*.
7–9. Plotinus' circle and methods of teaching.
10–12. Plotinus' personal merits, as evidenced by conflicts with opponents, feats of insight and distinguished friendships.
13–14. Methods, qualities and antecedents of Plotinus as philosopher, with indication of the prominence of Porphyry.
15–16. Success of Plotinus and his outstanding pupils (i.e. Porphyry and Amelius) in confuting misapprehension and disparagement of his philosophy.
17–21. Testimony of Longinus to the originality and genius of Plotinus.
22–23. Testimony of the gods, with corrective commentary from Porphyry.
24–26. Plan and justification of Porphyry's edition of the *Enneads*.

Hitherto no biographer had set out to accomplish such a variety of objects. For that matter since the fourth century B.C., when the earnest Xenophon had penned his *Memorabilia of Socrates*, no surviving

---

96 See further Edwards (1997) for an attempt to distinguish true *bioi* from biographic literature.
97 See now the translation and commentary by Cameron and Hall (1999).

account of a philosopher was written by his pupil.[98] Xenophon enjoyed a certain vogue among Greek sophists of the Empire,[99] but no biographical writer of the fourth century A.D. would have wooed his audience with a similar concatenation of anecdotes, withholding all that he knew about the first and final years of his protagonist or the works that he left behind him. Could the Sophists provide a better model? Porphyry, to whom verisimilitude mattered more than ornament, was not disposed to imitate the long travelogues and picturesque orations of the *Life of Apollonius*; he does, however, credit his master with miracles of clairvoyance and a Pythagorean reverence for his teacher, Ammonius Saccas. He also casts himself in a role akin to that of Damis, whose memoirs of his companion Apollonius were cited (and most probably invented)[100] by Philostratus as the source of his own account. It is difficult to see what Plotinus gained by joining the expedition of Gordian in 243; Porphyry contends that he was setting out, in the footsteps of Apollonius, to acquaint himself with the wisdom of the Indians and Chaldaeans. Far too many historians of philosophy have believed this explanation, or modified it only by the less plausible conjecture that Plotinus was attracted by the Manichaean religion which had lately sprung up in Persia.[101] Nothing in the *Enneads* favours any such hypothesis, and nothing in the field of human experience requires us to assume that a philosopher must always have a philosophical reason for his acts.

It is not a bold conjecture that it was in the hope of personal or political advantage that Plotinus joined the retinue of Gordian. Which was uppermost we cannot say: it would not be safe to argue, for example, that, as Gordian was the favourite of the senate, Plotinus also must have espoused the interests of that venerable but ineffective body.[102] Indeed, we might draw the opposite conclusion from the fact that, once in Rome, he caused a senator to forsake his duties on the very eve of

[98] Though accounts of philosophers by contemporaries were known to Diogenes Laertius, e.g. at 9.61–2 on Pyrrho the Sceptic.

[99] See e.g. the proem to Eunapius, *Sophists*, which alludes to the proem of Xenophon's *Symposium*.

[100] Following Bowie (1978), 1653–71, though Anderson (1986), 155–73 attempts to find evidence of Damis elsewhere.

[101] See Edwards (1994) against Puech (1978), 61 and De Blois (1989). My arguments are distilled in the notes to *Plotinus,* chapter 3.

[102] Harder (1960) has impressed many subsequent scholars. On the senator Rogatianus see *Plotinus* 7.

taking up his new responsibilities as a praetor. Should we surmise instead that he was a friend of the royal adventurer, and that this was the reason for his flight to Antioch in the wake of Gordian's death? This would be a fair inference if we were sure that "death" meant "murder at the hands of his compatriots", which might then entail reprisals against his former partisans. Much evidence suggests, however, that Gordian fell in battle, and it is certain that the end of his life coincided with a military disaster. It is possible that Plotinus fled with a portion of the army, and that Porphyry's allusion to the Emperor's death is merely an infelicitous example of his habit of dating everything in the life by regnal years. Those who accept this theory will not need to ask how Plotinus could have gone to Rome and settled there in the reign of Philip the Arab, who was commonly alleged to have been Gordian's assassin. Nor will they be astonished by his friendship with the wife of the later Emperor Gallienus, who lived on terms of cordial hostility with the senate. Porphyry is not concerned to supplement the lacunae in our knowledge of Roman history in the third century, but to furnish dates for a narrative. Historical fact is one of the determinants in this narrative; another is his own view that philosophers should live better lives than other men, yet still enjoy the patronage of kings.[103]

NEOPLATONISM AFTER PORPHYRY

Between Porphyry and Proclus the most distinguished figure in the Neoplatonic tradition is Iamblichus of Chalcis. To his successors he was always "the divine Iamblichus", and in his life his pupils thought him capable of such preternatural feats as levitation.[104] His commentaries on Plato have not survived, but his extant works include a *Protreptic to Philosophy* (much indebted to Aristotle), a treatise *On the Common Science of Number* (richly larded with Pythagorean learning) and the compendious dissertation, both biographical and expository, *On the Pythagorean Life*. Most celebrated of all (if it is really his)[105] is the huge tract *On the Mysteries*, which purports to be an answer, in the name of the Egyptian priest Abammon, to the question raised by Porphyry in his

---

103 See again Edwards (1994) and notes to *Plotinus*, chapter 3.
104 Born as early as 245, if we follow Cameron (1968). On his levitation (rumoured rather than witnessed) see Eunapius, *Sophists* 458.30–40 Boissonade-Dübner.
105 See Saffrey (1971) in defence of the authenticity of the treatise.

Letter to Anebo. Abammon advances three new doctrines which could justify the use of incantations, sacrifice and material artefacts to facilitate human intercourse with the gods. Firstly, he asserts that matter is not merely the formless nothingness at the vanishing-point of being, but an immediate emanation from the first principle, which makes possible the emergence of a manifold from its unitary source. Secondly, he denies that even the rational part of the soul remains immune to the pains and intrigues of the body, though it of course remains impassible in itself. Thirdly, he alleges that the activity of gods in the present world is mediated by inferior manifestations of divinity – the heroes below the daemons, the latter below the angels – and the nearer such powers are to our condition, the more readily they allow themselves to be seen and to be affected by the sympathetic forces of the material domain.[106]

It is obvious already from this summary that Iamblichus is a systematic thinker. He could call himself a Platonist because magic is only part of his philosophy, a catalyst, not a substitute, for ratiocination. The fragments of his commentaries on Plato show that he earned his fame by a scrupulous consistency, which required him to be inventive in his handling and didactic in his arrangement of the texts. Moreover the Pythagorean life, as he conceives it, is free of sacrifices and involves a higher species of theurgy whose only instruments are those of mathematics.[107] Logic, not revelation, caused Iamblichus to imagine a one above the One of Porphyry and Plotinus: he argued that the One in which every unity participates cannot escape all contact with plurality, and that this paradox can be transcended only if we posit a more sublime One that is unparticipated (*amethektos*). In fact it would be possible to elicit from the *Parmenides* a descending triad: first the One or God and any deities superior to the intellect; then the One participated in intellect and the intellectual gods; then the lesser beings (heroes, daemons) who are one by virtue of this

---

106 On matter in Iamblichus see *Myst.* 8.3 (197 Des Places) with Shaw (1988); on the soul and theurgy see *Myst.* 1.10–11 (57–62 Des Places); on heroes, daemons etc. see *Myst.* 2.1–3 (77–82 Des Places).

107 See Dillon's edition (1973) for the fragments of commentaries, known chiefly from Proclus. On mathematics as the purest form of divination see *DVP* 93. See also *DCMS* 8 33.22–3 Festa) on the superiority of intuitive to discursive apprehension. Lewy (1956), Excursus iv argues that Iamblichus excludes ritual from the highest theurgy; I am not wholly convinced by the rejoinder of Smith (1974), 97–9.

participation.[108] For Iamblichus, as for Plato, the existence of the manifold arises from the conjunction of dynamic and static principles; for example, in the triadic constitution of the intellect the foundation of productivity is being, the productive motion is life and the product is the objectified intellect or mind-in-act. The vocabulary is borrowed, with a small emendation in deference to Plato, from the *Chaldaean Oracles*,[109] and as in this collection the intelligible triad is but one of a series, in which each member exercises a demiurgic function. There is one demiurge for the intellect, one for the imperishable universe, and one for the shifting play beneath the moon.

These doctrines became the orthodoxy of later Neoplatonists. Iamblichus had brought the gods back into Platonism, thus cementing the alliance between philosophy and popular religion that had been briefly intercepted by Plotinus. For him as for any Platonist, theology and ethics were one subject, since the universe was a house that the gods had fashioned for the discipline and correction of the soul. Every personage, human or divine, in Plato's dialogues is a symbol of some power or disability in the soul, and the entire shape of a dialogue may be an image of the world from the point of view of an observer who has reached a particular level of understanding. A dialogue should be approached, not as a timeless conversation, but as a personal transaction between the author and the reader; if the latter is properly equipped for its perusal, the text without will both reflect and shape the soul within.[110] As commentary releases us from the literal construction of the words, so meditation and the corresponding actions will release us from the gross envelope of flesh. The complete annihilation of the body is not the aim, for the soul retains a tenuous vehicle, which is not a crude accretion from some bodily existence but the indefeasible substrate of

---

108 Fr. 2 Dillon on *Parmenides*, with commentary at Dillon (1973), 208. The source being Proclus, *Parm.* 1054 Cousin, we cannot be sure that there is a true anticipation of the doctrine of henads in the reference to superintelligible gods. On the multiplication of Ones see Dillon (1973), 29–33, citing a fragment of the *Commentary on the Chaldaean Oracles*, book 28.

109 See Hadot (1967) for the *Oracles*; Iamblichus, Fr. 65 on *Timaeus*, with commentary at Dillon (1973), 349–50. The change from "power" to "life" is dictated by Plato, *Sophist* 248e, where life is a property of the Forms.

110 See the anonymous *Prolegomena to Plato* (sixth century), with Larsen (1972), 438–42 and 449–55 for Iamblichus' maxims on the exegesis of the dialogues, which may have left some vestiges in Christian interpretation of scripture.

its own. Iamblichus may have been the earliest Platonist to take this view; at the same time he found a justification of astrology, which sets limits both to the freedom of the soul and to the tyranny of the powers that reign in matter. Every soul that comes into this world has a constellation as its overlord (*oikodespotês*), according to the lot that it has chosen; this overlord furnishes, but is distinct from, the ideal state or paradigm which the soul, if it makes the right use of its capacities, is destined to achieve.[111]

We do not know exactly when Porphyry or Iamblichus died, but we know that their successors had to practise in a less auspicious climate. In 324 the eastern and western portions of the Empire, divided in 284 by Diocletian, were united again by Constantine, a Christian who was not ashamed to trumpet his hostility to pagans. Though he may not have abolished public sacrifice, his successors did; and as the Bible drove out Plato, Christians ousted pagan teachers even from the schools of classical rhetoric and philosophy. The current was momentarily reversed in 361 by the Emperor Julian, one of Constantine's descendants and reputedly an apostate from his faith.[112] If he was converted, it was not to any one of the pagan cults but to a medley of Platonism with religions old and new, for all of which he undertook to supply a rationale in seven tedious orations. The fourth is to the Sun, the fifth to the Mother of the Gods – the former an ancient patron of Roman Emperors, the latter a name of power in classical times and now perhaps an intended antitype to Mary, whom the Church had graced with the title Mother of God. Julian palliates the obscenities of her cult and myth with the argument – reminiscent of Iamblichus – that such external blemishes force the mind to look for truths beneath the veil that would otherwise escape conjecture. He and his friend Sallustius, whose tract *On the Gods and the World* is a compendium of defences for the myths, are the only Platonists who represent this period; and both manifestly adhere to the Iamblichean, rather than the Plotinian branch of this philosophy.

The most vivid illustration of this allegiance is an anecdote in the *Lives of the Philosophers* by Eunapius, a document as typical of the

---

111 See Finamore (1985) on this vehicle in Iamblichus. On the *oikodespotês* etc. see *Myst.* 9.

112 Athanassiadi (1981) doubts whether he was ever a Christian. Smith (1995) shows that he is too eclectic, both in his philosophy and in his religion, to be labelled a strict Iamblichean, Mithraist etc.

fourth century as Philostratus' *Lives of the Sophists* is of the second. The term philosopher could now extend to include those connoisseurs of showpiece declamation who had hitherto preferred the name of sophist, and also to the adepts of a different art, who in the second century would still have ranked as charlatans or sorcerers, and therefore, says Philostratus, were not men of the type to which a true "divine man" such as Apollonius would belong.[113] One such professor, a certain Maximus, gained such a reputation as a philosopher that the Emperor Julian was inclined to engage him as a tutor. His counsellor Chrysanthius was so disturbed that he told him an admonitory tale of the man's vulgarity. An associate of his had once been present when Maximus was praying to Athena. He had gone so far as to ask her statue to smile, and such was his meretricious skill that the goddess had complied. The warning had a contrary effect to the one intended, and Julian sought out Maximus forthwith. The man who records this anecdote is not a superstitious ignoramus, but a fair specimen of the late fourth-century intellect, whose *Chronicle* still commands respect among historians of late antiquity.[114] He is also our only source (whether reliable or not) for information about Plotinus which we do not find in Porphyry, as well as an alternative account of Porphyry's life that is too often judged to be worthless merely because it contradicts him. In our present state of knowledge, we can only observe that Porphyry had rivals, and not everyone was happy to contemplate him on his self-erected throne.

The most ferocious enemies of Porphyry were the Christians, who replied to his books, then burned them and began to use the adjective "Porphyrian" as a term of vilification in their internal controversies. Hostility increased after Julian's reign, as the royal philosopher had also issued a book against the Christians, forbade them to teach the classics and punished those who flagrantly refused to tolerate his toleration. Eunapius' contemporary, the Emperor Theodosius I (r. 379–95), was an ardent Christian.[115] He renewed the laws against public sacrifices,

---

113 See Raynor (1984) on Philostratus' rebuttal of the depiction of Apollonius as a sorcerer in the earlier biography by Moiragenes. For the term *theios anêr* see *Apollonius* 1.1–2 etc.

114 Eunapius, *Sophists* 475 Boissonade-Dübner. See Hahn (1990) on his antecedents and motives. For his information on Plotinus and Porphyry see especially my notes to *Plotinus*, chapters 1, 3, 11 and 16.

115 See Salzman (1993) on the history of legislation in the fourth century, and Porphyry, Frs 38T and 39T Smith for the epithet "Porphyrian".

winked at the destruction of pagan temples, removed the financial privileges of the priesthoods and restricted public offices to members of the Church. Nevertheless the literature of paganism flourished, and so did the trade in bile between the parties. Christians to Eunapius were fools in black who had at heart the extinction of Greek culture; one would never guess that his tutor Prohaeresius had been one of them. The use of offensive sobriquets for the hated sect can hardly have been designed to conceal his meaning, which must have been transparent to every reader. It is a literary convention born of literary scruple: there was more than one pagan author of late antiquity who clung to his ancient models and fastidiously expelled from his vocabulary a name so redolent of a barbarous age.

PROCLUS AND THE ATHENIAN REVIVAL OF NEOPLATONISM

In the fifth century, harsher disabilities were imposed on worshippers of the ancient gods. Philosophers had time to resent, but no power to avenge, such an atrocity as the murder of Hypatia the mathematician by an Alexandrian mob in 415. During the minority of the Emperor Theodosius II (r. 408–450), attempts were made to restrain such crimes, but once the young sovereign came of age, he proved himself a champion of militant orthodoxy. Heretics suffered more than pagans, but the latter were deprived of civil and judicial office and the privilege of serving in the army. In 423 he doubted in an edict whether any followers of the old religion still existed.[116] His boasting was evidently premature, for in 435 he was obliged to renew and extend the ban on pagan sacrifices that had already been imposed by more than one of his predecessors. Now it was illegal even to sprinkle incense or to pour libations, but the very frequency of such legislation is a sign that it was widely disobeyed.[117] Like his greater namesake, Theodosius connived at the fall of temples, yet he acknowledged their survival in a law of 435 which enacted that

---

116 See Damascius, *Isid*. 105 (Hypatia), *Theodosian Code* 16.2.42 against the assassins of Hypatia; *ibid*. 16.10.21 for the expulsion of pagans from military, civil and judicial office; *ibid*. 16.10.23 on the scarcity of pagans.

117 *Theodosian Code* 16.10.25; see *ibid*. 16.10.1–20 for prohibitions by previous emperors. Trombley (1993), 309 suggests that the metaphor in Marinus, *Proclus* 1 implies that different types of sacrifice were observed in Athens even after 450; we must, however, allow for the possibility of tendentious or literary archaism.

such buildings as remained should be destroyed and superseded by a cross. Laws against magic had been in force since the late fourth century, but Christian witnesses from that time on complain that they were flouted even by many ignorant members of the Church.[118]

Nevertheless conditions in the eastern Empire favoured the cultivation of literature. No laws could have coerced so many pagans into the Church if they had been forbidden to bring their interests with them; after Constantine a Christian humanism supervened on the old distrust of Greek philosophy. Even in the time of Julian, Christians taught philosophy and rhetoric to pagans, and were not afraid to appropriate the vocabulary of Plato and his followers for the exposition of their cardinal doctrines. They continued to employ "Greek" as a synonym for "infidel", began to call themselves *Romaioi*, and promulgated their laws in Latin up to the mid-sixth century; yet there was no danger that the Greek world would be overshadowed by the west, for there the monarchy was in ruins. The surrender of Britain in 410 failed to prevent the sack of Rome; in 430 the Vandals conquered Africa, and once again Rome felt the aftermath. Byzantine rulers tried to recover Africa, but met with no success before the sixth century; meanwhile the last western Emperor was deposed by his barbarian protector, and Italy became a Gothic kingdom. The troubles of eastern Christendom were internal, and after the controversies which precipitated ecumenical councils in 431 and 451, the use of Greek was frequently regarded as a token of orthodoxy. The evangelisation of the rural areas, and of neighbouring lands, promoted the spread of Greek as a learned language;[119] the marriage between Christianity and the classics, forced though it was and lacking cordiality, was not to be dissolved.

Careers in law and medicine were still open to a pagan, and for a while there was no repression of the liberal arts, of which indeed the Emperor's wife Eudocia was a patron.[120] The old Greek cities did not lose their schools, their cults, their monuments or their pagan benefactors. The citizens of Athens, as she recovered from barbarian depredations of the third century, inherited both the wealth and the classical manners of their forbears; they continued, as in Plato's time, to honour

---

118 *Theodosian Code* 9.16.7; for Theodosius I's law against astrology see *ibid*. 9.16.8. For Theodosius II's legislation against temples see *ibid*. 16.10.15 (14 Nov. 435).
119 See especially Bowersock (1990).
120 Photius, *Bib*. 183–4 etc.

a host of deities, some traditional, some hitherto unknown. The name of Plutarch, known to us from more than one commemorative inscription, is also that of an eminent philosopher, who came of a line of priests. We cannot say whether this was the civic donor, nor whether he traced his ancestry to Plutarch of Chaeronea. His grandfather – still called long after his death "the great Nestorius" – left his writings on religious ceremonial and theurgy as a Book of Common Prayer to the Athenian Neoplatonists of the fifth century. Plutarch himself, whose acme we may date to about 400, was the most stringent commentator on Plato's dialogues since Iamblichus. The most interesting of the extracts from his work that have come down through later authors are concerned with the relation between the sensory and intellectual media of perception; but under his sway the syllabus of the revived Academy covered every topic in Platonic and Aristotelian philosophy, not excluding rhetoric. While nothing less would have been expected from a true Athenian, the writings of his pupil and successor Syrianus, whose name betrays his origin, declare an equally catholic range of interests. It is not so much in his few surviving treatises as in those of his successor and avowed disciple Proclus that his subtlest and most lasting contributions to philosophy appear.[121]

Born of affluent parents in Byzantium in 412, Proclus came to Athens around 430, just as Plutarch was approaching the end of life and had already bequeathed his cares to Syrianus. Proclus was only twenty-eight years old when he put his talents on display in a massive *Commentary on the Timaeus*.[122] Barely a fifth survives, and yet this fraction amounts to almost a thousand pages of print in the modern Teubner text. It justifies its length because the questions raised by the dialogue were numerous and the author never states his own opinion without canvassing the views of his precursors, from Speusippus to Syrianus. Here we meet in epitome the centuries of debate concerning the origin of the world and the relation between the demiurgic intellect and the Forms. On the first issue Proclus holds, like every Neoplatonist, that the works of the Demiurge cannot be arbitrary and must therefore be eternal; on the second he borrowed (here as elsewhere) a refinement of Platonic nomenclature from Iamblichus. The demiurgic intellect, he tells us, has two aspects: the higher or

---

[121] On these figures see *Proclus* 12, with my notes. Trombley (1993), 304 cites Nestorius as an example of tenacious religiosity in Athens.

[122] See Marinus, *Proclus* 12 on Plutarch, 13 on Proclus' *Commentary on the Timaeus*.

noetic is the intellect in its self-reflective purity, at one with thought and thinking, while the lower or noeric is the intellect that communicates its thought and forms a bridge between the higher realm and soul. The noetic intellect contains the Forms, while the noeric – Plato's Demiurge when he calls him "maker" but not when he calls him "father" – is the medium between the immobile paradigm and the mutable creation.[123] Those who find this treatment of the myth perverse will be even less disposed to accept the theological parable which Proclus foists on the story of Atlantis in order to make it consonant with the whole design or *skopos* of the *Timaeus*. According to him, the Atlanteans, as neighbours of the setting sun, represent the lower order of divine beings, and the passions to which such beings are exposed by their affinity with matter are both symbolised and punished by their immersion in the waves.[124]

Proclus was not incapable of taking Plato literally in his myths – although, conversely, there was hardly any character or statement in the texts that he could not invest with a figurative meaning. In a series of essays on the *Republic*, after disarming Plato's criticisms of Homer and the mythographers, he turns to the depiction of the afterlife in the tenth book of the dialogue, and concludes that we can be true to the letter only if we grant to the departed soul a body with some likeness to the one that it inhabited in its cycle of mortality. Adopting the same position in his commentary on the *Timaeus*, he makes peace between conflicting predecessors by allotting separate vehicles to the rational and irrational components of the soul. These doctrines leave a trace in chapter 3 of Marinus' *Proclus*, where the mortal shell is implicitly contrasted with the body that survives it; Marinus also cites, as an innovation of his master, a distinction between the cosmic and the supracosmic soul which may be analogous to that between the noeric and the noetic

---

123 On the eternity of the world, against Atticus and Plutarch, see *Tim*. 83f–87c (i, 276–85 Diehl). On the Demiurge as Father and Creator see *PTh* 5.27–28 (v, 99–105 Saffrey and Westerink). In fact there is a triad of intellectual principles (noetic, noetic-and-noeric, noeric), each of which is itself triadic. The adjectve *noeros* occurs occasionally in Plotinus (e.g. *Enn*. 5.3.6.20); for a formal distinction between noeric and noetic in Iamblichus see *Myst*. 1.19 (72 Des Places). Occurrences in the *Commentary on the Timaeus* begin with *Tim*. 1e (i, 3 Diehl); see especially *ibid*. 308 (iii, 224.22–32 Diehl).

124 See especially *Tim*. 54a–c (i, 174–5 Diehl), commenting on Plato, *Timaeus* 24e. Tempests of the soul are a ubiquitous image in Neoplatonic literature: cf. *Plotinus* 22 and *Proclus* 15. At 53b (i, 172 Diehl).

intellects.[125] These are niceties of exegesis rather than logical deductions; but had Marinus been a logician rather than a moralist – had his book been called *On Being* and not *On Happiness* – he could hardly have failed to mention Proclus' *Commentary on the Parmenides*, which was the apex of his metaphysical studies, as the dialogue itself was often judged to be the crown of Plato's thought. To modern eyes the most rewarding section is an excursus on the Forms, which recapitulates the queries and objections that the theory had excited, together with the defences, elaborations and refinements that a Platonist could offer in reply. Proclus of course does not suspect that any part of the dialogue is flippant or ornamental. He proposes that the speakers, who are characterised in the prologue by their several modes of argument, exemplify different orders of the daemonic or divine. As for the contradictory hypotheses or antinomies expounded in the second half, each is intended to acquaint the reader with a particular mode of unity at a certain level of being. Since the hierarchy has five levels – God, Mind, Soul, enmattered Form and Matter – and each of these is the subject of two antithetical theses, Proclus adopts a division of the text that raises the number of antinomies from eight or nine to ten.[126]

Every source of unity is a henad, and without these there would be no participation in unity below the One. In the *Elements of Theology*, where Proclus explained the basis of his system, we encounter henads of the noetic, the noetic-and-noeric, the noeric and the psychical – but a contrast is also drawn between the self-sufficient henads, which transcend the intellectual realm, and those that are realised in some lower substrate. Henads of the first (the self-sufficient) type are "gods"; and we must not assume that this term is a mere epithet or the flourish of an ingratiating pen.[127] The title of the *Elements of Theology* is well chosen, for while the higher essences of Proclus may not be personal in our sense, they are certainly divine. Their powers may be refracted through successive layers of being, they may seem (as in the *Cratylus*) to be

---

125 On the interpretation of the *Republic* see Sheppard (1980); on the vehicle of the soul see my notes to *Proclus* 3. On the supracosmic soul see Dillon and Morrow (1970), xv, as well as my notes to *Proclus* 23.

126 On the speakers see *Parm.* 628–9 Cousin (where they are related to Being, Mind and Life) and 663–70 (where some are more daemonic, some more godlike). On the antinomies of the *Parmenides* see *Parm.* 1063, with notes at Dillon and Morrow (1970), 418–9.

127 Dillon (1972) maintains that Proclus, *Parm.* 1066 Cousin traces the doctrine of henads to Iamblichus.

nothing but abstractions with a name attached, but still a benign intelligence is expected to respond to the adoration that the philosopher expresses in his seven fervent hymns. We are even told "as it were to hymn" the One in the second book of his *Platonic Theology*, where he illustrates the distinction between the apophatic and kataphatic approaches to the ineffable.[128] The former is the negation of every property; the latter achieves predication through analogies and metaphors. Yet whether we withhold or apply the predicates, the sense of awe remains, because the subject is not only the One, the Good or any other reified adjective; it is equally philosophical to call him God, and even to use mythological appellations. In his annotations to the *Cratylus* of Plato, Proclus says that the names of the gods have power in incantations because the gods themselves have revealed them to us through their intermediaries, and since these lesser beings are homonymous with the greater ones, it is they who come at the call of the theurgist. The task of the philosopher is to disengage the natural signification of a word – its form or *eidos* – from its matter, which is a variable conglomerate of sounds. This he achieves by mastering the art of the "theologians", who can also teach him how to parse the symbols that are vouchsafed to us by gods whom none can name.[129]

Proclus is the author of a number of works on providence, which are generally agreed to rank among the most profound deliberations on the subject. Two questions were particularly taxing for the godly Neoplatonist: how can powers impervious to sense and change be willing or even competent to attend to the affairs of transient creatures? And why, if the gods do exercise such vigilance, are evils so abundant in the world? To the first, Proclus answers that the gods have an immediate and synoptic understanding of the things that present themselves to us through dissipated knowledge; the second can be met with Plato's axiom that privation or affliction in the body do not compromise the happiness of a meritorious soul.[130] Providence is the thread that runs from the summit

---

128 Proclus, *PTh* 2.11 (ii, 65.6 Saffrey and Westerink). For the hymns see Saffrey (1994).

129 See *Crat.* 75.11 Pasquali on revelation through the lesser deities; 4.17–18 etc. on form and matter; 32.18, 65.17–19 and 66.17–20 on gods known only by symbols. On Proclus' attempt to derive a theory of natural language (and magic) from the *Cratylus*, see Hirschle (1979), 3–35.

130 See especially Proclus, *DD* 2.13–16 (22–23 Boese) on the knowledge of the gods; *ibid.* 6.33–7 (54–60 Boese) on the congruity of divine gifts with the character of the recipient. Trouillard (1982), 46–51 explains, with particular reference to Proclus, *Tim.* 107 (i, 352

INTRODUCTION

to the base of Proclus' world, and for the novice in philosophy its first disclosure is likely to be the wise and tactful governance of his tutor. This is the theme of Proclus' *Commentary on the First Alcibiades*, which serves as an introduction to his thought because he believed that Plato had composed dialogue as a preface to a systematic perusal of the corpus. Here, because the approach of Socrates to Alcibiades is portrayed as a sort of courtship, we find the most meticulous analysis of the different kinds of love in Platonic literature; and here, because Alcibiades aspired to be a statesman, Proclus can devise a cunning harmony between the three modes of oratory – forensic, epideictic and deliberative – and the three goals of philosophy – Justice, Beauty and the Good. He asserts that in his role as counsellor Socrates is a good daemon (*agathos daimôn*) to Alcibiades, though in himself he has the paradigmatic qualities of a god. Proclus, in the eyes of his admirers, was a new Socrates, who combined ancestral piety with unprecedented excellence of character.[131] It is therefore not by accident that the Alcibiades commentary has been consulted more than any other in my notes to Marinus' *Proclus, or On Happiness*, the second text translated in this book.

MARINUS AS BIOGRAPHER OF PROCLUS

Marinus was the successor to Proclus at the school in Athens, and left behind him a few remarks on Euclid, which are extant, as well as a dissertation on the *Philebus*, which is lost.[132] Although his name is a Roman one, its best-known bearer in Flavia Neapolis, his native town, was the

---

Diehl) that the five grades of knowledge are: unitive (in the gods), intuitive (in daemons), discursive (in rational natures), imaginative (in souls), sensitive (in the body and lower creatures).

131 See *Alc.* 11 (i, 9 Segonds) on the place of the *Alcibiades*; *Alc.* 30–37 (i, 24–31 Segonds) on varieties of love; *Alc.* 183–4 (ii, 244 Segonds) on the branches of rhetoric; *Alc.* 9 (i, 7 Segonds) and 174 (ii, 236 Segonds) on mystic rites; *Alc.* 198–9 (ii, 256 Segonds) on Socrates as *agathos daimôn*, and 158 (i, 222 Segonds) on his divinity. Modern authorities generally regard the *First Alcibiades* as spurious, but such doubts never troubled the Neoplatonists.

132 See the notice from the *Suda*, used here as a preface to the *Proclus*, as in the edition of Boissonade (1850), 150. Menge's text of the commentary on Euclid's Data, with the French translation of M. Michaux, are appended to Kenneth Guthrie's translation of Boissonade's text of the *Proclus* in the edition of Oikonomides (1977). See *ibid.*, 6–8 on the source of Marinus' name, which does not of course exclude his being Samaritan by birth, though Oikonomides rightly argues that we need not suppose that he was.

father of the Emperor Philip (244–249), who received divine honours there. Marinus' own contemporaries thought him a mediocrity, incapable of grasping the theological interpretation of the Platonic dialogues which his master had expounded. Perhaps he was out to shame them in a chapter of his *Proclus, or On Happiness*, where he tells us how, in the twilight of his master's years, he attended him on his sickbed and was privy to the composition of works that never saw the light of day (27). At the same time, his allusions to the illnesses of Proclus are too frequent to be attributed entirely to his vanity, or even to a sense of impending death which the notorious weakness of his own constitution may have fostered. Disease for him is not the prelude to apotheosis, as in Porphyry, but a gymnasium for the display of moral excellence. Justice, wisdom, temperance and fortitude are the four species of virtue, as in Plato, but, adhering to the scheme set out in Porphyry's *Sententiae*, Marinus held that each of them admits of four degrees. These belong respectively to the body (or the embodied soul), the soul in itself, the intellect, and – so he seems to hint – the "flower of intellect", a level of personhood beyond reflection or experience and hence amenable only to theurgy. One who has passed through all the grades of virtue in his span of years has attained the *eudaimonia* or happiness which Aristotle and many thinkers after him had identified as the goal of human life.[133]

Marinus' work is more than a biography of Proclus, for, notwithstanding his belittlement of rhetoric in chapter 11, he writes with the art and ardour of a sophist. As in panegyrics like the *Agesilaus* of Xenophon or the *Evagoras* of Isocrates, the name of his hero furnishes a title without the addition of the term *bios*; at the same time the second title, *On Happiness*, reminiscent of those bestowed by custom on the Platonic dialogues, betokens an intention to make biography a vehicle of philosophy. In the manner prescribed for orators, Marinus courts the favour of his audience, first for himself, then for his subject; the narrative succeeds the account of personal characteristics, reversing the order followed by Suetonius in his lives of the first twelve Caesars. Since Proclus, more than any man, had lived his own philosophy, there is no dichotomy between life and works such as we have noted in Diogenes Laertius – not even a separate catalogue as in Porphyry. Instead the plan of the treatise is as follows:

---

133 See my notes to chapter 3 on the division of the virtues.

1–2. Apology for the author and introduction to the work.
3–5. Virtues of Proclus proper to the embodied state (physical and ethical).
6–9. Early education and signs of promise in Byzantium, Lycia and Alexandria.
10–13. Philosophical studies in Athens under Plutarch and Syrianus.
14–15. Political conduct, including exile.
16–17. Cultivation of liberal arts and friendship.
18–20. The cathartic or purificatory virtues.
21–25. Contemplative virtues.
26–29. Theurgic studies and writings.
30–33. Tokens of Proclus' affinity to the gods.
34. Summary.
35–37. Death and horoscope.
38. *Envoi*.

We are not surprised to find Proclus represented by Marinus as an adept of theurgy; perhaps it seems perverse that a philosophy which led to this should commence with Aristotle. Nothing, however, would have appeared more natural in that epoch. A commentary on part of the *Metaphysics* is among the few remains of Proclus' tutor Syrianus, while Marinus himself is said to have instructed Isidorus in Aristotelian philosophy during Proclus' tenure of the Athenian chair.[134] The harmony of Plato and Aristotle was now a dogma,[135] though perhaps it was the sacerdotal tradition of his family that caused Plutarch of Athens to put their writings on the soul at the beginning of his curriculum. The religious and the intellectual past converge in such a man, as they also do in the topographical details which provide the scaffold of Marinus' narrative. Athens for him is not so much the centre of Hellenic civilisation as the place where the great philosophers are buried; the journey of his hero from the Piraeus to the Academy is marked by scenes reminiscent of the *Republic* and the *Phaedrus*; the location of his house on the southern slopes of the Acropolis is so carefully, though obscurely, indicated, that

---

134 See the notice from the *Suda* at the beginning of the *Proclus* in this volume.
135 Though the harmony is not always thought to be perfect. Hadot (1991) notes at p. 186 that Elias rebuked Iamblichus for suppressing all divergence, and at 182 that Platonists sometimes defined their own first principle as the Good, rather than as the "God" of Aristotle's *Metaphysics*.

INTRODUCTION   liii

the text is like a treasure-seeker's map to archaeologists, some of whom now believe that they have excavated the ruins of this splendid domicile.[136]

In Porphyry's recollections of Plotinus, it is only ingenuous rivals and disciples who associate particular localities with the gods. For Marinus, on the other hand – and the hymns of Proclus bear him out – a sense of place is inseparable from the piety of the great Athenian scholarch. Byzantium, his birthplace, is the city of a great goddess, whose identity is probably less important than the presence of her cult. Marinus' work is peppered with allusions, both direct and oblique, to this maternal figure: she may be the secret president of the Lydian mysteries in chapter 15, she is certainly the unnamed mother of Attis in chapter 33, and (though it is never mentioned) her temple, the Metroon, was a conspicuous site in Athens, where Proclus was punctilious in his orisons to the Mother of the Gods.[137] The deity who in Julian's *Fifth Oration* is little more than a grand conjecture was for Proclus an acquaintance to be visited, wherever any of her names was known. Almost as ubiquitous, and less fond of his anonymity, is Asclepius, the physician of the immortals. He or his intermediaries appear to the sage in dangerous bouts of sickness, and a vision of his offspring near a Lydian shrine is an index of his presence in that region. He is worshipped under his own name, though no doubt with other rituals, as a lion-headed god of Ascalon. In theurgy the queen of the rites is Hecate, virgin goddess of the underworld, whom Proclus draws to himself with the machinery of the *Chaldaean Oracles*. Athens had its own tutelary virgin, Pallas Athena, who visited Proclus of her own accord to take up residence in his house.[138]

Her arrival was a consequence of the Christian agitation that had expelled her from the Parthenon. Saffrey has conjectured that it was violence from this quarter against the temple of Asclepius that forced Proclus to make his journey into Lydia, which would therefore have fallen around the year 450.[139] If names and dates are lacking in Marinus where we should look for them in Porphyry, his reticence is sometimes the result of fear, or more often (as in Eunapius) of reluctance to

---

136 See my notes to chapters 12 (Plutarch), 36 (Athens), 29 (the house), 10 (the journey).
137 See my notes to chapter 6 (Byzantium) and chapter 33 (Great Mother).
138 See my notes to chapters 32 (Lydia), 19 (Ascalon), 28 (Hecate), 30 (Athena). For Hecate and Athena as aspects of the same goddess see Proclus, *Crat.* 94.29–95.2 Pasquali.
139 See Saffrey (1975) with my notes to *Proclus* 29.

acknowledge Christianity as a subject for his classicising prose. On the same principle, names of Christian sovereigns are excluded, and, notwithstanding the wealth and high connexions of the Athenian Neoplatonists, they cannot be represented as either having or desiring friends at court. Porphyry and Philostratus could flirt with such alliances, but a Greek patrician of the late fifth century was forced to exert his talents in the city, without repining for the larger world where glory was now vouchsafed to none but clergymen and military commanders. At least he was free to shine wherever men could understand him; he did not, like Socrates, think that he owed his life to his native soil because he now knew that the stars had inscribed his destiny in a language more ubiquitous than Greek. Marinus records the horoscope of Proclus, not so much to fix the exact date of his birth in 412[140] – though of course he does so adventitiously – as to build a centrepiece for his mosaic of pagan sciences. Some Platonists may have raised an eyebrow in memory of Plotinus, but in this generation Christians were the only strict opponents of astrology.[141] In the present instance their chagrin will have been compounded by the assertion that the death of Proclus almost coincided, like the crucifixion of Christ, with an eclipse.

The most profound eclipse was still to come. We have seen what Proclus suffered, and in his commentary on the Platonic *Alcibiades* he alleged that such eruptions spring from discord in the soul; even this conjecture was suppressed in the paraphrase of his disciple Olympiodorus.[142] History accords to the Emperor Justinian the honour of having closed the philosophical schools of Athens in 529. Our sources are not unanimous, and in one we read that the scholarchs fled the tyranny of Christendom on their own initiative, only to return in haste from Persia when they found that there was no relief at the court of King Chosroes. Furthermore, it is possible that the brunt of the legislation fell on the schools of jurisprudence, and that philosophy was only a casual victim of the measures designed to curb political

---

140 For discussion see notes to chapter 35.

141 Trombley (1993), 71 notes that Proclus could have been punished for the possession of a horoscope under *Theodosian Code* 9.16.8.

142 For Proclus' strictures on the "atheism" of "the many" see *Alc.* 264 (ii, 307 Segonds), with note by Segonds, 428 on Olympiodorus. Like Damascius, *Isid.* 105 Zintzen on Hypatia, Proclus employs the term *thorubos* ("tumult"); Marinus preferred a more picturesque metaphor.

insubordination.[143] In any case, Damascius, the pupil and biographer of Proclus' own disciple Isidorus, was the last of the Athenian Neoplatonists.[144] Some life remained in the school of Alexandria, where Hierocles, a student of Plutarch of Athens, was a scholarch; the city was also visited by the Athenian Simplicius, still admired for his commentaries on Aristotle.[145] After him came the Christian expositors, Elias and Stephanus, who made handsome use of Neoplatonic arguments; the most famous of the Alexandrian commentators on Aristotle, John Philoponus, was or became a Christian; but since he was an infamous heretic even in his day, he left no mark on posterity but his writings. In 640 the Arabs conquered Egypt in the name of Allah, and, even if the burning of the great library is not to be laid to their account,[146] they certainly appeared to have completed what Justinian had begun.

THE LONGEVITY OF NEOPLATONISM

Yet Neoplatonism survived its founders. By the year 400, it had already left its mark on ecclesiastics such as Gregory of Nyssa and Augustine, who may be called respectively the fathers of the Orthodox and Catholic traditions.[147] Around 500, an otherwise unknown disciple of Proclus, under the name of Paul's Athenian convert Denys the Areopagite, wrote treatises *On the Divine Names* and *On Mystical Theology*, which remain unmatched in their profound austerity by any other Christian work of contemplative literature.[148] Boethius, a Latin-speaking

---

143 The story of the expulsion is accepted by Cameron (1969) and Blumenthal (1978), though the latter (1996), 37–43 observes that Platonic commentary did not become extinct in Alexandria. I find the scepticism of Hallstrom (1994) rather extravagant, though he rightly draws attention to the disparities in our sources.
144 See now Athanassiadi (1999b), 20–64 on his education, exile and return.
145 These late Neoplatonists have only now begun to attract the interest of scholars: see Hadot (1978) for a clear and erudite survey and Schibli (1993) on the eschatology of Hierocles.
146 On the role ascribed by legend to Philoponus in the destruction or partial preservation of the library see Butler (1978), 401–28.
147 See Meredith (1990) on Gregory, Theiler (1933) on Augustine's use of Porphyry and Hadot (1968) on Marius Victorinus as an intermediary. Beatrice (1989) contends that Augustine derived almost the whole of his knowledge of Porphyry from a single work, which subsumes those that we call *On the Regression of the Soul* and *Against the Christians*.
148 See Saffrey (1966) on the word *theandritês* (*Proclus*, chapter 19). Ritter (1994), 4–30 reviews the many theories about the identity and aims of the Areopagite, who may have

Christian of the same period, wrote commentaries on Porphyry's *Isagoge*, while in his theological discourses he combined a belief in immaterial forms with the categories of Aristotle.[149] The Latin schoolmen of the middle ages learned their logic from this Platonising scholar; in the application of Aristotelian arguments to the proof of God's existence and the discovery of his virtues, Europe was indebted to Islamic thinkers, who also came to Aristotle by way of Porphyry.[150] The handful of Latin writers who desired to restore the harmony of the eastern and western churches could not fail to be attracted by a creed that had subsumed the best of many competing systems; John Scotus Eriugena in the ninth century made copious (and as many thought, heretical) use of Neoplatonic texts in his majestic work *On Nature (Periphuseon)*.[151] Intercourse between Italy and Byzantium grew more frequent as the eastern Empire tottered to its ruin.[152] To the Florentine Marsilio Ficino, who translated them in the fifteenth century, Porphyry and Plotinus ranked with Plato as springs of ancient (hence authoritative) wisdom; Pico della Mirandola convened the same authorities, with others, to proclaim his new religion of the "dignity of man".[153] Humanists of a more orthodox persuasion, like Erasmus, could admire the ascetic vein in Platonism.[154] Those who despise the world will not be afraid to leave it suddenly, and it was Porphyry's brief conspiracy against his own life that stirred the

---

been a heretic, a champion of orthodoxy, a Christian apologist for philosophy, an evangelist to the pagans or even a pagan of Christian sympathies. A defence of his Neoplatonism has been felt necessary since the sixth century, as Rorem (1998), 99–137 shows; for a recent one, differentiating his thought from that of pagan Platonists, see Rist (1992).

149 See Ebbesen (1990b) on the value and influence of Boethius' commentaries. At 389–90 he finds Boethius saner than Iamblichus and sometimes more Porphyrian than Porphyry.

150 See Walzer (1967) on Porphyry, and Rosenthal (1975), 151–61 for excerpts from Arabic translations of Proclus and other authors, not always traceable to surviving Greek originals. Dillon (1989) notes that Jewish philosophy also was indebted to the Arabic tradition.

151 See Dillon (1992c) on his use of Porphyry and other Neoplatonists.

152 On Pletho and Bessarion as precursors of the Italian Platonists see Wilson (1992), though he suggests that the importance of Pletho has been exaggerated.

153 On Ficino's knowledge of the Neoplatonists see Allen (1984); on his rejection of Pico's synthesis of Plato and Aristotle see Allen (1989), 9–48. On the manifold varieties and causes of the Platonic revival see Hankins (1990), 3–26.

154 See Screech (1980) on Erasmus' debt to the ascetic mysticism of the Christian Origen (185–254 A.D.) For a subtle consideration of Platonic echoes in the latter see Rist (1964).

imagination of the melancholic Giacomo Leopardi near the end of the nineteenth century. He assumed a poet's licence in his *Dialogue between Porphyry and Plotinus*, inventing many unattested arguments and turning the scale in favour of suicide.[155]

English Protestants turned to Platonism, not only as an alternative to Popery, but as an antidote to secular philosophies that quenched the soul and deified the world. Edmund Spenser's Elizabethan hymns to heavenly love and heavenly beauty were the works of a believer; so was Herbert of Cherbury's defence of the pluralistic faith of Porphyry in his *Dialogue between a Teacher and a Pupil*, which, like many of his other heterodoxies, saw the light long after his death (1734). Donne's lampoon on the doctrine of transmigration in *The Progress of the Soul* outshines the ceremonious prose of the Cambridge Platonists – Ralph Cudworth, Benjamin Whichcote, John Smith and Henry More – but even they can count among their associates such poets as Milton, Vaughan and Traherne.[156] Time and incomprehension have not staled the reputation of the versatile George Berkeley, whose last and (to his mind) greatest work, the *Siris* (1744), comes to an end with a catena of famous passages from Plato. Like him, many poets and artists of the nineteenth century held that it was impossible to give a complete description of reality on mechanistic premises. To free the creative intellect, to reanimate the cosmos, to catch a reverberation of the ineffable – these were typical aspirations of Romanticism, and Plato became an oracle to those who could remember any Greek.

The poet Shelley – famous for his quotable line, "The One remains, the many change and pass" – was a disciple of the ancients in his vegetarianism.[157] A disciple in everything was Thomas Taylor, who styled himself "the Platonist" in defiance of the prevailing Anglicanism.[158] His translations of Plotinus, Porphyry, Proclus, Marinus, Iamblichus and

---

155 In *Pensieri*, translated by Thomson (1905), 276–90. For the symptoms of Leopardi's persistent ill-health see Thomson, 39 etc.

156 Important studies include Patrides (1969), 33–39, with Hunter (1959) on Milton and Marks (1966) on Traherne. For a recent collection of essays on these and other authors see Baldwin and Hutton (1994).

157 In an essay from 1900 on "The Philosophy of Shelley's Poetry", Yeats (1961), 82 cites Taylor's translation of Porphyry's *Cave of the Nymphs*.

158 For his writings see Raine and Harper (1969), and for his possible influence on William Blake see Raine (1963), 4–5.

Pythagorean literature were generally the earliest, and are sometimes even now the only English versions of them. Two authors who paid the tribute of allusion to his rendering of Porphyry's *Life of Plotinus* were the novelist John Meade Falkner (1895) and the greatest name in Irish poetry, William Butler Yeats. Neither was a philosopher in the modern sense, though both could have passed as such in the Renaissance or in late antiquity. They lived at a time when God and science were equally out of fashion, and for some it had become a sign of culture to entertain a learned interest in astrology, alchemy, witchcraft and the summoning of spirits. In Falkner's *The Lost Stradivarius*, the death of the hero is precipitated by an attempt to repeat the evocation of the guardian daemon at *Plotinus* 10, though now it is not a god but an evil genius who emerges.[159] Yeats (though his critics often fail to see this) was more Iamblichean than Plotinian in his mysticism,[160] and looked for immortality through the sublimation rather than the desertion of the body. Works of art – his own and those of his magian predecessors – were for him the only walls that could withstand the siege of time. Perhaps it is for this reason that in his elegant paraphrase of the Delphic Oracle on Plotinus, the progress of the sage becomes more arduous and the assistance of the ancients is required to bring him nearer to his goal:[161]

> Behold that great Plotinus swim
> Buffeted by such seas;
> Bland Rhadmanthus beckons him,
> But the Golden race looks dim,
> Salt blood blocks his eyes.

Yeats wrote most of his poems (though not this) before his fellow-Romantic and compatriot Stephen Mackenna made the first complete translation of the *Enneads* into English (1928). A catalyst to the

---

159 See Wilson's (1954) edition, xxi–xxii on Falkner's occult interests, and 180, 184, 185 and 190 on his acquaintance with Neoplatonism. The name *Porphyrius philosophus* appears in the final paragraph (p. 166 of this edition).

160 Thus Ritvo (1975) makes him thoroughly Plotinian, even in *A Vision* (1925), where the cycle of transmigration is inescapable, and the highest state is that of a work of art. The frequency of circular motions in Yeats's poetry (e.g. "The Gyres" at 340 and "The Second Coming" at 235 of the Allt and Alsprach edition) may bespeak an acquaintance with the *Chaldaean Oracles* in Taylor's rendering.

161 Allt and Alsprach (1989), 320, giving the date of composition as 1931. "The Tower" (1925–7), at 244 and "News from the Delphic Oracle" (1939) at 385 are openly disparaging or satirical, though Wilson (1958), 220 contrives to find a "moving tribute" to Plotinus.

academic study of Plotinus had been provided in two courses of Gifford Lectures, delivered in 1911 and 1912 by Dean Ralph Inge, a combative apologist for Protestant Christianity, who deserves to be called the last of the Cambridge Platonists. For English-speaking readers the doyen of Plotinian scholarship in the twentieth century is Hilary Armstrong, whose work spans sixty years from 1930 to 1990, and whose edition of the life (based on the Oxford text of Henry and Schwyzer) is the one translated here. There has been no complete edition of Proclus in this century, though E.R. Dodds' edition and annotation of the *Elements of Theology* may be counted among the glories of Classical scholarship in England. Dodds was another Irishman, as are such recent students in the field as John O'Meara, Dominic O'Meara, Denis O'Brien, John Dillon, Andrew Smith and Kevin Corrigan. Dillon's *The Middle Platonists* remains after twenty years the indispensable *vade mecum* for the interval between Plato and Plotinus. Important contributions on Plotinus and Middle Platonism have come from North America in the writings of John Whittaker, Frederick Schroeder and Lloyd Gerson. Two other Americans, Gregory Shaw and John Finamore, have done much to elucidate the doctrine of salvation in Iamblichus, while two scholars based in London, Richard Sorabji and Lucas Siorvanes, have claimed for Proclus an honourable mention in the history of science.[162] Both are strict philosophers, but Anne Sheppard has elucidated Proclus' thought in areas that would now be deemed superfluous to that discipline. Many British readers may have made their first acquaintance with the earlier Neoplatonists, whether Christian or pagan, through the numerous books and articles of John Rist.[163]

The works translated here have largely escaped the notice of English-speaking scholars, except as sources of historical information.[164] In Italy, where Leopardi thought the life of Plotinus worth translating (1982), Masullo (1985) has now furnished that of Proclus with a commentary as well as a new edition. Damascius' life of Isidorus now survives in

162 See Sorabji (1983), 33–45 on theories of time from Iamblichus to Damascius, 52–66 on the science of divisibles in the Athenian school and 210–31 on Philoponus and the infinite. Siorvanes (1996) shows that Proclus' views on the planetary system were highly original and even anticipate the Copernican theory.

163 See bibliography for books and articles by the authors named in this and the following paragraph.

164 Cox (1983) and Blumenthal (1978) are notable exceptions. Guthrie's fine translation of the *Proclus* (1925) has been reprinted in Oikonomides (1977).

fragments and the epitome of Photius; it has been edited most recently, with an excellent translation into English and copious notes, by Polymnia Athanassiadi (1999b), herself a professor at Athens. In France a number of distinguished scholars have pooled their labours, under the guidance of Luc Brisson, to produce a two-volume commentary on the life of Plotinus, as monumental in quality as in scope (1982, 1992). I have consulted all these books, together with the commentary on Porphyry's work by Kalligas (1991), and where I am indebted to them I am careful to record it. To indicate at every point how far I agree or disagree with each would be of interest only to a reader who was proposing to write a monograph on the subject, and such a reader would of course have all editions and commentaries to hand. There is a peculiar fitness in having Liverpool University Press as the publisher of the present book, for it is at this university that Tony Lloyd and Henry Blumenthal have conspired with Hilary Armstrong to perpetuate the study of Plotinus and his followers in Britain. In the series of Translated Texts for Historians this volume may be regarded as a companion to Gillian Clark's translation of Iamblichus' *On the Pythagorean Life*. Like hers, it is intended to introduce a great tradition to a wider public, and also to remind scholars that the technical dissertation was not always the only vehicle of philosophy. We have something to learn from a period when this discipline was not yet academic in our sense of the word "academic", and the merits of its professors were estimated, not by their writings, and still less by their reading, but by the quality of their lives.

ON THE LIFE OF PLOTINUS AND THE ARRANGEMENT OF HIS WORKS

1. Plotinus, the philosopher who lived in our time,[1] seemed like one who felt ashamed of being in a body.[2] Feeling as he did, he could not endure to talk about his race, his parents or his country of birth.[3] Painters and sculptors were unendurable to him[4] – so much so indeed that, when Amelius begged him to have a portrait done of himself, he said "Is it not enough to carry the image that nature has put about me?"[5] Did Amelius think that he would agree to leave a more enduring image of the image[6] as though it were some piece worthy of display? So he said no and refused to sit for this purpose; but Amelius had a friend Carterius, the best of the painters living then, whom he got to enter and attend the meetings – it was, in fact, open to anyone to come into the meetings – and

---

1 The phrase *kath' hêmas gegonôs*, possibly a trick of speech inherited from Longinus (chapter 20), may here be used to draw a tacit contrast between the immortal soul and its temporary sojourn in the body. See n. 2 and cf. *Vita Platonis* 6.12–15 Westermann on the distinction between being and *genesis*.

2 All Platonists saw the soul as an immortal, and therefore temporary, tenant in the body. Though many of his successors held that even in heaven the soul possesses a rarefied body (see introduction), Plotinus is generally thought to have adhered to the older notion that the perfect state is incorporeal.

3 See chapter 3.

4 Edwards (1993b) argues that the purpose of this prologue is to reveal the limitations of Amelius' understanding (cf. chapters 3, 10 and 19), and also to imply that this biography will give a truer image of Plotinus than would a visual portrait. Cf. Isocrates, *Evagoras* 4 and 74; Cicero, *Orator* 8–9; Tacitus, *Agricola* 46.2–3. Plutarch's *Sulla* commences with a portrait, but it is easier to represent a statesman's passions than a philosopher's soul.

5 Plotinus, *Enn.* 5.8.1 admits the inspiration of the artist, but deplores the translation of his idea into plastic form. See Rich (1960); Dillon (1986) finds a theory of transcendent imagination in Plotinus.

6 Alluding to Plato, *Rep.* 597d–e, where the painter is said to fashion merely the image of an image. For Plotinus the soul is a self-fashioning *agalma* (*Enn.* 1.6. 9; cf. Plato, *Phaedrus* 252d); if it forgets itself it becomes an *eidôlon* (*Enn.* 3.9.3), the word used here. *Enn.* 2.9.10 notes that the Gnostics used the same phrase (*eidôlon eidôlou*) of the world created by their Demiurge. Pépin (1992), 326 cites Clement of Alexandria, *Protrepticus* 98, which is less pejorative (*eikôn eikonos*).

accustomed him, by being present more and more, to retain more vivid impressions[7] of what he saw. Then Carterius drew a sketch from the figure that was stored within his memory, and Amelius helped to make a better likeness of the outline. Carterius had the talent[8] to produce, without the knowledge of Plotinus, a very faithful portrait of him.[9]

2. Though often afflicted with a disease of the bowels,[10] he would not endure an enema, saying that it was not for an old man to bear such treatments, nor would he consent to remedies taken from beasts,[11] saying that he would not accept nourishment even from the bodies of tame creatures.[12] He kept away from the bath and had himself massaged every day in the house; when those who massaged him died through an aggravation of the plague,[13] he gave up this sort of treatment, and soon succumbed to intense diphtheria.[14] This had not yet become apparent

---

7 Translating *phantasiai*, a term which in *Enn.* 1.8.15.18 signifies an "irrational strike from without". In Neoplatonism it is used pejoratively of sensory perceptions and their traces, though elsewhere (e. g. Philostratus, *Apollonius* 6.19) it denotes the creative imagination. See Watson (1988), Sheppard (1991), Edwards (1993b).

8 For qualified recognition of natural aptitudes see Alcinous, *Isagoge*, 183, and on the Stoic origin of this see Dillon (1993), 183–4. Damascius, *Isid.* 127 allows that one can be a musician by natural aptitude, and uses *euphuês* as a term of praise at 36 etc. Carterius may have possessed *euphuia doxastikos* (*ibid.* 32); all Platonists, however, would agree that philosophy requires discipleship as well as talent.

9 Porphyry's term *eikôn* is less pejorative than *eidôlon;* in *Plotinus*, Mind is an *eikôn* of the One. L'Orange (1951) claims to have identified a portrait of Plotinus, on the evidence of "Oriental features", a transcendental gaze and the high quality of the picture, which he assumes to be commensurate with the greatness of its subject. See Kalligas (1991), 200–201 on other possible survivals.

10 Porphyry here commences his account of Plotinus' death, which occupies this early and prominent place in the life because, according to Plato (*Phaedo* 64a), the whole purpose of philosophy is to prepare us for departure from the body. Its suffering is irrelevant to the happiness or dignity of the soul.

11 Kalligas (1991), 89 cites Galen, 14.298 Kuhn on the popularity of "theriac" remedies in second-century Rome.

12 *Enn.* 3.4.2 implies that Plotinus accepted the "Pythagorean" view that human souls migrated into animals; cf. Plutarch, *On Eating Meats* on this as a reason for vegetarianism. Porphyry may not have held this (Augustine, *City of God* 10.30). He does, however, argue in *Abst.* that animals have rational souls, and that both the killing and the eating of them brutalises human agents. See further Carlier (1998).

13 For plagues in Rome in the mid-third century see Zonaras 12.21 and Kalligas (1991), 90. Grmek (1992), 350 identifies this plague as typhus.

14 The symptoms have suggested elephantiasis to Oppermann (1929), 13–14 and Henry (1934), 26–9. Grmek (1992) argues for tuberculosis. We must allow for some assimilation to

while I was with him, but after my voyage[15] the affliction became so intense that – as I heard on my return from his friend Eustochius, who also remained with him until his death – the clarity and resonance of his voice were destroyed by hoarseness, his vision was blurred and his hands and feet were ulcerated.[16] Since his friends therefore avoided his company on account of his habit of greeting everyone with a kiss, he left the city and, having gone to Campania, took up residence in the house of Zethus, an old friend of his who had died.[17]

Necessary provisions were supplied by the estate of Zethus and also brought from that of Castricius at Minturnae,[18] for Minturnae was where Castricius had his property. As Plotinus was about to die, Eustochius – as he himself informed me – was living in Puteoli and took a long time to come to him; Plotinus said, "I am still waiting for you",[19]

---

the literary epidemic phthiriasis: Keaveney and Madden (1982). Death begins at the extremities for Socrates (*Phaedo* 118a) and also in Damascius, *Isid.* 218. Platonists were peculiarly vulnerable to protracted infirmity: see Marinus, *Proclus* and also Diogenes Laertius 4.3 on Speusippus and 4.61 on Lacydes, both of whom suffered fatal paralysis.

15 See chapter 11.

16 The astrologer Firmicus Maternus, *Math.* 1.20–21, while retaining the substance of this account, adds that Plotinus fell into a "cold torpor", that "a pest erupted through the whole of his skin", and that his entrails gradually dissolved. The thesis of Oppermann (1929) that he derived his information from Eustochius would be more cogent were it not for Maternus' errors (see next note), the vague and conventional style of his embellishments and his undisguised hostility to this notorious critic of his art.

17 Firmicus Maternus, *Math.* 1.14–17 says that Plotinus built himself a home in Campania, thus apparently confusing this retirement with the Platonopolis project. Either he misremembered Porphyry or he used a less accurate source. See Henry (1934) 25–43. On Zethus see chapter 7; it is probable that Plotinus spent his last days as a pensioner of his widow. Does chapter 7 imply that she was the daughter of Theodosius, or had Zethus taken a second wife, the daughter or sister of Castricius Firmus, who had once owned the estate and retained a tutelary interest in it after the death of Zethus?

18 See chapter 7, where Zethus too is said to have resided at Minturnae in property which Castricius must have either sold or given to him. Both men are clearly wealthier than Plotinus, living in Rome but possessing rural seats in the manner of Cicero and Catullus. Castricius, a loyal disciple of Plotinus here, survived him and is reproached at *Abst.* 85.1ff Nauck for his failure to keep to a vegetarian diet.

19 That is, waiting to die. The scene resembles the deathbed of Pherecydes, who had no-one but Pythagoras in attendance (Porphyry, *Pyth.* 24.11–14 Nauck). Socrates' dying utterance, "we owe a cock to Asclepius" (*Phaedo* 118a 7–8) was taken by Platonists to mean that death is the cure for the disease of life, since Asclepius was the patron of physicians (Damascius, *Phaed.*, 205.24–7 Norvin). For a (malicious) comparison with Socrates see Firmicus Maternus, *Math.* 1.20.

adding that he was trying to raise the divine in himself to the divine in the all.[20] As a snake crept under the bed in which he was lying and slipped out through a hole that was there in the wall,[21] he gave up the ghost.[22] He had lived, according to Eustochius, sixty-six years, this being the end of the second year of Claudius.[23] Now when he died, I Porphyry was staying in Lilybaeum, Amelius in Syrian Apamea, Castricius in Rome,[24] and Eustochius alone was with him. If we reckon back from the second year of the reign of Claudius to sixty-six years before, the time of his birth falls in the thirteenth year of the reign of Severus.[25] He did not tell anyone either the month in which he was born, nor his natal day,[26] nor did he ask anyone either to sacrifice or feast on his birthday,[27] even

20 Henry (1953) notes that manuscripts offer three variants here. Plotinus was saying either: "Try to raise the divine in yourselves to the divine in the all"; or "Try to raise the god in yourselves to the divine in the all"; or "I am trying to raise the god in me/us (*hêmin*) to the divine in the all". I prefer the last because: (a) it seems more natural to read the infinitive *peirasthai* as reported speech than as an imperative; (b) Plotinus speaks of the "god in us (*hêmin*)" at *Enn.* 6.5.1; (c) he is represented elsewhere in the *Plotinus* as using the first-person plural of himself (e.g. chapter 15), but has no reason to use the second-person plural here; (d) the change from first to second person is easily accounted for by the fact that the phrase became proverbial (Synesius, *Epistle* 138), but the reverse would be more difficult to explain. "The divine in the all" would be a highly unusual designation for the One, but if Plotinus were alluding to intellect (as probably at *Enn.* 2.3.9.15 and 4.8.1), the aspiration would be, if anything, humbler than the achievement described at *Enn.* 4.8.1, where all but the highest plane of intellect is transcended.
21 In his edition of the *Enneads* Bréhier (1924), 2 n.1 suggests that this is Hermes Trismegistus, widely venerated in Eustochius' native Alexandria. I suspect that this would mean less to Porphyry than the association of serpents with the god Asclepius (n.16); he may also be sneering at Heraclides Ponticus, an eccentric Peripatetic, who concealed a snake in his shroud in the hope that it would be taken for his soul quitting the body (Diogenes Laertius 5.6.89).
22 The phrase is (perhaps intentionally) reminiscent of Mark 15.37 and Luke 23.46.
23 That is in 270. See appendix.
24 To prove himself a legitimate successor, a pupil had to explain his absence from the master's deathbed. See Plato, *Phaedo* 59b, Owen (1983), 12.
25 204–5, if we take April 193 as Severus' year of accession and date his second year from mid-193. Plotinus must in fact be born in 204 to be 66 in 270.
26 Eunapius, *Sophists,* 455.34–5 Boissonade-Dübner claims to know that he was an Egyptian from "Lyco" (unknown). The *Suda* gives his birthplace as the large town of Lycopolis, and Zucker (1950) builds a speculative article on this claim. The city certainly produced philosophers, such as the anti-Manichaean writer Alexander (c. 300), on whom see Van der Horst and Mansfeld (1974).
27 As, for example, Epicurus did (Cicero, *On Goals* 2.101–2); contrast also the horoscope of Proclus (*Proclus* 35) and the (metaphorical) statement of Eunapius, *loc. cit.,* that

though he sacrificed and feasted his friends on the traditional birthdays of Plato and Socrates,[28] when those of his friends who had the skill were required to read a speech to the gathering.[29]

3. The following is, however, what he himself told us unprompted, as he was wont to do in conversation.[30] He used to run to his nurse, even when he was going to grammar-school, right up to the eighth year of his birth, uncovering her breasts and craving to suck them. But when he heard that he was an irksome child, he was abashed and stopped. Next, in his twenty-eighth year,[31] he conceived a bent for philosophy and went to hear the leading celebrities of the time in Alexandria; but he came away from hearing them despondent and full of grief, and went so far as to tell a friend of his disappointment. The friend, perceiving what his soul desired, led him to Ammonius,[32] with whom he was hitherto unacquainted. But when he attended his class and heard him, he said to his friend, "This is the man I was seeking".[33] From that day on he remained continuously in the company of Ammonius, and achieved such proficiency in philosophy that he was also eager to acquaint himself with the corresponding practices of the

---

the altars of Plotinus are still smoking. The Christian Origen shared a similar prejudice against birthdays (*Homily on Leviticus* 8.3), but fear of astrologers may have been a motive for Plotinus' reticence (see chapter 10).

28 *Vita Platonis* 6.10ff Westermann says that Plato's birthday fell on the day of Apollo (the seventh of the month Thargelion) and that of Socrates on the day of Artemis, which immediately preceded it. Plotinus' sacrifices were no doubt meatless like those of Pythagoras: Porphyry, *Pyth.*, 36.8–10 Nauck.

29 See further chapter 15.

30 Contrast the only autobiographical passage in the *Enneads* (4.8.1, sixth treatise), which alludes to an intellectual rapture. From this anecdote we may surmise that Plotinus' family was not poor, and had perhaps retained his nurse to feed his younger siblings.

31 That is, 232–3. Other claims to have done the rounds of the philosophical schools occur in Lucian, *Menippus* 3 and Justin Martyr, *Trypho* 2–9 (both mid-second century).

32 The fourth-century historian Ammianus Marcellinus, 22.16.15–16 says that he came from Bruchion in Alexandria. The fourth-century Christian philosopher Nemesius of Emesa (*On Human Nature* 3.20), who quotes him on the "unconfused commingling" whereby the incorporeal soul coexists with a body but is not degraded by it: see Rist (1988). Another Christian, Theodoret, in the fifth-century, calls him Ammonius Saccas (a name derived from carrying loads), and indicates a date of birth c. 170 (*Remedies* 6.61). Langerbeck (1957) reconstructs his thought; see Dodds (1960) for his influence on Plotinus.

33 Antisthenes spoke similarly on discovering Socrates: Jerome, *Against Jovinian* 2.14.34.

Persians[34] and the way that was followed in India.[35] And as the Emperor Gordian was preparing an expedition against the Persians,[36] he gave his services as a soldier and went along with them, being already in his thirty-ninth year.[37] For he had remained as a student with Ammonius for eleven whole years. But when Gordian perished near Mesopotamia,[38] he escaped with difficulty to Antioch and survived.[39] And when the Emperor Philip assumed power, he went up to Rome, being forty years of age.[40]

Now a pact had been made between Herennius, Origen[41] and

---

34 On Greek interest in Zoroaster and the Magi see Bidez-Cumont (1938), Kingsley (1990). *Vita Platonis* 4.7–11 Westermann states that war prevented Plato from visiting them, while Porphyry, *Pyth.* 23.8–9 Nauck says that Pythagoras studied with "Zaratas" (Zoroaster). Puech (1978), 61 suggests that Plotinus had heard of Mani, founder of the dualistic Manichaean religion, who accompanied King Sapor on his campaigns. Since, however, Plotinus (unlike Porphyry) shows no interest in alien wisdom, Edwards (1994) argues that he wanted to go to Rome after failing to become head of Ammonius' school.

35 On ancient knowledge of India see André and Filliozat (1986). Since Alexander's campaigns, the Indian "naked sages" had enjoyed a high reputation, augmented in the third century by an embassy to the emperor Elagabalus (218–222), commemorated by Porphyry at *Abst.* 256 Nauck. This may have been the inspiration for the fictitious visit of Apollonius of Tyana to India at Philostratus, *Apollonius* 3. Porphyry (*On the Styx*, Fr. 376 Smith) records a miracle witnessed by Apollonius in that region; his admiration for the Brahmins is revealed here and at *Abst.* 256; compare Numenius, Fr. 1 Des Places. At *City of God* 10.32 Augustine reports that Porphyry coupled Indians with Chaldaeans as masters of theurgy. On the other hand, Plotinus, as Armstrong (1936) notes, never reached India.

36 Gordian III (238–244) was the favourite of the Senate after a period of anarchy and usurpation. His expedition against the resurgent Persian Empire began in north Africa.

37 That is, 243–4. See appendix.

38 An area corresponding roughly to modern Iraq. Sapor claims to have killed him in battle: Olmstead (1942), supported by Eadie (1996), 144–5. He is also said to have been killed by his successor Philip the Arab and/or other conspirators: *Sybylline Oracles* 13.20, *Augustan History, Gordian* 29.2ff. Porphyry does not imply any personal motive for the flight of Plotinus, which is easily explained as it coincided with the defeat and rout of the Roman army. See Edwards (1994), against the theory of Harder (1960) that Plotinus was attached to the senatorial interest represented by Gordian.

39 This passage, together with the silence of Sapor's inscriptions, seems to refute the statement of the notoriously unreliable *Augustan History* (*Gordian* 26.5) that Antioch fell to the Persians in 242/3. See further Eadie (1996), 143–4.

40 The year is 244. Potter (1990), 210 notes that if Plotinus had been a friend of Gordian, Rome might not have been safe for him under Philip, the beneficiary and alleged author of his death.

41 Named as a fellow-philosopher of Porphyry, who left some written works, by Eunapius, *Sophists* 457.10 Boissonade-Dübner. This is not the Christian Origen (185–254), who

Plotinus that they would not reveal any of the doctrines which Ammonius had elucidated for them in his meetings.[42] Plotinus carried on seminars with some of those who came to him, but avoided the exposition of the doctrines taught by Ammonius. Herennius was the first to break the pact,[43] then Origen followed the precedent of Herennius, though he wrote nothing except the treatise *On Daemons*[44] and, in the reign of Gallienus, *That the King is the Sole Creator*.[45] Plotinus, for his part, refrained from writing for a long time, although he based his classes on his seminars with Ammonius; and thus he went on for a whole ten years, holding seminars with some but writing nothing. Now his classes, since he urged those who were present to conduct the inquiry, were full of disorder and a great deal of nonsense, as Amelius informed me.[46] Amelius joined him in the third year of his residence in Rome, in the third year of the Emperor Philip, and he remained in his company for twenty-four whole years until the first year of the reign of Claudius.[47] When he arrived he owed his education to seminars with Lysimachus, but he surpassed all his contemporaries in assiduity in that he had transcribed and collated all the writings of Numenius and had almost the

---

died near the beginning of Gallienus' reign, having written many volumes. Porphyry, cited by Eusebius, *HE* 6.19, records that he too was taught by an Ammonius, whom most (following Theodoret) assume to be Saccas. But Goulet (1977) suggests that Porphyry merely confused the two Origens, while Dörrie (1955) posits two Ammonii. Edwards (1993a) argues that the Christian was taught by the Peripatetic Ammonius (see chapter 20).

42 Often described as a Pythagorean pact, because novices were sworn to secrecy: Schroeder (1987), 518–9. No doubt the story illustrates the humility of the three disciples – though the term *akroasesin* ("meetings") hardly implies that they were intimates of Ammonius: on *akroatai* see chapter 7.

43 Perhaps because he became the master of Ammonius' school. Nothing is known of him, though there was a wealthy family of Herennii in Africa: Apuleius, *Apology* 67.

44 Numenius, Fr. 37 Des Places may suggest that this was an interpretation of the Atlantis myth in the *Timaeus*. The Christian Origen gave a pejorative sense to the word daemon like all his co-religionists.

45 Possibly not a compliment to Gallienus' poetry, but an (?anti-Gnostic) affirmation of the view that Plato's highest principle (styled the "king of all" in his Second Letter) was the world-creator or Demiurge of his *Timaeus*. This treatise was probably written after 263, as Longinus' letter in chapter 20 makes no mention of it; it is therefore futile to emend the name Gallienus in order to make it possible for the Christian Origen (d. 254) to have written it.

46 On his life and writings see Brisson (1987a) and chapter 7. He was evidently the star of the school before (and perhaps after) the arrival of Porphyry.

47 That is, from 245 to 269. Because Philip succeeded Gordian early in 244, his first year ends in mid-244, his third begins in mid-245. Claudius' first is 268–9.

whole by heart.[48] And having made notes of the seminars,[49] he put together some hundred books of notes, which he dedicated to the Apamean Hostillianus Hesychius,[50] whom he adopted as his son.

4. Now in the tenth year of the reign of Gallienus,[51] I Porphyry, having come from Greece with Antonius the Rhodian, found Amelius in the eighteenth year of his association with Plotinus,[52] though he had not yet ventured to write anything but the notes, which did not yet come to a hundred in total. In the tenth year of Gallienus, Plotinus was about fifty-nine years old, and I Porphyry began my association with him when I myself was thirty years of age.[53] Since the first year of Gallienus, however, Plotinus had been urged to put in writing the speculations that cropped up, and by the tenth year of Gallienus' reign, when I Porphyry first made his acquaintance, I find that he had written twenty-one books, which I also received,[54] though they had been distributed only to a few people. For there was as yet no ready and accessible distribution; it was not done simply and on easy terms, but with the keenest scrutiny of the recipients. These were also the writings to which he himself supplied no titles, so that everybody gave a different rubric to each of

---

48 For Lysimachus the Stoic see chapter 20. Numenius of Syrian Apamea (fl.150) was a pioneer in the allegorical reading of Greek literature, who married a systematic account of Plato's metaphysics with doctrines derived from other cultures, mystery religions and the "Pythagorean" tradition. See Dodds (1960), Des Places (1973) and chapter 17 below.

49 A parallel with the picture (chapter 1) suggests itself. Since most of our fragments of Numenius, *On the Good* come from Eusebius, *PE* 11, and this work also quotes Plotinus from a non-Porphyrian version (*PE* 15.22), Amelius may have been Eusebius' source for both.

50 The adoption of this otherwise unknown person suggests that Amelius took up residence as a teacher in Apamea, perhaps succeeding to the school where his admired Numenius had once presided.

51 That is, 262–3. Gallienus was proclaimed co-Emperor with his father Valerian in 253.

52 Antonius is otherwise unknown. The calculation fixes 246 as Amelius' first year with Plotinus. Porphyry had studied with Longinus (*Plotinus* 20 and Eunapius, *Sophists* 456.8–18 Boissonade-Dübner) and records his actions on the feast of Plato: Eusebius, *PE* 10.3.1, Bidez (1913), 30n.

53 Yielding 232–3 as his date of birth.

54 Armstrong writes: "I found that he had written twenty-one treatises, and I also discovered that few people had received copies of them". Thus he renders *heurisketai* (literally "were found") and *kateilêpha* ("discovered" in Armstrong) as near-synonyms. But Porphyry is not prone to elegant variation, and I have therefore assumed that change of verb denotes an important change of meaning. His self-aggrandisement is typical.

them. The following titles are the ones that eventually prevailed. I shall add also the opening words of the books, so that each of the books I refer to will be easily recognised from its opening words:[55]

1. *On Beauty* [1.6]. Of which the opening is: "The beautiful is primarily visual".[56]
2. *On the Immortality of the Soul* [4.7]. Of which the opening is: "If the individual is immortal".
3. *On Destiny* [3.1]. Of which the opening is: "All that comes to be".
4. *On the Essence of the Soul* [4.2]. Of which the opening is: "The essence of the soul".
5. *On Mind, the Ideas and Being* [5.9]. Of which the opening is: "All men from the beginning".
6. *On the Descent of the Soul into Bodies* [4.8]. Of which the opening is: "Many times waking".
7. *How what is after the First comes from the First; and on the One* [5.4]. Of which the opening is: "If there is something after the First".[57]
8. *Whether all Souls are One* [4.9]. Of which the opening is: "Just as soul".

---

55 Plotinus is the only philosopher of antiquity whose works can be arranged in an undisputed chronological order. Some have seen a progress in his thought from a dualistic beginning to the more harmonious "Neoplatonism" of his maturity, perhaps with the attack on the Gnostics (33) as a watershed. Close studies of the texts, however, have failed to confirm any theory of smooth development, and we must remember (a) that Plotinus wrote nothing before the age of 40; (b) that according to chapter 16 he wrote not one, but numerous refutations of the Gnostics; and (c) that candid thinkers often sway back and forth between opinions throughout their lives.

56 It would be possible to see the first nine treatises as an attempt to create a "system", the first being an appeal to quit the world of sense for that of philosophical inquiry, while the ninth culminates in the encounter with the One. Both surpass the later treatises in their echoes of Numenius, a somewhat pessimistic Platonist of the previous century suggesting that he was, at that time, the chief source of discussion. This would account for Amelius' adherence to Plotinus and the charges of plagiarism in chapter 18.

57 Maijer (1992), 35–52 argues that Plotinus' thought underwent a sudden refinement, between the writing of this treatise and that of no. 9 (*Enn.* 6.9), where the first principle is styled "the One" and is stripped of its intellectual or noetic attributes. The term "First" is not Platonic: its source may be the (spurious) *Second Epistle* of Plato, dear to Pythagoreans, which speaks (312) of a "second" and "third" principle, though not explicitly of a first. Plutarch, *Isis and Osiris* 352a may be even earlier.

9. *On the Good or the One* [6.9]. Of which the opening is: "All that exists".
10. *On the Three Primary Hypostases* [5.1]. Of which the opening is: "What is it that has made souls".[58]
11. *On the Generation and Order of the things after the First* [5.2]. Of which the opening is "The One is all".
12. *On the two Kinds of Matter* [2.4]. Of which the opening is: "What is called matter".
13. *Various Considerations* [3.9]. Of which the opening is: "Mind, says [Plato], sees indwelling ideas."[59]
14. *On the Circular Motion* [2.2]. Of which the opening is: "Why it moves in a circle".[60]
15. *On the Spirit to which we are Allotted* [3.4]. Of which the opening words are: "Some things have their substance".[61]
16. *On Departing Rationally* [1.9]. Of which the opening is; "You shall not draw it out that it may not go out".[62]
17. *On Quality* [2.6]. Of which the opening is: "The existent and essence".
18. *Whether there are Ideas of Individuals* [5.7]. Of which the opening is: "If there are of the individual".
19. *On Virtues* [1.2]. Of which the opening is: "Since evils are here".
20. *On Dialectic* [1.3]. Of which the opening is: "What art or way".

---

58 The *hypostasis* is the mode in which a transcendent principle is able to "subsist", either at its own or a lower level. It is Porphyry, not Plotinus, who speaks expressly of three *hypostases*, perhaps with an ironic allusion to Christianity (Origen, *Commentary on John* 2.10 etc.).

59 An early treatise on Plato, *Timaeus* 39e, which was also used as a proof-text by the Gnostics (*Enn.* 2.9.6.17–19). Perhaps this is another of the "numerous refutations" (chapter 16), of which *Enn.* 2.9 (the 33rd treatise) is now the sole named survivor.

60 The circular or perfect motion is ascribed to the heavens in Plato's *Timaeus* and *Epinomis*, and Aristotle's *On the Heavens*.

61 See chapter 10. My translation aims at a literal rendering of the Greek, though Armstrong's "On our Allotted Personal Daemon" is closer to English idiom and to Plato's original meaning in *Republic* 620b and *Timaeus* 90a.

62 A short essay against suicide. If we believe Cumont (1919), a later edition of this work will have been produced by Porphyry after Plotinus dissuaded him from taking his own life (see chapter 11 and note). As it stands it is fragmentary, and opens with an allusion to the so-called *Chaldaean Oracles* (Michael Psellus, *Exegesis* 1125c–d), a theosophic collection valued by later Neoplatonists. See Dillon (1992a) on verbal parallels between Plotinus and the *Oracles*.

21. *How the Soul is said to Mediate between Undivided and Divided Being* [4.1]. Of which the opening is: "In the intelligible cosmos".

These, then, twenty-one in number, were found to have been written when I Porphyry first came to him, Plotinus being then in his fifty-ninth year.[63]

5. I began to associate with him in that year, and after that for another five years; for I Porphyry arrived in Rome a little before the tenth anniversary [of Gallienus],[64] and Plotinus was enjoying a summer vacation, though maintaining conversation with his students. During these six years,[65] many discussions occurred in the seminars, and, when Amelius and I begged him to put them in writing, he wrote:

22–3. Two books *On what it means for Being to be everywhere wholly present, One and the Same* [6.4–5]. The first of these has as its opening: "The soul then is everywhere". And the opening of the second is: "To be one and the same in number."

And next he wrote another two, of which one is:

24. *On the fact that what is beyond Being does not Think, and What is the Primary Thinking Agent, and what the Secondary one* [5.6]. Of which the opening is: "There is the case where one thing thinks another, and the case where the same thing thinks itself".

And the other is:

25. *On the Potential and Actual* [2.5]. Of which the opening is: "Some things are said to exist potentially".
26. *On the Impassibility of Incorporeals* [3.6]. Of which the opening is: "Not equating perceptions with affections".
27. *On the Soul I* [4.3]. Of which the opening is: "All the problems that must be raised about the soul".
28. *On the Soul II* [4.4]. Of which the opening is: "What then is one to say".
29. *On the Soul III*, or *On How we See* [4.5]. Of which the opening is: "Since we have proposed".

---

63 Confirming the date as 262–3 (Plotinus, born in 204, being now 58).
64 The Decennalia occurred in 263.
65 Meaning perhaps five years and somewhat more: he does not say "six whole years", but see appendix.

30. *On Contemplation* [3.8]. Of which the opening is: "Speaking playfully at first".
31. *On Intelligible Beauty* [5.8]. Of which the opening is: "Since we have said".
32. *On Intellect, and that the Intelligibles are not outside the Intellect, and on the Good* [5.5]. Of which the opening is: "Intellect, the true intellect".
33. *Against the Gnostics* [2.9]. Of which the opening is: "Since we have concluded". [66]
34. *On Numbers* [6.6]. Of which the opening is: "Plurality is".
35. *How Things seen far off appear Small* [2.8]. Of which the opening is: "As for things seen far off".
36. *Whether Happiness depends on a length of time?* [1.5]. Of which the opening is: "Being happy". [67]
37. *On Total Commingling* [2.7]. Of which the opening is: "Of the so-called total".
38. *How the Multitude of Ideas has come to Exist and on the Good* [6.7]. Of which the opening is: "God, sending into generation".
39. *On the Voluntary* [6.8]. Of which the opening is: "There is in the case of the gods".
40. *On the Cosmos* [2.1]. Of which the opening is: "Affirming the cosmos to be everlasting".
41. *On Perception and Recollection* [4.6]. Of which the opening is: "Perceptions are not impressions".
42. *On the Kinds of Being I* [6.1]. Of which the opening is: "What and how many kinds of being there are".
43. *On the Kinds of Being II* [6.2]. Of which the opening is: "Since, concerning the aforesaid".
44. *On the Kinds of Being III* [6.3]. Of which the opening is: "As to being, where it appears".
45. *On Eternity and Time* [3.7]. Of which the opening is: "Eternity and time".

---

66 It is only during the time of his acquaintance with Plotinus that Porphyry notes that certain works are logically consecutive and acknowledges this in his ordering of the *Enn.* But here it seems that Porphyry has disguised the continuity between this and the three preceding treatises, which is so complete that Harder (1936) treats all four as a single *magnum opus* (*Grossschrift*), while Cilento (1971) regards them as an "anti-Gnostic training". See further chapter 16 and 25; the latter gives a new title characterising the opponents.

67 Strictly: "If happiness increases". See chapter 24.

These twenty-four books are all the ones that he wrote in the six-year period when I Porphyry was in his company, commencing his speculations from problems as they arose,[68] as I have shown in the headings of each book. Adding the twenty-one composed before my sojourn with him, the total comes to forty-five.

6. During my stay in Sicily – for I went there about the fifteenth year of Gallienus[69] – Plotinus, having written these five books, sent them to me:

46. *On Happiness* [1.4]. Of which the opening is: "To live well and be happy".
47. *On Providence I* [3.2]. Of which the opening is: "To mechanical operation".
48. *On Providence II* [3.3]. Of which the opening is: "What then are we to conclude about this?"
49. *On the Knowing Hypostases and what is Beyond* [5.3]. Of which the opening is: "That which thinks itself must be complex".
50. *On Love* [3.5]. Of which the opening is: "As to love, whether it is a god".

These, then, were the ones he sent in the first year of the reign of Claudius.[70] At the beginning of the second, in which he also died shortly after, he sent these:

51. *What are evils?* [1.8]. Of which the opening is: "Those who seek the origin of evils".[71]
52. *Whether the Stars are causes* [2.3]. Of which the opening is: "The course of the stars".[72]
53. *What is the Living Creature?* [1.1]. Of which the opening is: "Pleasures and pains".
54. *On Happiness* [1.7]. Of which the opening is: "Should one posit another".[73]

---

68 Hence these writings often deal with problems (e.g. 22–3, 27) or engage in refutation of other thinkers (33 against the Gnostics, 37 against the Stoics, 42–4 against Aristotle).
69 267–8; see chapter 11.
70 268–9.
71 Called *Whence are Evils?* in chapter 24.
72 Presumably chapter 15 alludes to this work.
73 See chapter 24 for a different title and a longer excerpt.

When these later writings are added to the earlier forty-five the total is fifty-four. But some were written in his earliest phase, some in his prime and some in the period of his bodily sickness, and the treatises show a corresponding variation in genius. For the first twenty-one are works of lesser genius, not yet sufficiently developed for well-toned writing. Those which belong to the second period of publication display the maturity of genius, and are the twenty-four most finished, apart from the short ones.[74] The last five, however, were written when his genius was already failing; that is true at any rate of the last four, more than of the earlier five.

7. Now while he had many hearers, his followers,[75] who frequented his seminars for the sake of philosophy, were Amelius from Tuscany, whose family name was Gentilianus,[76] but the Master[77] presumed to introduce an "r" and call him Amerius, saying that it was more fitting that his name should derive from *amereia* (indivisibility) than from *ameleia* (indifference).[78] Another of them was a certain doctor from Scythopolis, Paulinus, to whom Amelius gave the nickname Mikkalos,[79] because he was so prone to misunderstanding. But there was also another doctor, the Alexandrian Eustochius, who made his acquaintance near the end of his life and continued to attend on him until his death, acquiring the character of a true philosopher by his exclusive adherence to the school of Plotinus.[80] Another was Zoticus, a poet and critic, who emended the

74 The period coincides with that of Porphyry's acquaintance with Plotinus.
75 A distinction appears to be made here between hearers (*akroatai*) and the more intimate "followers" (*zêlôtai*); Pythagoreans similarly contrasted the *acousmatici*, who obeyed the precepts literally, with the *mathêmatici*, who applied them with understanding. Although the seminars (*sunousiai*) did not exclude the "hearers" (see chapter 1), we may assume that only the *zêlôtai* spoke.
76 Taran (1984), confirming Amelius' Etruscan pedigree, notes that Eunapius, *Sophists* 457.10 Boissonade-Dübner writes Amerius. But the letters "r" and "l" were easily confounded by speakers with a lisp (Aristophanes, *Wasps* 45) and puns on name abound, both in the *Plotinus* and in Plato's dialogues: *Symposium* 198c, *Gorgias* 481d–e etc.
77 Porphyry uses only the pronoun *autos*, as Pythagoreans did when quoting the founder of their sect.
78 Significant etymologies were often sought for the names of gods on the authority of Plato's *Cratylus*. Indivisibility is the characteristic of the Platonic Ideas, because they contain no matter.
79 Replacing the Latin root connoting smallness for a Greek one of the same meaning. Cf. Maximus and Megalos in chapter 17.
80 Eustochius is credited with having produced his own edition of Plotinus' works, no doubt anticipating that of Porphyry. See Schwyzer (1951), 488 and scholiast on *Enn.* 4.4.29.

works of Antimachus and turned the *Atlanticus* into poetry of a high order; however, he lost his sight and died a little before the death of Plotinus.[81] Paulinus was another whose death anticipated that of Plotinus. Among his friends there was also Zethus, an Arabian by race: he took to wife the daughter of Theodosius, who had become one of Ammonius' friends.[82] This man too was a doctor and extremely dear to Plotinus. But he was a man of the political class with political aspirations, which Plotinus kept trying to curb.[83] Plotinus was very intimate with him, so that he even used to visit him at his rural seat, six miles from Minturnae, the former property of Castricius, surnamed Firmus. The latter was of all our contemporaries[84] the greatest lover of beauty,[85] venerating Plotinus and serving Amelius as a loyal retainer in all capacities, while to me Porphyry he acted in all things the part of a true brother. He was another who combined his veneration of Plotinus with the choice of a political career.

His hearers also included not a few members of the Senate, of whom Marcellus, Orontius and Sabinillus were the ones who made most progress in philosophy.[86] There was also another senator, Rogatianus,

81 Antimachus was an epic poet of the third century B.C. well known for his turgid prolixity; the *Atlanticus* is the *Critias* of Plato, which contains a long, though incomplete, account of the topography and history of this imaginary domain. The *Critias* is the sequel to the *Timaeus*, which gave rise to many essays in this period on the relation between the Demiurge, or Creator, and the Good (see notes on Origen in chapter 3, *Enn.* 3.9 in chapter 4 and the Gnostics in chapter 16).

82 This may imply that Theodosius came to Italy with, or in the wake of, Plotinus; or Zethus could have met his father-in-law in Alexandria, as his friendship with Plotinus might be taken to imply. John Dillon observes, in an unpublished paper, that the original name of Zethus the Arab was probably Zayd.

83 As Socrates did that of Glaucon: Xenophon, *Memorabilia* 3.6. In Roman times philosophers did not have the same access to, or interest in, the arts of government as in the era of the city-state, and most would have agreed with Porphyry (*Sent.* 32) in his low valuation of the practical virtues.

84 *Ton kath' hêmas* seems to me to mean something more than members of his own circle; cf. *kat' auton* ("in his time") in chapter 16. As *Enn.* 5.5.12 makes clear, the lover of beauty has not reached the highest level of philosophy. See chapter 2 on Plotinus' death at Minturnae.

85 See Plato, *Phaedrus* 248d and notes on the pursuit of beauty in chapter 23.

86 All otherwise unknown. The Senate was traditionally the ruling council of Rome, composed of men of the wealthiest class. As riches were hereditary, so usually was office, and members of such families considered it as much an obligation as a privilege. However, the Emperors greatly curtailed the power of this body, sometimes putting senators to death if their opposition was too vigorous, and under Gallienus (253–68) they were excluded from

whose conversion[87] from that life was so complete that he renounced all his possessions, manumitted the whole of his household[88] and even renounced his title. When he was about to go forth as a praetor,[89] in the presence of the attendants he neither went forth nor paid any attention to his magistracy; electing not even to live in his own house, he went the rounds of his friends and associates, dining here and sleeping there, though eating only every other day. The consequence of his renunciation and indifference to life was that, though he suffered so much from gout that he had to be carried on a litter, he recovered his strength and, though he was unable to stretch out his hands, he used them much more ably than those who engaged in manual trades. Plotinus made him welcome and, heaping the highest praise upon him, constantly held him up as an example to those who engaged in philosophy. Another disciple was the Alexandrian Serapion,[90] who was at first a rhetorician, but later also came to hear philosophical discussions; however, he was unable to renounce a weakness for money and for lending it at interest.[91] And also among his closest friends he had me Porphyry the Tyrian,[92] and he also requested me to edit his writings.

---

military command at a time when the army dominated politics. In maintaining such relations both with senators and with Gallienus (chapter 12), Plotinus showed the tact which was conventionally admired in private men: Nepos, *Atticus* 6 and 8.4 .

87 Philosophy, being a way of life, not merely a system of doctrine, was expected to revolutionise the ambitions and pursuits of its adherents. See Jaeger (1948), 426–61 and Nock (1933). But philosophical senators (Cicero, Brutus, Seneca, Helvidius Priscus) had hitherto upheld republican institutions, and Plotinus' seduction of individual politicians may not have endeared him to the Senate as a whole.

88 Under the Empire, it was common for dying (and even living) masters to release their slaves, not only out of compassion but to relieve the estate of a financial burden.

89 The praetorship was an office which could lead to the consulate or military command. After Augustus it was the function of the praetors to administer the treasury, perform some judicial functions and preside at public games. The attendants in this narrative are the lictors, who carried the rods of office when it was assumed by the incumbent.

90 Note the predominance of Alexandrians – Eustochius, Theodosius, Serapion – the last of whom, like Origen and Ammonius, has a "theophoric" name derived from an Egyptian deity.

91 In the second and third centuries, the profession of sophist or showpiece orator was a lucrative one, and some, like Herodes Atticus, were notorious for their wealth. The quarrel between philosophy and rhetoric begins with the *Phaedrus* and *Gorgias* of Plato, and, though the two disciplines were always mutually dependent, a sharp distinction was still drawn in the third century, as in Philostratus' *Sophists*.

92 Announcing his non-Greek origin, which is by no means incompatible with becoming "Greek by culture". See Swain (1996).

ON THE LIFE OF PLOTINUS

8. Plotinus, when he had written something, could never bear to revise it,[93] not even to read over and go through it, because his vision did not serve him for reading. When he wrote he did not aim at elegance in forming the letters, nor did he divide the syllables clearly, nor had he any concern for spelling, paying attention only to the sense;[94] to the amazement of us all, this practice of his continued up to his death. For, having completed the inquiry in his own mind from the beginning to the end, he then committed to writing the results of his inquiry, and as he thus wove together, in the course of writing, what he had deposited in his soul, it seemed as if he was transcribing what he wrote from a book. Even when he was in dialogue with someone and sustaining a conversation, his mind was on the inquiry, so that he simultaneously did what was necessary for the conversation and carried on thinking without interruption about the subjects of the inquiry. When his interlocutor went away, he did not take up what he had written, since (as I have said) his sight was not equal to this, but would introduce the next point directly, as though there had been no interval of time during which he was holding the conversation. Thus he communed at the same time with himself and with the others, and as for his internal concentration, the only time when he was ever wont to relax this was in sleep. This too he would reduce by his meagre diet[95] – for often he did not even touch bread – and by his continuous reversion to his own mind.[96]

---

93 Or "copy" if one accepts the emendation by O'Brien (1982) of *metalabein* to *metabalein*.

94 The contrast with Serapion, though unstated, could not be more profound. See further chapter 13.

95 Abstinence from food (as opposed to selective diet) had not formerly been a practice of philosophers, though Iamblichus, *DVP* 16 records that Pythagoras neglected to eat and drink in a three-day reverie. Porphyry, *Abst.* 117 Nauck, remarks that, all things being shameful in comparison with the intellect, the use of food is merely a concession to nature. It is also in the third century that regular, rather than occasional, fasting becomes the hallmark of a Christian saint: see Eusebius, *HE* 6.19 on Origen. The Antiochene Bishop John Chrysostom (d. 428) is said to have gone for three days without food when engaged in study: George of Alexandria, in Photius, *Bibl.* 96 (80b Migne; 54 Henry).

96 The notion of being "turned to oneself" (Plotinus, *Enn.* 1.2.4.16) becomes a paradigm of the philosophic life in Proclus, *Alc.* 19.21ff (i, 16 Segonds), where (following *Enn.* 3.9) he urges that we should turn from looking below to looking within, and hence to looking above.

9. Among his fervent devotees there were also women: Gemina, who owned the house he lived in,[97] her daughter Gemina, who shared her mother's name, Amphicleia who had married Ariston the son of Iamblichus,[98] all fervently devoted to philosophy. Moreover, many men and women on the point of death, people of the highest rank, brought their own children, male as well as female, and entrusted them to him with the rest of their goods, as though to a holy and divinely-endowed custodian. As a result, his home was full of boys and unwed girls. These included Potamon,[99] whose education was Plotinus' concern: he would listen to him often even when he was merely repeating a lesson. He consented to see the accounts when they were submitted by those in charge of them, and took pains to be accurate, saying that, while they were not engaged in philosophy, they needed to have their possessions and revenues preserved intact. And yet, though he protected so many from the concerns and cares of life, he would never in waking hours relax his mental concentration. He was kindly[100] as well, and ready at hand for anyone with whom he had the slightest association. Therefore, though he stayed in Rome for twenty-six whole years, and played the arbiter for many in their disputes with one another,[101] he did not once make a foe of anyone in the political class.

10. On the other hand, one of those with pretensions to philosophy, the Alexandrian Olympius,[102] who had briefly been a pupil of Ammonius, treated him contumeliously out of desire for precedence.[103] So far did his assaults on Plotinus go that he even used magic in an attempt to

---

97 A freeborn widow could inherit her husband's property if she remained unmarried, though the law might require her to have at least a nominal guardian. It was by no means uncommon for intellectuals to enjoy the patronage of wealthy women: see Kelly (1975) on the fourth-century Saint Jerome.

98 In Rome both sons and daughters tend to inherit the parent's name; in eminent Greek families eldest sons were called after their paternal grandfathers, producing a regular alternation of two names.

99 Another name that appears to be of Egyptian provenance, containing the name of Ammon-Ra.

100 Lucian, *Demonax* 9 shows that the virtue of being *praos* (attributed to God by Plato, *Republic* 500a) was admired even in a Cynic. It recurs in Damascius, *Isid.* 18 and in Plotinus, *Enn.* 1.2.5.10.

101 An act of civic involvement, even if not performed in any official role.

102 Another case of an Alexandrian following the philosopher to Rome.

103 Porphyry, *Regr.* 16 Bidez describes another such contest provoked by envy. Plotinus believed in, though he did not fear, the power of magic over the body (*Enn.* 4.4.43), but argues that the higher soul dissolves its power by "counter-charms"; cf. Porphyry,

injure him through the stars. But when he perceived that the attempt had recoiled upon himself, he said to his associates that Plotinus' soul possessed great power, because it was able to turn back the assaults on him against those who were making the attempt to harm him. The attempt of Olympius did in fact produce a reaction in Plotinus, and he said that at that time he suffered spasms of the body "like purse-strings being drawn tight",[104] as his limbs were forced together. Since, however, Olympius was often in danger of suffering more himself than he inflicted on Plotinus, he gave up. For Plotinus did have something more by birth when compared with others.[105]

In fact, there was a certain Egyptian priest who arrived in Rome and through some friend became acquainted with him. Wishing to give a demonstration of his own wisdom, he asked Plotinus to come to a visible conjuration of the personal daemon abiding with him.[106] He readily agreed, and the conjuration took place in the temple of Isis, this being, as the priest said, the one pure place that he had found in Rome.[107] When the daemon was conjured to appear, a god came forth,

---

Nymphs, 80.17 Nauck. Armstrong (1955–6) is probably right to maintain against Merlan (1944) that he did not practise ritual magic. See further Taormina (1984), 59–66.

104 Plato, *Symposium* 190d: having cut the primaeval humans in half, Zeus sewed up the wounds like *suspasta balantia*. To judge by his other allusions to this fable – *Enn.* 4.3.12.6 (191b) and *Enn.* 6.5.1.16 (192e) – his words here are intended to convey a painful feeling, rare in him though not in others, of estrangement from the unity of being. A victim of astrology or magic is called a *neurospastos*, i.e. puppet: Aulus Gellius, *Attic Nights* 14.1 Cf. Porphyry, Fr. 269 Smith (on victims of imagination or *phantasia*).

105 Cf. Aelian, *Miscellaneous Histories* 4.17 on the divine origin of Pythagoras. Ammianus Marcellinus, *Histories* 22.16.16, ranks Plotinus with Hermes Trismegistus and Apollonius of Tyana as the possessor of a personal genius. But unlike Pythagoras (Porphyry, *Pyth.*, 18.10 Nauck), Apollonius (Philostratus, *Apollonius* 1.7) or Christ, Plotinus is not presented here as the son of a god. See Cox (1983), 20.

106 Or possibly: "a vision of the so-called [*kaloumenou*] personal daemon abiding with him". Socrates was the first to claim the guidance of a *daimonion* or divine assistant (*Apology* 31c etc.), but the *oikeios daimôn* is more at home in Egyptian astrology, where, according to Iamblichus (*Myst.* 9.5) he is the "paradigm" assigned to us by the ruler of our star. Porphyry preferred to speak of a natal or *genethlios daimôn* at *Marc.* 274 Nauck etc. My translation here, however, reflects the fact that the episode is described as a conjuration [*klesis*], and the daemon is said to have been conjured [*klêthenta*].

107 Purity was the watchword of the rites of the Egyptian goddess Isis, whose cult was patronised by freeborn Roman women in the early Empire (Propertius, 2.33.15–16), and by the mid-second century A.D. had such "converts" as Apuleius (*Metamorphoses* 11). She subsumed the names and characters of other female deities, promising salvation from misfortune

not one of the daemon-kind. The Egyptian[108] therefore said, "Blessed art thou who hast as the daemon abiding[109] with thee a god[110] and not one of the lesser race." There was, however, no opportunity to ask a question or to see the apparition any longer, for the friend who was a fellow-observer strangled the birds which he was holding for protection, either through jealousy or indeed through fear of something.[111] Having, then, one of the higher class of daemons abiding with him, he for his part continued to direct his godlike gaze toward that being. There is, at any rate, a book written by him on some such occasion, *On the Daemon to whom we are Allotted*, in which he tries to give reasons for the variety of companions.[112] When Amelius became fond of sacrifices and travelled

---

and the consequences of sin. There were about a dozen Isiac sites in Rome; the most famous was in the Campus Martius, on which see Apuleius, *ibid.* 11. 28 and Witt (1971), 60–61.

108 This, the only ethnic designation in the life, had connoted guile, effeminacy and enmity to Rome since the days of Cleopatra. Priests seldom come off well in their encounters with men of true religious insight (cf. Amos 7.10, Mark 14.62, Philostratus, *Apollonius* 4.18.2), and the Isiac priest was a byword for hypocrisy: Josephus, *Antiquities* 18.65–80. Porphyry extols the wisdom of Egypt at *Abst.* 135.4 and 155.20 Nauck, but it was his *Anebo* that forced Iamblichus to defend Egyptian rituals in *Myst.* It has been suggested that the priest here is the "Egyptian" who appears in *Abst.* 175.6f Nauck as an expert on the penalties of suicide, though Festugière (1936) thinks it more probable that this passage alludes to an Hermetic source.

109 I take "abiding" [*sunonta*] with *daimôn* as in the earlier sentence, though Armstrong writes "and not a companion of the subordinate order". Like other Greeks, Porphyry sometimes speaks of daemons as a lesser race of gods and sometimes as a different species. On Egyptians as exorcists see e.g. the Christian Origen, *Against Celsus* 1.68, written about 248 A.D.

110 Proclus, *Alc.* 73.6 (59 Segonds) interprets this as a vision of a divine (*theios*) daemon, of the kind that enjoys the closest affinity to the gods (71.5). He goes on to explain that when a soul has chosen the life that is proper to the deity whom it followed in heaven, a daemon of this kind cements the fellowship.

111 He may have been Porphyry's informant, but the motives are conventional (cf. Tacitus, *Annals* 1.11.7), and repeated in chapter 12. A sacrifice may have been intended: see Porphyry, *Pyth.* 36.10 Nauck on the legitimacy of sacrificing cocks, and Eitrem (1942), 64–5 on "Egyptian" parallels in magical papyri. Brisson (1992), 471–2 cites *PGM* 12.15 and 4.814 to show that the strangulation is meant to protect the celebrants. Sheppard (1980), 159 notes a passage in Proclus, *On the Hieratic Art*, where a malignant daemon is exorcised by the sacrifice of a cock.

112 This work was written before he met his biographer, and does not imply that a daemon could be evoked. Alt (1993), 240 n. 252 cites a passage on daemonic apparitions from *Enn.* 1.6.7.20, but admits that it has no bearing on *Enn.* 3.4. The pretext for the latter is Plato's claim that the intellect is a daemon allotted to us by the gods (*Timaeus* 90a) and by

around the temples on the new moons and feast-days,[113] he once asked if he might take Plotinus with him. The latter answered, "It is they who should come to me, not I to them".[114] What was in his mind[115] when he made this lofty statement we ourselves were unable to divine, nor did we dare to ask him.

11. His insight into character was extraordinary,[116] particularly so after the theft of a valuable necklace from Chione,[117] who lived with him, accompanied by her children, chastely maintaining her widowhood.[118]

---

the statement in *Republic* 620b that the soul, when quit of one life, chooses its own lot in the next. For Plotinus the daemon is the state of being above our present one; when he himself attained godhood (*Enn.* 4.10), his daemon was the one. See Rist (1963) on the origins of the treatise; Edwards (1991) on Porphyry's misuse of it; Trigg (1991), 50–1, on features common to this anecdote and Christian documents.

113 Cf. Col. 2.16 for this definition of spurious religion. Amelius belonged to a race notorious for the gruesome sacrifices that it practised in the name of divination, and it is hard to see how he can have abstained from flesh in his eclectic piety. See Porphyry, *Abst.* 96 Nauck on sacrifice as a pretext for eating meat, and 133–45 for the refutation.

114 Already at *Enn.* 6.9.9 (ninth treatise), Plotinus speaks of *nous* begetting gods, as in fact does Porphyry, *Sent.* 32 (33 Lamberz). Fowden (1986), 122 cites a similar aphorism, expressing the same disdain for sacrifice, from the alchemist Zosimus of Panopolis in Egypt (c. 300 A.D.).

115 Porphyry uses the noun *dianoia*, rather than the more common *ennoia* (Proclus, *Alc.* 111.9 at i, 91 Segonds etc.) to indicate that Plotinus always spoke from deep and continuous reflection. Practical atheism – the refusal to participate in popular cults – had never been the norm among philosophers. Since the second century it had been regarded as a vice of Christians, many of whom had suffered in 251 when the Emperor Decius commanded universal sacrifice as a test of loyalty. Both Plotinus and his pupils therefore knew that he had taken a dangerous resolution.

116 Philosophers were more likely to work miracles of clairvoyance than of healing or of interference with the order of nature. Thus Pythagoras divined the previous lives of many people (Porphyry, *Pyth.*, 30.12 Nauck); Apollonius discerns the causes of personal distress and public plague. Cf. also John 2.25 and 6.70 on the sagacity of Jesus.

117 The Greek name probably indicates Greek parentage; she may have had an antecedent connexion with Plotinus. As the slaves in the house are hers, it would appear that Plotinus did not possess his own domicile, like those in which earlier Platonists had held their lessons: Dillon (1979). He was thus less wealthy than scholarchs tended to be, though his eleven years with Ammonius cannot have been cheap.

118 Though women retained their property even in marriage and could inherit from their husbands, it was generally assumed that they required a man's assistance in the management of finances. Treggiari (1991), 499–500 shows that permanent widowhood was a choice that pagan Romans seldom approved, and Plotinus therefore seems to have saved Chione from the disgrace of being an independent woman.

The household slaves were assembled under the eye of Plotinus, who, after gazing upon them all, pointed to one man, saying, "This is the thief". This man was flogged, and though at first he denied it repeatedly, he subsequently confessed and returned the stolen item with his own hand.[119] And he was wont to prophesy how each of the children in his company would turn out; for example he said how Polemon would fare, that he would be amorous and short-lived, which proved indeed to be the case.[120] And once he discerned that I Porphyry was thinking of expediting my departure from life. All of a sudden he came to me as I was keeping to my house, and saying that this urge did not arise from an intellectual resolution but from a kind of melancholic illness,[121] told me to go abroad. I complied with him and went to Sicily where I heard that a man of repute called Probus[122] was living near Lilybaeum.[123] For my part, I was delivered from this urge, but also I was prevented from being with Plotinus up to his death.

12. Plotinus received the warmest honour and veneration from the Emperor Gallienus and his wife Salonina.[124] Making full use of his friendship with them, he asked them to restore a certain city of

---

119 Courts applied torture to slaves to make them incriminate their masters, but generally only in less trivial cases and with more supporting evidence (Justinian, *Digest* 48.18.1). The law did little, however, to restrict the power of owners over slaves, and Plotinus clearly shared the assumptions of his class.

120 Perhaps he practised physiognomy, the art of divining a person's character from his countenance, to which Peripatetics attached much weight (Aristotle, *Prior Analytics* 70b7 etc.).

121 For diagnosis and history of this "melancholic state" see Toohey (1990). Dillon (1994) suggests that an intellectual justification of suicide is hinted at even in the *Enneads* at 1.4.16.

122 Otherwise unknown. The name is Roman, like those of Plotinus and his friend Castricius Firmus.

123 A maritime town in Sicily. See Goulet (1982a) on the many discrepancies between this account and that in Eunapius, *Sophists* 456.24–36 Boissonade-Dübner, where Porphyry goes to Sicily of his own accord and Plotinus has to follow to prevent his suicide. Eunapius claims to base his account on a treatise produced by Porphyry, which Cumont (1919) endeavours to reconstruct from Macrobius, *Dream of Scipio* 1.13.9–10 and *Enn.* 1.9. The subject recurs in *Nymphs* 80, and Eusebius, *PE* 6.19 alludes to the journey to Sicily in a way that suggests the use of a hostile record like the one preserved by Eunapius. The latter, of course, does not make Porphyry's absence the result of his master's command.

124 Possibly true, but see Rawson (1989) on the literary custom of assigning philosophical advisers to the ruler. As for signs of Plotinus' influence, De Blois (1976) presses speculation as far as it can go.

philosophers which was said to have existed in Campania, but at all events had later gone to ruin.[125] He also asked for a grant of the neighbouring land to the city when it had been founded, that those who were going to settle there should live by the laws of Plato,[126] and that the name of Platonopolis should be given to it; he undertook to decamp[127] there with his friends. And the wish of the philosopher would easily have come to pass, had not persons close to the ruler court stood in his way, whether through jealousy or resentment or some other vicious motive.[128]

13. In his seminars he spoke ably enough, and showed an outstanding ability to identify and examine what was pertinent, but he made mistakes with some words. For he would say not *anamimnesketai* ("remembers"), but *anamnemisketai*, and there were certain other verbal errors which he would also commit in writing.[129] But when he spoke his mind was manifest even in his countenance, which radiated light; lovely as he was to see, he was then especially beautiful to the sight.[130] A little sweat trickled, and his kindliness shone forth, and his affability displayed itself in answering questions, as did his [intellectual] vigour. For example, when I Porphyry spent three days asking Plotinus how the soul is present to the body, he kept explaining, causing a certain newcomer called Thaumasius to say that he wanted to hear him laying down

125 The city of the philosophers is probably fabulous, though Pythagorean communities were established in south Italy in the fifth century B.C. and seem to have wielded strong political influence. Porphyry may have been misled by reading of an imaginary commonwealth (comparable to those of Plato, Zeno the Stoic and Cicero) just as, conflating Plotinus' retirement to Minturnae in chapter 2 with the present chapter, the astrologer Firmicus Maternus thought that Plotinus' city in Campania had been built: *Math.* 1.14–17.

126 That is, the code in Plato's last and longest work, the *Laws*. Platonopolis means city of Plato.

127 *Anachôrein*, a technical term for philosophical retirement, later used by Christian "anchorites" who left the city for the desert.

128 The phrase, reminiscent of that applied to the friend at the Iseum in chapter 10, betrays Porphyry's ignorance. De Blois (1989) traces the opposition to an anti-senatorial faction; Edwards (1994) suggests that the impoverished Gallienus may have been glad of reasons not to finance this project.

129 This may be the first case of dyslexia on record, with a slight touch of aphasia. Henry (1938), 120 suggests that symptoms are still detectable in the MSS of the *Enneads*.

130 Cf. the transfiguration of Jesus (Matt. 17.2 etc.), of Moses (2Cor. 3.7) and of the angelic teacher in the (?third-century) work of Egyptian theosophy, *Poimandres* (*Hermetica* 1.4), as well as parallels cited at Marinus, *Proclus* 4.

universal principles with reference to texts,[131] and would not put up with Porphyry's responses and inquiries. But Plotinus said, "If we[132] do not resolve Porphyry's difficulties when he questions us, we shall not have anything that we can put straight into a text".

14. His writing is concise, his thought compact, his brevity more rich in sense than words; often he goes into raptures and speaks emotionally from the depths of feeling rather than from tradition. Nevertheless in his writings there is a discreet admixture of both Stoic[133] and Peripatetic doctrines; they are densely packed above all with the content of Aristotle's *Metaphysics*.[134] Indeed no geometrical speculation was unknown to him, nor any in arithmetic or mechanics or optics or music, though he himself was not prepared to make a professional study of these. In his seminars a scholarly discourse was read to him, which might be from Severus[135] or else from Cronius or Numenius[136]

---

131 I accept the translation of *eis biblia* proposed by Lim (1993), as also his demonstration that *katholou logoi* are neither "general statements" not statements of account. After some thought, I have adhered to my own construction of the sentence.

132 Note the authoritative use of the first-person plural, as also perhaps in his dying words (chapter 2).

133 See Graeser (1972) on Plotinus' debt to this philosophy which, originating in Athens in the fourth century B.C., became popular in the Roman world because of its unconditional pursuit of virtue. Stoics were also famous for their logic and their doctrine of a ruling principle (*logos*) immanent to the world.

134 Aristotle (384–322 B.C.) founded the Peripatetic school in Athens, and is undoubtedly, after Plato, the precursor to whom Plotinus is most indebted. None the less Porphyry's statement seems extravagant. The *Metaphysics* makes being the subject of the "first philosophy", but says nothing of a principle beyond it, suggesting rather that being and unity are identical. It posits a God who so transcends the world that he moves all nature without an act of thought or will, but, since this God is still the "thought of thoughts", he does not evade all definition like Plotinus' One. It agrees with Plato that the immaterial essence is more truly an object of our understanding than the material particular, but denies that the idea is separable from the particular. Porphyry himself attempted to harmonise the doctrines of Plato and Aristotle, but Plotinus drew a sharper line; see esp. *Enn.* 6.1–3.

135 See Dillon (1977), 262–4 on this second-century commentator who wrote works on the *Timaeus* (Proclus, *in Timaeum* iii, 212.8 Diehl) and *On the Soul* (Eusebius, *PE* 13.17).

136 On Numenius of Apamea see chapters 3 and 17. Cronius is cited as an allegorist by Porphyry at *Nymphs*, 55.17 Nauck. It is remarkable that, unlike the group of Platonists cited in Eusebius, *HE* 6.19 (on the Christian Origen), this list does not include Moderatus of Gades, a Pythagorean to whom Dodds (1928) plausibly ascribes the first conception of the "Neoplatonic One".

or Gaius[137] or Atticus,[138] or the work of a Peripatetic such as Aspasius, Alexander, Adrastus[139] or any others who came to hand. Yet nothing that he said came straight from these books; on the contrary, he was his own man, independent in his scrutiny, and applying the doctrine of Ammonius to the investigations. He digested everything rapidly, and having in a few words given the sense of a deep speculation, he left off. Once Longinus'[140] *Basic Principles* and *Back to Basics*[141] had been read out to him: "Longinus is a philologist," he said, "but no philosopher at all".[142] And when Origen dropped into a seminar,[143] he

137 A second-century Platonist whose works are lost. On his school in Rome see Praechter (1916).

138 Another Platonist (fl. 175), who maintained against Aristotle that the world was created in time, that virtue sufficed for happiness, and that the soul can be immortal without a body. Since Plotinus denied the first thesis, his use of Atticus illustrates the eclectic content of his seminars.

139 Alexander of Aphrodisias, the great commentator of the second century, is the only one of the three whose works are extant. His theory that the pure or "active" reason of human beings is identical with the self-thinking mind of God may have helped Plotinus to form his own view that "the intelligibles are not outside the intellect" (*Enn.* 5.5). See his *Mantissa* and Armstrong (1960), 406–414.

140 Cassius Longinus (c. 213–72/3), the former tutor of Porphyry, and according to Eunapius (*Sophists,* 456.3 Boissonade-Dübner) a "walking library", is the author of a fragmentary treatise applying the Aristotelian categories to the art of rhetoric. Modern scholars generally deny that he wrote the great treatise *On the Sublime* which is ascribed to "Dionysius or Longinus", but those who date this writing to the first century must explain how it comes to cite the Greek Old Testament (9.9) and make a reference to imagination (*phantasia*: 15.1) which seems more at home in the third century. See Boyd (1957) for further discussion.

141 This somewhat playful rendering aims to preserve the phonetic likeness between the titles *Peri Archôn* and *Philarkhaios*. *Archê* is a word of many meanings, and the latter work may profess a "love of antiquity" as Armstrong indicates, or may be a (punning) defence of the "principles" expounded in the former. The title *Peri Archôn*, not attested in classical antiquity, was also employed in the lifetime of Longinus by two Christian authors, Clement of Alexandria and Origen; but here it is often assumed to belong to a commentary on the *Timaeus*.

142 Porphyry, *Abst.* 87.5–12 explains that philologists prefer "practical and common" to philosophical arguments. Longinus' analysis of a Platonic sentence makes him both philologist and critic in the eyes of Proclus, *Tim.* i.14.7 Diehl. Proclus also thinks that he slights the philosophy of the dialogue by pronouncing certain flights of style to be purely ornamental: *ibid.*, 59.12 and cf. 68.3.

143 If, as Goulet (1977) opines, Porphyry confused the two Origens, this will be the meeting to which he alluded in his work *Against the Christians*, cited by Eusebius, *HE* 6.19. But see below, chapter 20.

blushed deeply, and wanted to leave off. When, however, Origen begged him to speak, he said that it dampened the ardour of a speaker to see that what he is about to say will be addressed to those who already know it. And therefore, after a little discussion, he got up to leave.

15. At the feast of Plato I read a poem entitled *The Sacred Marriage*,[144] and because many things were mystically and enigmatically stated in a rapturous style, someone exclaimed that Porphyry was raving; but he said in the hearing of all, "You have proved yourself simultaneously a poet, a philosopher and a teacher of sacred truth".[145] On the other hand, when the rhetorician Diophanes read a defence of Alcibiades in the *Symposium* of Plato,[146] contending that, for the sake of instruction in virtue, one ought to submit to intercourse with a teacher who desired sexual relations, he repeatedly got up and made as if to leave the gathering;[147] he restrained himself none the less, and after the completion of

---

144 If not a Pythagorean meditation on the number 3 (*Theology of Arithmetic* 16), this will be an allegory based on a myth about the union of two deities. Such couplings (whether licit or illicit) included: (a) earth and heaven (as in Hesiod); (b) Aphrodite and Hephaestus (art and grace, as in Cornutus); (c) Aphrodite and Ares (love and strife, as in Empedocles and Lucretius); (d) Zeus and Hera (as in *Iliad* 13); (e) Eros and Psyche (as in Apuleius, *Metamorphoses* 4–6); (f) Zeus and Demeter/Rhea (as in the Eleusinian mysteries); (g) Zeus and Semele (as in the myth of Dionysus); (h) Osiris and Isis (mind and soul, as in Plutarch). On (b), (c) and (d) in Proclus and Homer see Sheppard (1980), 62–74.

145 "Teacher of sacred truth" renders the Greek *hierophantês*. Plotinus is alluding to the three species of divine madness – prophetic, initiatory and poetic – distinguished by Socrates in Plato, *Phaedrus* 244a–245a, but says nothing of the fourth and highest species, the erotic. The last is the truly philosophical inspiration in Plato and Plotinus, though clearly not in the hands of Diophanes. Porphyry's ambition to write philosophic poetry may have been fired by a compilation of philosophic verses called the *Chaldaean Oracles*, attributed to the gods but originating in the late second or early third century. The *Thirteenth Sibylline Oracle* and the *Oracle on Plotinus* (chapter 22) are the most interesting specimens of Greek verse from this epoch, in which both Greek and Latin poetry emitted few signs of life.

146 Evidently a hearer, not a follower of Plotinus, Diophanes concurs with the early speakers in the *Symposium*, Plato's dialogue on love, who maintain that homosexual unions, even pederasty, offer more incentives to virtue than domestic marriage. As soon as Socrates has finished arguing that ideal beauty, not carnal intercourse, ought to be the goal of the philosopher, the party is broken up by Alcibiades, his aristocratic pupil, who describes the comic failure of his attempts to seduce his master. A rhetorician would naturally side with Alcibiades rather than Plato, whose attacks on statesmen are reprimanded by Aelius Aristides (second century) in his *Oration on the Four*.

147 Exhibiting the Roman distaste for homosexuality which recurs in his disparagement of the Gnostics (*Enn.* 2.9.17.28–9), and which Platonists had already been taught to feel by

ON THE LIFE OF PLOTINUS 27

the lecture he enjoined me Porphyry to write a response. Since Diophanes refused to hand over his script, in writing my response I rehearsed his arguments from memory. I read it before the same gathering which had heard the original, and gave such pleasure to Plotinus that in the course of the seminar itself he kept on quoting:

Strike thus, that unto men thou may'st be light.[148]

Now when Eubulus, the incumbent of the Platonic school,[149] wrote to him from Athens and sent him writings on some Platonic questions, he caused them to be given to me Porphyry, requesting me to look over them and bring him what I had written.[150] He also turned his attention to the lore of the stars – not much at all to the science of astrology,[151] but more keenly to the calculations of the horoscope-casters.[152] And having exposed the uncertainty of their predictions, he was not afraid to refute many of the statements in their writings.[153]

---

the *Amatorius* of Plutarch. Unlike Plutarch and the novelists (Longus, Heliodorus, Apuleius, Achilles Tatius), the celibate Plotinus did not choose to throw the halo of philosophy round the heterosexual practice.

148 *Iliad* 8.282, changing the word "Greeks" to "men". Plato excepted, Homer is the author most often quoted in the *Enn.*, which otherwise exhibit no great knowledge of Greek poetry.

149 Possibly, though not probably, the writer on Zoroaster cited at *Nymphs*, 60.5 Nauck. All philosophers were assumed in late antiquity to have passed on their authentic teaching through successors or *diadochi*. Teachers at the Athenian "Academy" claimed unbroken descent from Plato, though Dillon (1979) contends that from Antiochus of Ascalon (fl. 86 B.C.) to the establishment of an official chair in the late second century, teaching in Athens may have been series of "one-man shows".

150 The "Questions" of which we hear in ancient philosophy (e.g. Plutarch's various *Questions*, Porphyry's *Symmikta Zetemata*) were answered by the authors; these seem to be challenges, like those which grammarians and sophists presented to one another in this period.

151 Either *mathêtikôs*, "like a disciple", or *mathêmatikôs*, "mathematically". *Mathêmatikôs* often denoted an astrologer, and *Against the Mathematicians* by the second-century Sceptic Sextus Empiricus was an arsenal for subsequent polemics, especially those of Christians.

152 A person's horoscope was the key to his destiny. It was treason to cast that of the emperor (though Tiberius had retained the Pythagorean Thrasyllus as his astrologer), and we can understand why someone might conceal his birthday because and not in spite of his belief in the efficacy of this art.

153 Arguments like those rehearsed in *Enn.* 2.3 sufficed to make a vehement enemy of Firmicus Maternus (*Math.* 1.14–20), who rightly perceives that Plotinus exempted only

28 PORPHYRY

16. There were in his time[154] Christians of many kinds, and especially certain heretics[155] who based their teachings on the ancient philosophy.[156] They were followers of Adelphius and Aculinus,[157] who possessed a lot of writings by Alexander the Libyan,[158] Philocomus, Demostratus and Lydus,[159] and also brandished apocalyptic works of

---

the strong, not everyone, from the power of destiny (*Enn.* 2.3.15). Even the philosopher has his own star (*Enn.* 3.4.6). Similar views were held by his younger Egyptian contemporary Zosimus of Panopolis (*Treatise on the Omega* 8; see chapter 16) and by Iamblichus (*Myst.* 9.5 etc.). Porphyry himself wrote an introduction to the astrological textbook of Claudius Ptolemaeus, showing a sympathetic interest in the science while learnedly exposing the contradictions of its practitioners. Perhaps it was the superficiality of *Enn.* 2.3 that made him count it among the least of his master's works.

154 The Gnostics recapitulate the errors of all Plotinus' other rivals. They practise magic (*Enn.* 2.9.14.1ff), traduce the stars (2.9.13.7) and claim a precedence in philosophy (2.9.6), disparaging the world with their unfounded claims to purity (2.9.15.32). Opposing spurious documents to the canon of Plotinus, they adopt an unphilosophical construction of Plato's work (2.9.6.17–19). Thus a well-founded contrast between the freedom of the spirit and the subjection of the body is marred by a superstitious demonology (2.9.14.24–5) and an inane conviction that they are close to God (2.15.33–6).

155 Not "Christians and others, and sectarians", as Armstrong writes. The construction, paralleled in *Enn.* 2.9.10.1 (Plotinus' treatise against the Gnostics) is explained by Igal (1982). *Hairetikos* had been in common use among Christians in the sense of "heretic" since Irenaeus (fl. 170), though among pagans it still denoted merely a "choice" (*hairesis*) of philosophical allegiance.

156 Or "who had abandoned the old philosophy", as Armstrong writes. Their deviation from the "ancient Greek way" is censured in *Enn.* 2.9.6. But as Porphyry styles them Christian heretics, it would be odd for him to accuse them of having fallen away from any creed that he would call a philosophy. No doubt he ignored the affinities between their doctrine and that of Numenius (Fr. 11 Des Places), who also seems to postulate a temporal creation, in pre-existent matter, resulting from a schism in the divine.

157 Or Aquilinus. Eunapius, *Sophists* 457.12 Boissonade-Dübner calls him a fellow-philosopher of Porphyry, and says that he left no works; but the Byzantine John Lydus quotes a writer of the same name on the Aristotelian (and Plotinian) concept of "intelligible matter". He could easily have been one of the "friends" regretted in *Enn.* 2.9.10.3. See Edwards (1993b).

158 Perhaps the writer attacked in Tertullian's *On the Flesh of Christ* 16–17 (post 200), though Tertullian locates him in Carthage rather than Libya. Puech (1960) argues that the Platonising school of Valentinus (fl. 140 A.D.) is the one represented here, though the treatises named by Porphyry would generally be assigned now to the more pessimistic, "Sethian" branch of the Gnostic family. Other attempts to identify the Gnostics have been made by Schmidt (1901), Elsas (1975) and Edwards (1990a).

159 Unknown authors. Some would reduce the number by reading "Demostratus the Lydian".

Zoroaster,[160] Zostrianus,[161] Nicotheus,[162] Allogenes, Messus[163] and others of that kind. Deceiving many and themselves deceived, they claimed that Plato had not reached the depths of intelligible being.[164] Therefore, having himself produced many refutations in his seminars,[165] and having written the book which we have entitled *Against the Gnostics*,[166] Plotinus left it to us to pronounce on what remained. Amelius reached a total of forty books in his response to the book called *Zostrianus*, while I Porphyry have produced numerous refutations of the book of Zoroaster, proving the book to be entirely spurious and recent, a fabrication of those who upheld this heresy to make it seem that the doctrines which they had chosen to acclaim were those of the ancient Zoroaster.[167]

160 See chapter 3 on the Magi, whose teacher Zoroaster was said to be. Edwards (1988) notes that the Book of Zoroaster was the prototype of the *Apocryphon of John*, a text which Schmidt compared with the teaching of Plotinus' Gnostics, and which was subsequently discovered in new versions at the Egyptian site of Nag Hammadi in 1945. Like many other texts found in the same hoard (but unlike the *Zostrianus*) it is clearly, in its present form at least, a Christian work. The provenance and purpose of the hoard remain obscure.

161 Another text discovered at the same site. It is clearly a descendant of the treatise known to Porphyry, as it contains the myth narrated in *Enn*. 2.9.10. It also knows the "intelligible triad" (being, life, mind) which is generally assumed to be the innovation of Porphyry himself or a later author. On the likely direction of influence see Majercik (1992).

162 We learn most about "the hidden one" from the alchemist Zosimus, *Treatise on the Omega*, though he is also mentioned in the tract *Marsanes* from Nag Hammadi. See Jackson (1990).

163 The tract in the name of Allogenes, also found at Nag Hammadi, is addressed to his son Messos. The name itself ("another-born") may be a title for Seth, the first man after Adam (cf. Gen. 4.25).

164 Though Christians could extol the depth or *bathos* of God's riches (Rom. 11.33), it was heresy to pretend to understand them. The second-century Gnostic sect whose enemies styled them Naassenes made frequent use of the term (Hippolytus, *Refutation* 5.6ff). The Valentinians did not pretend to know God the Father, whom they represent as the ineffable *Buthos* or Abyss.

165 See note 59, chapter 4 on *Enn*. 3.9.

166 Porphyry's title; but Iamblichus, *De Anima*, 357 Wachsmuth, speaks of the Gnostics as a group of philosophers who held a pessimistic view of the present condition of the human soul (cf. *Enn*. 2.9.10). The term is otherwise found only in Christians, who, as Edwards (1990a) observes, do not bestow it so profusely as their modern readers. In general it applies to those groups who justify the subtitle of the treatise, "That the creator of the cosmos is evil".

167 Clearly the *Zostrianus* and *Zoroaster* were not one book, as Doresse (1950) maintained, though the seal of the *Zostrianus* alludes to the Persian sage. *Nymphs* is a prime

17. When those in Greece[168] began to accuse Plotinus of passing off Numenius' teachings as his own, this was reported to Amelius by Trypho, the Stoic and Platonist,[169] and Amelius wrote a treatise which we have entitled *How Plotinus differs from Numenius in his Doctrine*.[170] This he addressed to me as Basileus [King], and this was indeed my name, because I Porphyry was called Malkus in the dialect of my homeland,[171] this being also the name of my father,[172] and Malkus has the meaning "King" if one elects to turn it into the Greek tongue.[173] That is why, when Longinus addressed his work *On Impulse*[174] to Cleodamus and to me Porphyry, his preface began "Cleodamus and Malchus". It

---

source on philosophical Mithraism, supposedly the religion of Zoroaster: on the anti-Gnostic tenor of the work see Edwards (1996).

168 Porphyry contrasts the originality of his master with the Gnostic appeal to fabricated sources. The critics referred to here may be Eubulus and his friends, perhaps claiming the authority of Longinus.

169 Stoicising Platonists included Severus as well as Plotinus (chapter 14); we also know of Platonising Stoics, like Posidonius of Apamea. Trypho himself, however, we do not know, nor in what way he professed a dual allegiance. See next chapter for Longinus *On Impulse* and Thrasyllus.

170 Ancient authors exploited (or transcribed) their predecessors with scant acknowledgment. Hostile criticism (of which Porphyry himself has left a specimen: Eusebius, *PE* 10.3) did not distinguish plagiarism from influence, allusion, imitation, candid borrowing and tacit criticism. Plotinus in his earliest treatise certainly reads the *Odyssey* in the allegorical manner of Numenius (*Enn.* 1.6.8; cf. Numenius, Frs 30–35 Des Places); he may also be indebted to Numenius for the famous words "the flight of the alone to the alone" (*Enn.* 6.9.9; cf. Fr. 2.12 Des Places), which Porphyry placed at the end of the *Enn.* Nevertheless, Numenius had no place for the One, and where Plotinus wrote of three *hypostases* (the One, Mind, Soul), the "three gods" of Numenius (Fr. 25) were two minds and the world.

171 That is, Phoenicia. The Semitic root *mlk*, meaning "king" is the origin of the name Malcolm. The name Porphyry is itself a pun, denoting the "purple" of royalty. That Porphyry had a Phoenician name, and knew what it meant, is no proof that he was fluent in that language; he read the *Phoenician History* of Sanchuniathon in Greek. Jones (1940), 36 notes that Phoenicians adopted Greek names as early as the third century B.C. Millar (1997) doubts whether the Phoenician language had survived by the third century A.D.

172 Unusual in Phoenicia, as in Greece: the family had adopted a Roman practice without a Roman name. The Plutarch who appears in Marinus, *Proclus* 12 had a father and grandfather with the same name, Nestorius. See also Lewis (1957) on Moschos, son of Moschion, a freed Jew of the third century B.C.

173 At John 18.10 it is transcribed as Malchus; the aspirate may not have been evident in pronunciation.

174 The title suggests an interest in Stoic theories of action, *hormê* being conceived as the initial impulse, subject to our rational approval or restraint.

was Amelius who, translating the name as Numenius turned that of Maximus into Megalos,[175] turned Malchus into Basileus, writing thus:

> Amelius to Basileus, good health. You know that on their own account I should never have said a word to those worshipful sirs who, as you say, have been badgering you with claims that our friend derived his doctrines from Numenius the Apamean.[176] For it is obviously the consequence of their cherished orotundity and quickness of tongue that they say now that he is a great windbag, then that he is a plagiarist, and then again that in any case he has plagiarised the feeblest of existing [arguments];[177] it is clear that they are censuring him for the pleasure of abuse. Nevertheless, I have deferred to your opinion that we should use this as an occasion, first to put our own beliefs in a more memorable form, and next to make more widely known the things that have admittedly been famous for a long time, thus securing for our friend the renown that is due to the greatness of Plotinus. And therefore I am now in a position to present you with the labours which, in accordance with the promise that you remember, I have completed in three days.[178] The compilation and selection here do not follow the order of their compilations,[179] but

---

175 The first name means "Greatest" in Latin; the second means "Great" in Greek. But in fact it was only Greeks who would use the name Maximus by itself; thus Maximus of Tyre was a second-century Platonist, and is possibly the person intended here.

176 A common designation of the great Numenius. It is generally assumed that he is the same man as "Numenius the Roman" (Fr. 57 Des Places); if so, he may have founded the school over which Plotinus presided. The presence of the Gnostic (chapter 16) supports this conjecture, as they may have invoked his teachings.

177 Amelius writes pretentiously; but I do not see, with Armstrong, an allusion to Plotinus' use of negatives to characterise the principles of being. It is possible that Amelius has misunderstood an allusion to the Demiurge, who, according to Diogenes Laertius, 5.1.63 was called *phaulos* ("simple" rather than "feeble") in the Platonic tradition. The accuser might then be Longinus (see below), who doubted whether the Demiurge could come immediately after the One (Proclus, *Tim.* i.322.24–8 Diehl). But probably the phrase is simply compounding the charge of plagiarism by hinting that the author is using sources that he would not care to disclose. Cf. Irenaeus, *Against Heresies* 1.30.15 on the Valentinian heresy.

178 Is this to be taken literally, or is it a Semitism (cf. Hosea 6.2)? If the latter, Amelius the Italian may be mocking one of Porphyry's Phoenician mannerisms.

179 It appears that this term often denotes a series of indictments against one adversary: cf. the *Syntagma* of the second-century Christian Justin Martyr against the heretic Marcion. (Irenaeus, *Against Heresies* 4.6).

have been republished as I first encountered them and as each one came to hand; I have a right to your indulgence, if only because the meaning of the one who is being arraigned for the beliefs that he shares with us is not very easy to apprehend, seeing that he adopted different approaches at different times as he saw fit. I know well that, if I have falsified any of the things that come from our own hearth,[180] you will be kind enough to put it right. But even at this distance from the master's teachings, it seems that I am bound, by what the tragedy somewhere calls my "love of meddling" to engage in rectifications and denials.[181] This, you see, is what it means to desire to be of service to you in everything. Farewell.

18. I have thought it right to insert this letter, not only as a proof that people of that time, who were his contemporaries, thought that he was striking airs on the basis of plagiarisms from Numenius, but also that they reckoned him a great windbag and despised him because they did not know his teachings, and because he was quite unsoiled by the pompous apparatus of the sophists.[182] In his seminars he seemed like one engaged in conversation, and the cogent reasonings that his discourse contained were not immediately apparent to anyone. Thus it was that I Porphyry made an error of this kind when I first heard him.[183] For this reason I took it upon myself to write against him, showing that the object of the intellect is outside it.[184] He had Amelius read this to him, and when he had read it, said with a smile, "It is for

180 Meaning the school of Plotinus.
181 No-one knows the meaning of this sentence, which I render at my own peril. I do not know whether the works to be rectified are his own, those of Plotinus or those of his adversaries, nor which is the tragic element, nor whether "distance" means remoteness in place or intellectual alienation.
182 Porphyry may be thinking of Plato's *Phaedrus*, which disparages written speeches because they cannot answer for themselves (see 230a–b and 275a). At the same time, he is justifying his decision to turn his master's "conversations" into the written prose that had been the standard vehicle for philosophy since Aristotle.
183 Plotinus is thus to be contrasted with those, including Ammonius, who won over their greatest pupils at one hearing. Cf. the conversions of Zeno and Polemon: Diogenes Laertius 7.1.2 and 4.316.
184 The opinion of Longinus, as we shall see, distinguishing the Demiurge of the *Timaeus* from the paradigm which he contemplates in creating the world. *Enn.* 5.5 maintains the contrary position.

ON THE LIFE OF PLOTINUS 33

you, Amelius, to resolve the difficulties into which he has fallen because he did not know our opinions".[185] Amelius wrote a book of no mean length *Against the Difficulties of Porphyry*, and I in turn wrote another against what he had written, and Amelius replied to this also: then, having at the third attempt, and with difficulty, understood what was being said, I Porphyry changed my position and read in class the palinode that I had written.[186] After that the treatises of Plotinus were entrusted to me, and I urged the master, for his own reputation, to articulate his doctrines and expound them at greater length. Not only that, but I quickened a zeal for writing in Amelius as well.[187]

19. As for the opinion that Longinus had of Plotinus, chiefly from what I told him in my letters to him,[188] this will be apparent from a portion of a letter which he wrote to me and which runs as follows. Requesting me to return to him in Phoenicia from Sicily,[189] bringing the treatises of Plotinus, he says:

> And you for your part send these when it suits you, or rather bring them with you; for I shall not relax my constant prayer that you will choose to come to me rather than go to any other place. If there is no other reason – for what wisdom would you expect to derive from me by coming? – there is our old acquaintance and the fact that the air will be extremely temperate for the bodily infirmity that you speak of.[190] And in case you should have thought otherwise, do not expect any novelties from me, nor

---

185 Thus Amelius could at first assume the role Plotinus himself had to perform on a later occasion (chapter 14). *Enn.* 5.5 is the eleventh treatise written after Porphyry's arrival, so clearly Plotinus made his doctrines known to his associates long before he wrote them down.

186 Porphyry covers his embarrassment by alluding again to the *Phaedrus* (243a–c), where Socrates produces his great myth as a "palinode" to his former speech.

187 The *scholia* of Amelius would perhaps not have justified the verb *sungraphein*. In any case, Porphyry makes it clear that no-one else can be credited with the publication of Plotinus' thoughts.

188 Introducing a higher authority than Amelius, soon to be succeeded by the gods, and at the same time making himself, not Amelius, responsible for the writer's information. His defensive remarks in chapter 21 suggest that Longinus was popularly regarded as a critic of Plotinus.

189 Therefore the letter is written after Porphyry left Rome in 268, Longinus having now moved from Athens to Phoenicia – probably to Porphyry's native city of Tyre.

190 Porphyry has clearly been reticent about his health; see chapter 11.

even [copies of] those former writings which you say you have lost. For such is the present scarcity of scribes here that – by the gods – although I have been assembling the remnants of Plotinus' writings all this time,[191] I have barely got hold of them by diverting my amanuensis from his wonted tasks and bidding him attend to this one thing. I have indeed obtained everything so far as I know, including the ones that you have now sent to me,[192] but I have obtained them in a half-finished state. They are indeed more than a little defective, though I thought that our friend Amelius was going to remove the lapses of the scribes. He, however, had other business more pressing than this. Therefore I do not have any way of making myself familiar with them, dearly though I long to examine the works *On the Soul*[193] and *On Being*.[194] For these, I must say, are particularly defective.

I should be glad indeed to receive from you accurately written copies, just to read them in parallel and then send them back. So again I shall make the same petition, that you do not send them but rather, I pray, come bringing these as well as any others that may have escaped Amelius; for what he brought I have enthusiastically received. How was it possible that I should not obtain the man's writings when they were worthy of the highest respect and honour?[195] This after all is what I have told you in your presence and by letter when you were far away, and again when you were staying in Tyre, that, while I was not able to accept a great many of his theses, I love and applaud the manner of writing, the density of the man's thoughts and his extraordinarily philosophical way of treating the inquiries, and I would say that inquirers

---

191 I take this to mean that Plotinus is dead, which also explains why Longinus can expect Porphyry to prefer him to any other destination. Thus the date is 270 or later.

192 Since Porphyry left Rome before Amelius, these can only be different copies of the same works.

193 Probably the present *Enn.* 4.1–3 (then undivided), though it may also be 4.8, since one of Longinus' best-known theses (rebutted by Porphyry) was that when the soul descended it entered seed of a quality corresponding to its destiny: Proclus, *Tim.* i.51.9–12 Diehl.

194 Perhaps *Enn.* 6.1–3 (so Henry and Schwyzer) or else 6.4–5 (Armstrong).

195 Professions of *aidôs* (respect) had, since Plato, *Republic* 595b (on Homer), implied a firm intention to differ; cf. Plotinus, *Enn.* 2.9.10.3 and Taran (1984). Longinus had already attacked the doctrines of Plotinus, and this time even Porphyry suspects that he was not well disposed to him.

ought to rank this author's works among the most distinguished.[196]

20. I have cited these remarks at length to illustrate how Plotinus was judged by the foremost critic of our time, one who was rigorous in his strictures on almost all his other contemporaries. Yet at first he maintained a disparaging attitude towards him because of the ignorance of others. The reason why, on receiving what he obtained from Amelius, he supposed it to be defective, was that he did not know the man's customary style. For if ever there were correct copies, they were those of Amelius, which were produced from the very manuscripts of Plotinus.[197] It is necessary to make a further citation of what he wrote about Plotinus and Amelius and the other philosophers of his time, giving in full the judgment passed on them by this most distinguished and rigorous man. The treatise of Longinus against Plotinus and Gentilianus Amelius[198] bears the title *On the End*, and has the following preface:[199]

> Marcellus,[200] there have been many philosophers in my time, and not least in my early youth – for as to the present time, one can hardly say how lacking it is in this respect. But when I was an adolescent, there were not a few outstanding professors of philosophy, all of whom I had the opportunity to hear because from childhood on I made visits to many places with my parents, and as I encountered numerous peoples and cities I associated with those who were still there at the same time. Now some of them made the effort to set out their opinions in writing, allowing posterity to get

---

196 This cautious estimate, dwelling on form while disowning the content, seems to justify the Neoplatonic estimate of Longinus as a philologist rather than a philosopher (see chapter 14). The next sentence calls him *kritikôtatos*, using the superlative of the epithet later conferred on him by Proclus, *Tim.* i.14.7 Diehl, and raising afresh the possibility that he was the author of *On the Sublime*. See Heath (1999) on echoes of this treatise in the Neoplatonists.

197 Implying perhaps that Porphyry's were only "copies of copies", as Plotinus (chapter 1) said of a picture.

198 Longinus seems to treat him as a collaborator rather than a disciple, as was natural after such a long association. In any case, he was responding directly to Amelius.

199 The date must be 263–4, as Porphyry is said in chapter 21 to have been at the beginning of his studies with Plotinus. See further n. 222.

200 Not known, but if he was a sympathiser with Plotinus, as the laudatory tone of this introduction may imply, he may have been an auditor at the school in Rome, perhaps even the brother of the Marcella whom Porphyry later took as his wife.

a measure of benefit from them, while others thought that all they needed to do was to guide their associates to an understanding of their doctrines. Among those who took the first way were the Platonists Euclides and Democritus and Proclinus,[201] who lived in the area of the Troad, as well as Plotinus and Gentilianus Amelius, his familiar friend, who up to the present time are teaching publicly in Rome. Among the Stoics there were Themistocles and Phoebion with Annius and Medius, who only recently attained their peak; and among the Peripatetics the Alexandrian Heliodorus.[202] Platonists who took the second way were Ammonius and Origen, men whose lectures I attended regularly for a very long time, and who far excelled their contemporaries in understanding.[203] There were also the Athenian successors Theodotus and Eubulus.[204] For if any of these men did write anything, as Origen wrote his *On Daemons*[205] and Eubulus his *On the Philebus and Gorgias and Aristotle's Objections to the Republic of Plato*,[206] these are not of a kind to make us reckon them among those who have produced writings; this was an incidental pursuit of theirs, and they had in general no disposition to write. The Stoics included Hermaeus and Lysimachus,[207] as well as Athenaeus and Musonius who lived in the town.[208] The Peripatetics included Ammonius and Ptolemaeus, who were the greatest philologists of their

201 Unknown, like most of the others in this catalogue.

202 Nothing but the name connects this figure with the sophist of Philostratus' time (*Sophists* 2.32) or with the author of the Ethiopian story, though neither identification is impossible.

203 Treating Origen as a teaching friend of Ammonius (which the Christian Origen can hardly have been), and evidently judging both superior to Plotinus at this time.

204 See chapter 15 on Eubulus and the succession at the Academy. Turcan (1975), 23–43 suggests that he is the expositor of Mithraism cited at *Abst*. 253.19 and *Nymphs* 66.5.

205 Which Longinus may have answered incidentally in his response to Amelius on the *Republic* of Plato: Proclus, *Tim*. i.31.19–20 and i.63.25 Diehl.

206 He does not allude to Origen's treatise *On Daemons* or anything by Eubulus on the Mithraic mysteries. Either he is not aiming to give a full account, or the works were still to be written – or, in the latter case, it may have been another Eubulus who wrote on Mithraism. *Pace* Goulet (1977), it is clear at least that if Porphyry read this preface c. 264, he could not have imagined when he composed his treatise *Against the Christians* (after 270), that the Origen described here was the prolific Christian author.

207 The teacher of Amelius in chapter 3.

208 Probably meaning in Athens. Armstrong suggests that the usage is archaic, but it may be that Longinus is writing from that city.

time,[209] and especially Ammonius, for there was no-one who excelled this man in breadth of learning.[210] For all that, they wrote no technical works, only poems and showpiece lectures, which I therefore imagine to have been preserved without the authority of these men, who could hardly have wished to become known to posterity through such works when they did not care to invest their thoughts in writings of a more serious nature.

Of those who did write, some did little more than collate and reproduce the compositions of their elders, as Euclides and Democritus and Proclinus did,[211] while others, recalling extremely small issues in the inquiries of the ancients, undertook the composition of treatises on the same topics. Such were Annius, Medius and Phoebion, the last of whom desired to be known more for the elegant construction of his language than for the coherence of his thought. To this class one might also assign Heliodorus, as he too added nothing to his orderly discourses but what his elders had said in their lectures. But those who have demonstrated their zeal for writing by the number of problems they address, while employing their own method in the consideration of them, were Plotinus and Gentilianus Amelius. The former, as I believe, has produced a clearer exposition of Pythagorean and Platonic principles than any of his precursors, for there is nothing approaching the accuracy of Plotinus' writings in those of Numenius, Cronius, Moderatus[212] and Thrasyllus[213] on the same matters. As for Amelius, his

---

209 Applying the term to exegesis and using it in a less pejorative sense than Plotinus (chapter 14), though the similar praise of Origen and Ammonius Saccas for their "understanding" implies that Longinus too perceived a difference between philology and philosophy.

210 See Philostratus, *Sophists* 2.27.6 for another contemporary testimony to Ammonius' learning. The names Ammonius and Ptolemaeus both suggest an Egyptian provenance. Edwards (1993a) suggests that this Ammonius taught the Christian Origen, himself more a philologist than a practising philosopher; in that case Longinus' subsequent remarks may contain a slighting reference to the *Harmony of Jesus and Moses*, which Eusebius attributes to Ammonius the teacher of Origen at *HE* 6.19.

211 As Platonists (including Plotinus) often claimed to be doing up to the time of Proclus (d. 480).

212 Of Gades (Cadiz). Porphyry himself is our chief informant on the contribution made by this second-century Pythagorean to the doctrine of the One: see Dodds (1928).

213 Of Rhodes, astrologer to the Emperor Tiberius (14–37). See Tarrant (1993) on the work of this neglected Pythagorean, once again best known to us from Porphyry, who

intention was to follow in the other's footsteps, and he holds many of the same doctrines, yet he is prolix in his treatment and in his rambling expositions he pursues the opposite goal to that of Plotinus. These are the only ones whose writings I think worthy of examination. For why should anyone look up the others if he leaves unread the authors from whom these men derived these doctrines, adding nothing on their account even in argument, let alone in the cardinal issues, not even bothering to collect the opinions of the majority or to judge which is the best?[214]

This has therefore been my procedure in other writings,[215] such as my response to Gentilianus on Plato's notion of justice[216] and in my examination of Plotinus *On the Ideas*.[217] As for the friend that they and I have in common, Basileus of Tyre,[218] who has himself made no small effort to imitate Plotinus, and, preferring to take him rather than myself as his mentor, has undertaken to show in a treatise that his opinion about the Ideas is better than the one that I embrace, I think that in my answer I have convicted him, though in measured terms, of singing too hasty a palinode.[219] And in this work I have addressed not a few of these men's opinions, as also in my letter to Amelius, which has the dimensions of a treatise, and replies to some of the points that he raised in a letter to me from Rome, which he entitled *On the Philosophical Method of Plotinus*. For my part, I was content

---

arranged the Platonic dialogues in tetralogies, gave them second titles and developed a doctrine of the immanent *logos*, or ruling principle in the cosmos. Porphyry (chapter 14) neglects the last two figures in this list.

214 Both the syntax and the foregoing comments seem to me to imply this rendering, rather than that of Amstrong, who understands the Greek to mean that they did nothing else.

215 I take this to mean: "I have preferred to give my attention to these authors".

216 Proclus, *Tim*. i.31.18–27 Diehl reports Longinus' view that political, rather than psychic or cosmic, justice is the true theme of the *Republic*.

217 Henry-Schwyzer and Armstrong suggest *Enn.* 6.7, but the doctrine of 5.5, that "the intelligibles are not outside the intellect", is surely the principal ground of controversy.

218 Chapter 17 states that Longinus called him Malchus, while Amelius rendered this as Basileus; Longinus' correspondent, or his wider audience, must have been more familiar with the Greek name.

219 See chapter 17.

simply to give a generic title to my treatise, calling it *An Answer to the Letter of Amelius*.

21. In these words of his at that time, then, he has confessed that of all his contemporaries Plotinus and Amelius took the palm for the "number of problems", and that they above all were "employing their own method", and that they did not plagiarise Numenius and give precedence to his teachings, but followed the teachings of the Pythagoreans, which he also adopted, and that "there is nothing approaching the accuracy of Plotinus' writings in those of Numenius, Cronius, Moderatus and Thrasyllus on the same matters".[220] And while he has said of Amelius that "he walks in the footsteps of Plotinus, but is prolix in his treatment and in his rambling exposition pursues the opposite goal to that of Plotinus",[221] he none the less makes mention of me Porphyry when I was still at the beginning of my association with Plotinus,[222] saying "the friend that they and I have in common, Basileus of Tyre, who has himself made no small effort to imitate Plotinus". He wrote this because he was perfectly aware that I had in all respects avoided the unphilosophical ramblings of Amelius and was looking to the same goal as Plotinus in my writing.[223] It is enough that a man of such stature, whose pre-eminence as a critic is acknowledged to this day, writes about Plotinus in such a way that, if it had also been possible for me Porphyry to join him when he invited me, he would not have written against him in the way that he ventured to write before acquiring an accurate knowledge of the doctrines.[224]

---

220 This is patently a paraphrase interspersed with direct quotation and explicative comment, rather than a continuous quotation, as the Oxford text and Armstrong's translation imply.

221 Here the quotation is almost exact, except for slight omissions.

222 It is not clear whether this means that the letter itself was written at the beginning of Porphyry's studies, or merely that it refers to this early phase. But Igal (1982), 112 prefers the second interpretation only because he erroneously deduces from the end of the chapter that this letter was written after Porphyry left Rome for Sicily.

223 The frankest criticism of his colleague in the *Plotinus*.

224 This convoluted assertion does not imply that Longinus ever gained such knowledge; nor does it imply that Longinus wrote against Plotinus after Porphyry rejected his invitation. It certainly does not suggest that the letter in chapter 20, which is probably the preface to a treatise against Plotinus, was of a later date than the invitation to Porphyry in Sicily (chapter 19). That was written after Amelius came to Apamea, whereas the letter excerpted in chapter 20 states that Amelius is still in Rome. Longinus died in 272 at the

22. But what is all this talk of mine about a tree or a rock, as Hesiod says?[225] For if one must make use of the testimonies that come from the wise, who could be wiser than a god – the god indeed who said with truth:

> I know the reckoning of the sands, the measure of the sea;
> I understand the dumb and hear the one who speaketh not.[226]

Now Apollo was asked by Amelius where the soul of Plotinus had gone.[227] He was the one who had said so grandly of Socrates: "Of all men the most wise is Socrates".[228] Listen to the oracle that he gave to Plotinus' circle:[229]

> I am preparing to play a deathless hymn of song, weaving it about my gentle friend with the sweetest sounds beneath the golden

---

hands of the Emperor Aurelian; Porphyry appears to mean that had Longinus lived, he would of course have carried on writing, and, once Porphyry had verified his copies of Plotinus and explained them, would have replied again, but in a different vein.

225 Hesiod, *Theogony* 35.6–7, taking leave of the Muses who profess to speak both truth and falsehood. Porphyry hereby promises to speak only the truth. The formula recurs at *Iliad* 22.166–7 and *Odyssey* 19.163, cited by Plato, *Apology* 34d. For its other cognates and theories as to its meaning see West (1964) and Vadé (1977).

226 Herodotus 1.47. The words are spoken by the Delphic Oracle, which, according to Plutarch, was not strictly the voice of the god (*On the Pythian Oracles* 397c, 404b). They were none the less often assumed to come directly from Apollo, and were parodied on this assumption by the disbelieving Cynic Oenomaus, cited a little after Porphyry's time by Eusebius, *PE* 5.34.

227 Since it was widely held that the Greek Oracles were silent (Plutarch, *On the Decline of the Oracles*), or at least that the Pythia did not give oracles in verse (Plutarch, *On the Pythian Oracles*), Porphyry may not have meant to imply that this oracle, like the others which he quotes, emanated from Delphi. Possible sources, if it is not a forgery by some well-meaning pupil, would be the Asian sites of Didyma and Claros: see Brisson (1990), 87; Lane Fox (1986), 177–85; Parke (1985), 92.

228 Plato, *Apology* 21a, allegedly the motivation for Socrates' inquiries into the ignorance of others.

229 As the succeeding notes will show, these verses are saturated in the language of Homer, Hesiod and Empedocles. Even if we allow that it was the custom for learned priests to cast the mouthings of the Sibyl into hexameters, this denseness of allusion, coupled with the unusual length of the poem, must raise suspicions. See Goulet (1982b) for a comprehensive survey. Brisson (1990), 81–2 points out that Porphyry's glosses do not always represent the poem fairly; but that will not exclude his being the author if three decades intervened between composition and commentary. For the sceptic Amelius remains the principal subject: Igal (1984). Those who regard the oracle as "genuine" must think either that Apollo was its author or that Plotinus was more celebrated than any philosopher has a right to be.

plectrum of my well-toned lyre.²³⁰ And I summon the Muses to raise a common shout with me, mingling all their voices in triumphal anthems and all the harmonies in their strains, just as for Aeacides they were called to raise the dance with immortal ravings and Homeric songs.²³¹ But come, sacred chorus of Muses, let us unite in inspiration to reach the limits of all song, myself in the middle of you, Phoebus of the rich hair.²³²

Daemon, once a man,²³³ but now attaining the more divine lot of daemons, since you have loosed the bond of human necessity,²³⁴ and in the vigour of your spirit²³⁵ have swum²³⁶ from the roaring billows of the bodily frame towards the shore of a peaceful headland, in your haste to set going the well-turned course of a pure soul far away from the mob of sinners.²³⁷ There the light

---

230 The style and tenor of this introduction recall the *Odes* of Pindar, a favourite of Plato. The notion of wreathing the honorand in song is Pindaric, and is echoed at the end (again in the Pindaric manner) by the metaphorical "crest" of previous lives.

231 All this to refer to the *Iliad*, the first line of which invites the Muse to sing the "wrath of Achilles", here given his conventional patronymic because his ancestor Aeacus appears below.

232 This trope by which the poet first undertakes to sing and then invokes the Muses is Hellenistic (Apollonius Rhodius, *Argonautica* 1.23); the Homeric poets ask the Muse to sing. That Apollo should require these lesser beings to assist his memory or inspire his diction is a thought unparalleled before this poem.

233 The argument of *Enn.* 3.4 suggests that if a man has a god as his guardian, he himself will be a daemon; but Apollo underestimates Plotinus, who, in *Enn.* 4.7.10, makes the philosopher repeat Empedocles' boast that he is "a god, no longer a mortal" (Fr. 112.3 DK). This line recurs in the Pythagorean *Golden Verses* 71 (Hierocles, *CA* 483). Empedocles was himself a former *daimôn* (Fr. 115); whatever he intended, Plotinus means that he is a purely noetic being assimilated to Mind itself.

234 From *Republic* 620 on, philosophers had distinguished between the necessity which circumscribes our bodies and the freedom of our souls to pursue the Good.

235 Bréhier and Armstrong make *prapidessi* refer to the heart, but Empedocles Fr. 129 DK applies it to the discerning intellect of Pythagoras (cited by Porphyry, *Pyth.* 33.12 Nauck).

236 This passage is based on *Odyssey* 5.399. Although Numenius (cited by Porphyry, *Nymphs* 79.21 Nauck) had construed the return of Odysseus to Ithaca as a parable of the soul's return to a higher state, it is Maximus of Tyre, *Philosophumena* 11.10 Hobein, who supplies the precedent for the allegorical construction of the scene in which Odysseus swims from his raft.

237 Alluding to Plato, *Phaedrus* 247c–d on the proper course of the soul in the "supercelestial region", and also to *Odyssey* 24.12, which speaks of souls as a "mob of dreams". Numenius, Fr. 32 Des Places applies this to souls detained in the present world.

of god[238] shines forth, there are the righteous in purity, far off from unrighteous sin. And even then, as you leapt to escape from beneath the bitter wave of this blood-gorged life[239] with its noisome swirls,[240] in the very midst of the wave and the sudden billow, the nearby goal was frequently revealed to you by the blessed ones. Often, as the shafts[241] of your mind were set loose to run in veering paths by their own impulses, the immortal ones set them straight and raised them up to the spheres in their deathless course,[242] sending a frequent ray of light to enable your eyes to see through the maudlin gloom.[243] Nor did sweet sleep ever take hold of your eyelids,[244] but, pulling the heavy bolt of mist[245] from your eyelids, you in your eddying course beheld things many and fair, which no-one[246] could have seen easily among those who were after wisdom.

But now that you have put off the tabernacle,[247] and have left

238 A typical example of the indefinite use of *theos* in the singular, which does not entail monotheism.

239 Bidez (1913), 124 takes this as an allusion to the eating of meat, though it may refer more widely to the cruelty of existence in this period, as do related images in Marinus, *Proclus* 15 and Hierocles, *CA* 450. At *Enn.* 5.1.2.15 the wave is a symbol of the body; at Porphyry, *Nymphs* 32 (= Numenius, Fr. 33) it stands for the whole of material existence.

240 The turbulence of the embodied soul, as at Plato, *Phaedo* 79c. But there may also be an allusion to Charybdis, which almost destroyed Odysseus after he blinded the Cyclops.

241 Brisson and Flamand (1992), 585 note that *bolai* are characteristic of Apollo at Plato, *Cratylus* 405c etc. See also *Proclus* 22 with note on *epibolê*.

242 Or "raised them up to the sphere of the straight way and the deathless course", if we follow the Henry-Schwyzer Editio Maior reading of *orthoporou* instead of the *orthoporous* of the Editio Minor.

243 Cf. Numenius, Fr. 2 where the gods send shafts of light to the mind engaged on a voyage of contemplation. Edwards (1989) suggests that the author also has in mind the olive which greeted Odysseus on his arrival in Ithaca (*Odyssey* 13.104). This is interpreted by Porphyry, *Nymphs* 79.6 Nauck as the lamp of wisdom beckoning the soul.

244 As it did to Odysseus: *Odyssey* 13.79. The philosopher surpasses the hero of practical virtue, as Porphyry makes clear at *Nymphs* 80.7ff. The line may also be translated "sleep did not wholly seal your eyes".

245 As Athene, goddess of wisdom did to Odysseus: *Odyssey* 13.352. On the ability of the wise to discern the Ideas in the gloom of matter see Porphyry, *Nymphs* 59.18–25. This treatise is another allegorical essay on *Odyssey* 13.102–112; if Porphyry did not compose the oracle, he shared the author's thoughts.

246 A playful allusion to the name *outis*, which Odysseus gave to himself to prevent the Cyclops from revealing his identity: *Odyssey* 9.366–7.

247 Armstrong suggests an allusion to the word *skênos* at [Plato], *Axiochus*, 366a, though *skênê* is a metaphor more familiar from Christian writings: 2Cor. 5.1 etc.

the tomb of your daemonic soul,[248] you have already entered the daemonic band that exhales winds of delight,[249] where friendship is,[250] where there is desire to please the eyes; you are full of pure gladness and are constantly being filled with immortal currents from the gods, the source of the loves' enticements, of sweet breath and tranquil air. There dwell Minos and Rhadamanthus,[251] brothers of the great Zeus's golden race,[252] there the just Aeacus, there Plato, that divine and powerful man,[253] there glorious Pythagoras,[254] and all those who have set going the dance of immortal love,[255] all those whose lot it was to share a common race with the happiest of daemons,[256] where the heart has joy in festive gladness. O blessed one, what a great number of

---

248 See Plato, *Gorgias* 493a etc. for the "Orphic" notion that the body is the tomb of the soul. It is not a phrase that Plato seems to endorse without reserve.

249 Bidez (1913), 125 notes that this and some of the following phrases suggest the Isles of the Blessed (Pindar, *Olympian* 2.127), the seat of ideal Beauty (Plato, *Symposium* 197); we should not forget that Homer's Elysian fields (*Odyssey* 4.563–6) had been promised to philosophers since Lucretius, *On the nature of Things* 3.19–22.

250 Cf. *Iliad* 14.216 on the girdle of Aphrodite, which inspires love for Hera in Zeus and thereby consummates one kind of "sacred marriage" (see chapter 15). But whereas in Homer *philotês* means "endearment" and its presence in the girdle is a poetic conceit, in the *Oracle* it means "friendship", a cardinal virtue among Pythagoreans, and now it is literal, though too sublime for the present world.

251 Plato, *Apology* 41a adds Triptolemus to this list of upright men whom Zeus appointed to judge the dead. Plato, *Gorgias* 524a makes Rhadamanthus judge of Asia, Aeacus of Europe and Minos the supreme court of appeal. Note Porphyry's comment below.

252 The earliest race of mortals, according to Hesiod, *Works and Days* 115 and Aratus, *Phenomena* 132.

253 Literally "sacred power" (as in Armstrong): the phrase is Homeric.

254 The first appearance in the *Plotinus* of this semi-legendary figure, reportedly the earliest philosopher to found his own community, and the inventor of arithmetic and harmonics. He was best known for his doctrine that the soul survives the body, and is said to have recalled the past embodiments of his own. Porphyry's life of the sage is based on those by Aristotle and the second-century "Pythagorean" Nicomachus of Gerasa; he also believed that Empedocles, Thrasyllus, Moderatus and Numenius represented the same tradition.

255 Here as elsewhere in the poem, the love is the philosophical aspiration to the good celebrated in the *Symposium*, and the harmonious fellowship of the soul in its primal state, as described by Empedocles, Frs 17, 115, 137 DK etc.

256 Empedocles, Fr. 115.5 DK speaks of daemons, whose lot is immortal life. But the feasting is that of the Homeric gods at *Iliad* 1.595–600 etc.

contests you endured, you who now follow the saintly daemons, wearing a crest of doughty lives![257]

Muses, let us put an end[258] to our chant and the winding circle of the dance for Plotinus in his jubilation. This much, for my part, has my golden lyre to say of his good fortune.

23. It is said in these lines that he was gentle and mild, and especially kindly and charming; that he possessed these traits we knew by our acquaintance with him. And it is said that he was tireless, guarding the purity of his soul and always hurrying on to the divine, which he loved with the whole of his soul; also that he made every effort to be released, "to escape from beneath the bitter wave" of the present "blood-gorged life". Thus it was that the god who has neither shape nor form,[259] and is set above intellect and all that is intelligible,[260] appeared to this daemonic man as time after time he drove himself on towards the first and transcendent[261] god, with his own reflections[262] and according to the ways set forth[263] by Plato in the *Symposium*. I Porphyry testify that I once drew close to this god and was united with him, being in my sixty-eighth

---

257 A reference to the transmigration of souls and an echo of the weaving metaphor at the beginning.

258 Following Bidez (1913), 126, rather than Armstrong, who takes the verb to mean "set going". The god has said enough, though it is true that Homeric hymns often end with a promise to sing again.

259 A reminiscence of *Symposium* 210–11, though the subject there is the Beautiful, not "God". Plutarch (c. 100 A.D.) had already transposed the language of the *Symposium* to the same effect: Brenk (1992). The word *theos* in Greek is often a predicate rather than a proper name, and Plotinus was no more inclined than Plato to use it as a unique or exclusive appellation of the highest principle, though Rist (1962a) suggests that he sometimes made the same distinction between the One as *ho theos* and the mind as *theos* which some Christians found (and find) between God and the Word in John 1.1.

260 Porphyry, who is sometimes accused of conflating the One with intellect, is faithful here to the teaching of his master.

261 Translating the word *epekeina* from Plato, *Republic* 509c, where the Good (not God) is said to be beyond being. The notion of a first god may imply that mind is the second, as in Numenius.

262 Apparently discriminating between spontaneous insight and acquired philosophy, and in any case ignoring the Oracle's hint that, left to itself, the mind of the sage would have gone astray.

263 The participle *huphêgoumenas* may imply that Porphyry counted the *Symposium* as a "hyphegetic" dialogue, i.e. one that leads to positive knowledge: see Tarrant (1993), 41. The pursuit of the Beautiful is in fact the beginning of philosophy according to the first of Plotinus' treatises, though even here we are warned that it is inferior to the Good (*Enn.* 1.6.9;

ON THE LIFE OF PLOTINUS

year.[264] To Plotinus, at any rate, the "goal ever near" was shown, for his end and goal was to be united with and close to the god above all.[265] This goal he achieved four times, while I was with him, not virtually but in unspeakable actuality.[266] And in saying that the gods often set him right when he was veering, sending a frequent ray of light, it means that he wrote what he wrote under their inspection and invigilation.[267] And it says, "by your tireless vision, within and without, you saw with your eyes things many and fair, which no-one could have seen easily" among those who have studied philosophy.[268] For contemplation in humans may perhaps become better than human, but when compared with divine knowledge it may be fair indeed, but not able to grasp the depth as the gods grasp it.[269]

That, then, is what it tells us of his achievements while still clothed in a body; but after putting off his body it says that "he entered the daemonic band", and that in that place there is a commonwealth of friendship, desire, gladness and god-enkindled love.[270] It adds that he joins the ranks of those who are said to be judges of souls, Minos, Rhadamanthus and Aeacus, yet went to them not to be judged, but to join those

---

cf. 5.5.12). We may contrast Plotinus' reverent use of the *Symposium* with the rhetorical declamation of Diophanes (chapter 15).

264 The syntax, though ambiguous, seems to mean that he is 67 years old at the time of writing (i.e. it is 301–2), without implying that this was his age at the time of this event. This fleeting reminiscence is unique in its author's writings, as are 2Cor. 12.1–3, Plotinus, *Enn.* 5.8.1 and Origen, *Hom. Cant* 1.7, p. 49 Baehrens. Only in the fourth century did the ancients develop a literature of "spiritual experience".

265 For this title of the highest god cf. Porphyry, *Abst.* 163.15–16 and 176.9.

266 Thus this may not be the experience which Plotinus professes to have known "many times" at *Enn.* 4.8.1. The obscure antithesis between virtual and actual union indicates that a "science" of mysticism was already developing.

267 Palpably misconstruing the lines which imply a certain intellectual weakness in Plotinus, and thereby limiting the role of the gods. For all that, as Armstrong notes, divine assistance is still more prominent here than elsewhere in the *Plotinus*, let alone the *Enneads*.

268 The whole sentence, though it is a tendentious paraphrase, has the form of a quotation.

269 Plotinus penetrates the depth as the Gnostics (chapter 16) merely pretended to do.

270 Contrasting the earthly polity with that of the world "there", as the Christians did (Phil. 3.20)."In that place" (*ekei*) is a frequent term for the supercelestial or intellectual realm in the *Enneads*. Note that "god" appears once more in the commentary without precedent in the poem; the presence of a deity "there" is emphasised as that of the gods "here" is diminished.

whose society includes all other men of the highest virtue. These associates are Plato, Pythagoras and all the others who have "set going the dance of immortal love". And in that place he says the "happiest of daemons" have their generation and pursue a life replete with festivals and gladness, a life that goes on with the blessing of gods.

24. Such then was the life of Plotinus, as I have recounted it. But since he entrusted to me the task of ordering and editing his treatises, and I both promised this to him while he was alive and have announced to our other friends that I would do this,[271] [let me say] first that I did not think it right to leave the books in chronological order of their sporadic distribution, but have imitated Apollodorus the Athenian[272] and Andronicus the Peripatetic,[273] the first of whom brought together the works of the comic poet Epicharmus[274] and put them into ten volumes, while the other divided the works of Aristotle and Theophrastus[275] according to subject, bringing the relevant theses together under the same head. Thus I too, having fifty-four treatises of Plotinus, have divided them into six Enneads,[276] happy to discover the perfection of the number six[277] along with the nines,[278] and, putting the relevant matters into each Ennead,

271 Porphyry proceeds to the second subject promised in his title, possibly with a glance at the edition of Eustochius.

272 Born c. 180 B.C. and migrated to Alexandria, where he performed a number of scholarly labours.

273 Of Rhodes (first century B.C.). On his compilation of the *Topics* from disparate treatises, see Barnes (1995), 11, who cites this passage from the *Plotinus*. Theories that Andronicus has influenced the subsequent arrangement of Plato's works have little foundation: Tarrant (1993), 76–81.

274 A fifth-century Sicilian dramatist, less interesting than the spurious works attributed to him, which were alleged to be the source of Plato's doctrines. See Diogenes Laertius, 8.3.73.

275 Athenian polymath (371–287 B.C.), the most distinguished pupil of Aristotle and author of works on nature, both human and general.

276 Plato's works were commonly divided into tetralogies: Tarrant (1993), 58–109. Porphyry implies that he himself is not responsible for the division of the *Grossschrift* and the other consecutive treatises; it is likely enough that Plotinus had divided them already, but those who numbered books in a sacred corpus went to great lengths to produce a significant figure. Thus the books in the Hebrew Bible came to 22 (the number of letters in the Hebrew alphabet) or 24 (Greek alphabet), though we now reckon 39.

277 The first triangle (as sum of the first three numbers), the first perfect number (as sum of all its factors) and the product of the first two primes.

278 The square of three, the largest number within the decad and the last of Plato's harmonic ratios. A letter on the virtues of the number nine is attributed both to Pythagoras and

have then put these together, giving the first place to problems of less weight.[279] The First Ennead contains these, the more ethical treatises:[280]

1.1 *What is the living creature and what is man?* [53][281]. Of which the opening is: "Pleasures and pains".
1.2 *On Virtues* [19]. Of which the opening is: "Since evils are here".
1.3 *On Dialectic* [20].[282] Of which the opening is: "What art or way".
1.4 *On Happiness* [46]. Of which the opening is: "To live well and be happy".
1.5 *Whether Happiness depends on a Length of Time* [36]. Of which the opening is "If happiness increases".[283]
1.6 *On Beauty* [1]. Of which the opening is: "The beautiful is primarily visual".
1.7 *On the First Good and the Other Goods* [54]. Of which the opening is: "Should one posit a different good for each?"[284]
1.8 *Whence are Evils?* Of which the opening is: "Those who seek the origin of evils".[285]

---

to Thrasyllus, whose tetralogical ordering of Plato's writings was the most renowned, if not the first: Tarrant (1993), 246–7.

279 It was customary for editors of Plato to maintain that his dialogues were of different characters, each fitted to a certain stage in the pupil's education. The ordering of his works was thus a subject of perpetual debate, as can be seen from the discussions by Thrasyllus, Albinus, Theon and Dercyllus. The scheme explained in chapter 26 may owe something to Theon of Smyrna, who divided the education of the Platonist into five stages: ethics, science, *epopteia* or vision, politics and the godlike state. If so, Porphyry has conflated the first two and ignored the fourth, in which the philosopher takes up mundane affairs for the sake of others, as at *Republic* 519. See further n. 309 below.

280 No fewer than three of Plotinus' last four works (the weakest, in Porphyry's estimation) appear in the first Ennead; the ordering is clearly intended to indicate quality as well as purpose.

281 The earlier title has been expanded, perhaps to explain why this is included among the ethical treatises. Editors tend to prefer the titles in the second arrangement, because it is here that Porphyry quotes the opening words most accurately.

282 Perhaps a surprising title for so early a position, as dialectic was the summit of Platonic schooling (*Republic* 533).

283 Correctly quoting the first words, whereas the citation above is misleadingly truncated.

284 Substituting a new title for the original *On Happiness*, which has already been used in this Ennead, and quoting the first words at greater length.

285 Called *What are Evils?* above.

1.9 *On Departing Rationally from Life.* Of which the opening is: "You shall not draw it out that it may not go out".[286]

These, then, are the contents of the First Ennead, which includes theses of the more ethical kind. The Second contains a collection of topics in natural philosophy, and consists of the works on the cosmos or pertaining to the cosmos. These are:

2.1 *On the Cosmos* [40]. Of which the opening is: "Affirming the cosmos to be everlasting and to exist beforehand".[287]

2.2 *On the Circular Motion* [14]. Of which the opening is "Why it moves in a circle".

2.3 *Whether the Stars are Causes* [52]. Of which the opening is: "That the course of the stars is significant".[288]

2.4 *On the two Kinds of Matter* [12]. Of which the opening is: "What is called matter".

2.5 *On the Potential and Actual* [25]. Of which the opening is: "Some things are said to exist potentially, some actually".[289]

2.6 *On Quality and Form* [17]. Of which the opening is: "Existence and essence differ".[290]

2.7 *On Total Commingling* [37]. Of which the opening is: "Of the total".[291]

2.8 *How Things seen far off appear Small* [35]. Of which the opening is: "Do things far off appear smaller".[292]

2.9 *Against those who say that the Creator of the Cosmos and the Cosmos are Evil* [33]. Of which the opening is: "Since we have concluded".[293]

The Third Ennead again contains topics in cosmology, consisting of these works about considerations on the cosmos:

---

286 Again an expanded rather than different title.
287 Another expanded citation.
288 Another expanded citation.
289 Another expanded citation.
290 Both title and opening are expanded.
291 For once, an abbreviation.
292 Expanded citation again.
293 The alternative title is of a form resembling those conferred on Plato's dialogues by Thrasyllus, in order to identify the theme where the original epigraph revealed only the name of the interlocutor.

ON THE LIFE OF PLOTINUS 49

3.1 *On Destiny* [3]. Of which the opening is: "All that comes to be".
3.2 *On Providence I* [47]. Of which the opening is: "To mechanical operation".
3.3 *On Providence II* [48]. Of which the opening is: "What then are we to conclude about this?".
3.4 *On the Daemon to Whom we are Allotted* [15]. Of which the opening is: "Some things have their substance".[294]
3.5 *On Love* [50]. Of which the opening is: "As to love, whether it is a god".
3.6 *On the Impassibility of Incorporeals* [26]. Of which the opening is: "Not equating perceptions with affections".
3.7 *On Eternity and Time* [45]. Of which the opening is: 'Eternity and time".
3.8 *On Nature and Contemplation and the One*. Of which the opening is: "Speaking playfully at first".[295]
3.9 *Various Considerations* [13]. Of which the opening is: "Mind, says [Plato], sees indwelling".[296]

25. These three Enneads I have arranged in a single corpus in my edition.[297] And my arrangement of the Third Ennead includes the one *On the Daemon to whom we are Allotted*, because it is studied on universal principles, and the problem is one of those which are considered with regard to the generation of human beings.[298] The same is true of the study *On Love*. As for the one *On Eternity and Time*, it is assigned to this one because of what it says about time. And the one *On Nature and Contemplation and the One* is assigned to this one because of the section on nature. To the Fourth Ennead, coming after the writings on the cosmos, these works are assigned:

---

294 This, 2.3 and 2.9 are the only works for which the *Plotinus* suggests a circumstantial motive; all three fall within the "physical" group.
295 The expanded title supplies that of a book by Deck (1967). Porphyry's comment below implies that, as with 1.7, a new title was needed to justify the arrangement.
296 Omitting the word *ideas* from *Timaeus* 39e.
297 The word *sômation* (body) begins to be applied to books in the third century, as does the word *sômatopoiêsai* ("flesh out") for the making of them (Origen, *Against Celsus*, proem 6).
298 See chapter 15 on horoscopy and 13 on the demand of the novice for universal principles. These belong to physics, not, it seems, to the more empirical treatment of the soul.

4.1 *On the Essence of the Soul I* [4]. Of which the opening is: "What the essence of the soul may be".[299]

4.2 *On the Essence of the Soul II* [21]. Of which the opening is: "In the intelligible cosmos".[300]

4.3 *On Difficulties concerning the Soul I* [27]. Of which the opening is: "All the problems about the soul that must be raised and elucidated".

4.4 *On Difficulties concerning the Soul II* [28]. Of which the opening is: "What then is one to say".

4.5 *On Difficulties concerning the Soul III*, or *On Vision* [29]. Of which the opening is: "Since we have proposed for investigation".[301]

4.6 *On Perception and Recollection* [41]. Of which the opening is: "Perceptions are not impressions".

4.7 *On the Immortality of the Soul* [2]. Of which the opening is: "If the individual is immortal".

4.8 *On the Descent of the Soul into Bodies* [6]. Of which the opening is: "Many times waking".

4.9 *Whether all Souls are One* [8]. Of which the opening is: "Just as we speak of the soul of the individual".[302]

Thus the Fourth Ennead contains all the theses concerning the soul itself. Now while the Fifth contains those concerning the intellect, each of the books[303] also contains material in some passages on what is beyond and on the intellect in soul and on the Ideas. They are:

5.1 *On the Three Primary Hypostases* [10]. Of which the opening is: "What is it that has made".[304]

---

299 In fact this appears in the *Enneads* as 4.2. Porphyry once again gives a longer citation here than above.

300 In fact this is *Ennead* 4.1, with a different title, in order to create a double volume with the foregoing. See Schwyzer (1951), 389 and Henry (1938), 37.

301 This tripartite work has been kept together, but with a more informative title, since the whole of this *Ennead* concerns the soul. In 4.5 an abstract noun has replaced the indirect question in the subtitle, and in 4.3 and 4.5 the opening citation has been expanded.

302 Again an expanded citation. Porphyry's arrangement conceals the fact that this late group contains four of Plotinus' first nine treatises, the most "Numenian" and autobiographical. See chapter 4.

303 I make the books the subject of the clause, rather than the Ennead itself, as Armstrong does. He thereby treats the word *tisi* as a relative pronoun, and *hekaston* as a mere synonym for *panta*.

304 An abbreviated citation.

5.2 *On the Generation and Order of the things after the First* [11]. Of which the opening is: "The One is all".
5.3 *On the Knowing Hypostases and that which is Beyond* [49]. Of which the opening is: "That which thinks itself must be complex".
5.4 *How what is after the First comes from the First, and on the One* [7]. Of which the opening is: "If there is something after the first, it necessarily comes from it".[305]
5.5 *That the Intelligibles are not outside the Intellect, and on the Good* [32]. Of which the opening is: "Intellect, the true intellect".
5.6 *That which is beyond Being does not Think, and what is the Primary Thinking Agent and what the Secondary One* [24]. Of which the opening is: "Thought may have as its object".[306]
5.7 *Whether there are Ideas of Individuals* [18]. Of which the opening is: "If there are of individual".
5.8 *On the Intelligible Beauty* [31]. Of which the opening is: "Since we have said that one engaged in the contemplation of the intelligible".[307]
5.9 *On Mind, the Ideas and Being* [5]. Of which the opening is: "All men from the beginning".

26. Thus I have co-ordinated the Fourth and Fifth Enneads into a single corpus,[308] and made the remaining Ennead, the Sixth, a separate corpus, so that three have sufficed for all Plotinus' writings. The first corpus contains three Enneads, the second two, the third one.[309] These are the contents of the third corpus, the Sixth Ennead:

305 Adding a further clause.
306 An unhelpful curtailment of the earlier citation.
307 Another informative expansion.
308 In support of the following note, it should be observed that Porphyry has assigned almost all Plotinus' works on intellectual vision to this corpus, which was the bedrock of the so-called *Theologia Platonica,* on which see Schwyzer (1951), 501–6, who suggests that it borrows matter from Amelius.
309 A neat diminuendo, and these divisions make volumes of roughly equal length in the Oxford text. The division of philosophy into ethics, physics and logic is well attested: Hadot (1978). But in the second-century Platonist Albinus, *Isagoge* 6, the sequence is: elenctic works, to purify the soul; maieutic, to communicate "physical" knowledge; hyphegetic, to impart the positive doctrines which promote likeness to God in contemplation and action; and finally logical, to make knowledge indefeasible. If we divide the first *Ennead* from the next two, thus differentiating ethics and physics, we achieve a similar sequence here; as it stands, the threefold division in Porphyry seems closer to that of Origen, *First Principles*

6.1 *On the Kinds of Being I* [42]. Of which the opening is: "What and how many kinds of being there are".

6.2 *On the Kinds of Being II* [43]. Of which the opening is: "Since we have inquired concerning the aforesaid ten kinds of being".[310]

6.3 *On the Kinds of Being III* [44]. Of which the opening is: "As to being, where it appears".

6.4 *On what it means for Being, as One and the Same, to be wholly present everywhere at once I.* Of which the opening is: "Soul is everywhere present to the all".[311]

6.5 *On what it means for Being, as One and the Same, to be wholly present everywhere at once II.* Of which the opening is: "To be wholly present everywhere at once, while one and the same in number".

6.6 *On Numbers.* Of which the opening is: "Plurality is a defection from the One".[312]

6.7 *How the Multitude of Ideas has come to exist, and on the Good* [38]. Of which the opening is: "God sending into generation".

6.8 *On the Voluntary and the Will of the One* [39]. Of which the opening is: "There is in the case of the gods, if any inquiry about them is possible".[313]

6.9 *On the Good, or on the One* [9]. Of which the opening is: "All that exists exists by virtue of the One".[314]

4.2.4, where the literal, cosmological and mystical senses of scripture are said to be respectively its body, soul and spirit. In fact, Origen was familiar with Albinus' classification, as we see from his arrangement of the books of Solomon in the proem to *Cant.*, p. 75 Baehrens.

310 Expanded citation. These treatises attack the logic of Aristotle; Porphyry, as a Platonist, allots them to the third and final body of Plotinus' writings, rather than the prefatory position that the *Organon* held in the Aristotelian corpus. Perhaps he follows the second-century anti-Aristotelian Platonist Atticus, who divides philosophy into ethics, physics and logic at Eusebius, *PE* 11.2.1. See Weil (1951), 284 and 300 on Aristotle's objection to making logic a distinct branch of philosophy with its own objects.

311 Here and in the next we find an expanded citation after a rearrangement of the title.

312 Expanding the citation to make sense. The late position of this treatise justifies the numerological interests of the life.

313 Expanded citation. Many of these treatises are of more philosophical interest than 6.9, which has often been overrated because of the terminal position accorded to it in the Porphyrian recension.

314 Another expansion. The One being the origin, and the Good the end of all existence, this has to be the final treatise, leaving us with the "flight of the alone to the alone".

ON THE LIFE OF PLOTINUS 53

In this way, then, I have arranged the treatises, of which there were fifty-four, in six Enneads, and I have attached discourses to some of the works,[315] haphazardly produced on account of friends who urged me to write about such matters as they themselves desired to have clarified for them. Furthermore, I have composed chapter-heads for all of them,[316] except *On Beauty*, because they were missing in my copies,[317] and in this I follow the chronological order in which the treatises were distributed. But in this matter, not only have the heads been affixed to each book but summaries[318] also, which are numbered in sequence with the chapter-heads. But now I shall try, going through all the treatises, to add punctuation to them and correct the wording where there is any defect.[319] And whatever else has required my labour the work itself reveals.

---

315 For an attempt to trace the remains of these lost works, see Henry (1938), 312–32. They may have included the *hypomnēma* written by Porphyry on the subject of suicide: Eunapius, *Sophists* 456.48 Boissonade-Dübner.

316 I take this to refer to a table of contents which has perished. Armstrong understands it as referring to the rubrics for each treatise, but in that case I do not see why the treatise *On Beauty* should be an exception, nor what it means to say that he follows the chronological order.

317 Most translators appear to agree with Susanetti (1995), 29 that the treatise *On Beauty* was lacking to Porphyry; yet it figures in our recension and is divided into chapters. I take this to mean rather that Plotinus himself had already divided the treatise, which is not only the first in order of composition, but takes the form of a protreptic or exhortation to philosophy. In Peripatetic usage, this implies that it was an "exoteric" writing, intended for outsiders, and Christian plagiarisms seem to indicate that it circulated more widely than, and thus perhaps independently of, Plotinus' other works (Ambrose, *On Isaac* 79 etc.).

318 Literally "arguments" (*epikheirēmata*). Porphyry may mean that chapter 1 of each treatise is his own synopsis, or else that each head was accompanied by a synopsis of the chapter.

319 See chapter 8 on Plotinus' negligent methods of composition.

THE *SUDA* ON MARINUS[1]

Marinus of Neapolis,[2] a philosopher and rhetorician,[3] disciple and successor[4] of Proclus the philosopher, wrote a life of Proclus, his own master, both in prose and in epic form,[5] with certain other philosophical questions.

1 From the edition of Boissonade (1850), 150. The *Suda*, once ascribed to a notional author named Suidas, but in fact deriving its title from a Latin word meaning "fortress", is a Greek encyclopaedia of the late tenth century, arranged in the form of an alphabetic lexicon and drawing the greater part of its information from lost writings of the same kind – in this case, Damascius' *Life of Isidorus*.

2 Damascius, *Isid*. 141 makes it clear that this was Flavia Neapolis, otherwise Shechem, in Samaria, adding that Marinus was a convert from the Samaritan religion. Home to Justin Martyr (6. 165), who studied Plato before he became a Christian, c. 140, Flavia Neapolis may have had a local school of Platonism.

3 The term may signify either a teacher of rhetoric or a professional orator. Plato's *Gorgias* suggests that the aims of rhetoric are opposed to those of philosophy, and Philostratus seems to concur in his account of Dio Chrysostom. The antithesis was hardly recognised in Marinus' time, though he invokes it temporarily in chapter 11 below. Even Plato's *Phaedrus* seems to ascribe a higher form of rhetoric to Isocrates, and Aristotle thought the subject worthy of two treatises, the "esoteric" *Rhetoric* and the "exoteric" *Gryllus*. In the Latin-speaking world where rhetoric was an indispensable part of education, Cicero excelled in both pursuits. In the late fourth century Julian delivered his philosophy in orations, Eunapius applied the term "philosopher" to those whom Philostratus would have ranked as Sophists, and Themistius was celebrated both for his florid speeches and for his lucid commentaries on Aristotle.

4 Greek historians of philosophy tended to assume that from the earliest days philosophers had formed schools with a clear succession of leaders, whom they styled *diadochoi*. Blumenthal (1978), Glucker (1978), Dillon (1983a) and many others have doubted whether this was true of Plato's Academy, even after a chair was founded for it by the Emperor Marcus Aurelius c. 176 A.D. Oliver (1981), 316 notes that appointment to this and other chairs was originally entrusted to a *gerousia* or "senate", whose chief task was to promote the cult of Athena. Proclus seems to have taken both these duties on himself.

5 To judge by Quintus Smyrnaeus' *Posthomerica* and the voluminous work of Nonnus, narrative poetry in hexameters returned to fashion among the Greeks of the later Roman Empire. Marinus' choice of subject is unparalleled, but in structure his poem may have resembled Nonnus' paraphrase of the Gospel of John, while its contents may have included philosophical myths like those rehearsed in the *Dionysiaca* of the same author. We may also compare the panegyrics which Claudian, a poet of Greek origin, wrote in Latin hexameters on the Emperor Honorius and his general Stilicho at the turn of the fifth century.

Marinus. This man succeeded to the school of Proclus and instructed Isidorus the philosopher in Aristotelian doctrines.[6] When the latter came to Athens for a second time, after the death of their common master,[7] Marinus showed him a commentary of many lines which he himself had composed on Plato's *Philebus*,[8] asking him to study the book and pronounce as to whether it ought to be published. Isidorus, having read it carefully, made no secret of his own opinions, yet his words were not at all rude:[9] he said only this, that the master's commentaries were adequate to the dialogue. Marinus, however, understood

---

6 Isidorus, successor of Marinus, is the hero of a life written by Damascius, and this passage is a lengthened version of chapter 42. The teaching of the Athenian school was not confined to commentary on Plato, but extended to the works of Aristotle; Damascius, *Isid.* 79 speaks highly of Proclus' pupil Ammonius as an interpreter. Aristotle's doctrines had been assumed to coincide with those of his master since the time of Porphyry, and Hadot (1991), 180 cites *Tim.* i, 6–7 Diehl to show that Proclus admired those writings which concerned the physical world.

7 Damascius, *Isid.* 297 notes that Isidorus studied with Proclus in Athens while the latter was still sound of body. It seems that Marinus succeeded to the school before the death of Proclus because of his infirmity, yet was himself of such a weak constitution that Proclus had feared for his life while he was still an adolescent (Damascius, *Isid.* 142–52). Isidorus' devotion to the "common master" was such that he gave the name Proclus to his son: *Isid.* 301.

8 In order to prove that the human good is not pleasure but a mixed life of pleasure and reason, Plato introduces the key terms "limit" and "the unlimited" in this dialogue. Neoplatonists held that in the "unwritten philosophy" of Plato these were equated with the Monad and the Dyad, generative principles of all being in Pythagoreanism. As Frede (1992) shows, however, the *Philebus* has two ostensible goals: (a) a scientific taxonomy in which the limiting unity of the genus conditions the unlimited plurality of its contents; (b) a cosmology in which the indeterminate properties of matter are conditioned by stable measures of limits, mathematically defined. Under (b) Plato also posits a cause of mixture in addition to limit, the unlimited and the mixture itself. Readers, ancient and modern, have been divided as to whether the "Ideas" of classical Platonism, if they figure in this work at all, are to be identified with the limit, the mixture or the cause; nor is it clear how the final ranking of goods relates to the supreme Good of the *Republic* and other dialogues. Bury (1897) has one of the fullest discussions, with a review of scholarship.

9 The Greek word is *amousos*: cf. *Proclus* 6. Plato, *Phaedo* 61a, made Socrates speak of philosophy as the highest music, and was alleged to have founded his school as a "Museum" (Diogenes Laertius 4.1). The word occurs already in Damascius, *Isid.* 42; *Isid.* 41 ascribes to Isidorus a capacity for saying a word in season, though elsewhere we are told that he had little taste for rhetoric (35) and was sometimes choleric in criticism of perverse opinions (18). *Isid.* 10 describes another occasion when he said less than he thought.

and immediately destroyed the book by fire.[10] Moreover, by this time he had already sent Isidorus a letter communicating his view of the propositions and expositions in the *Parmenides*;[11] he sent him a compilation of his treatises, in which he urged that the dialogue is not about the gods but about the ideas.[12] Therewith he also composed commentaries, expounding the dialectical propositions of Parmenides on this principle. Isidorus, for his part, also responded to this letter with a composition showing by countless proofs that the more theological[13] exposition of the dialogue is the truest, so that, if the book had not already been published, this one too should be destroyed by fire. Perhaps, indeed, he was also deterred by the vision of the dream,[14] which Proclus claimed to have seen once, that commentaries on the *Parmenides* were going to be written by Marinus.

10 One could wish that Isidorus had been less critical, for the commentary of Proclus has perished, leaving us with only Damascius' commentary as a specimen of Neoplatonic scholarship on this dialogue.

11 In this, perhaps the most seminal of Plato's dialogues for the Neoplatonists, the philosopher Parmenides brings harsh criticisms to bear against the "Platonic" theory of ideal forms, and goes on to propound a series of contradictory theses on "the One" and its relation to the "Many". While modern scholars often treat this second part as a *jeu d'esprit*, or an exercise to test the bounds of logic, some Neoplatonists cited it as proof that the ineffable One was already a postulate of Plato's esoteric system. See Halfwassen (1993).

12 At *Parm.* 633–40 Proclus denies that the dialogue is a logical or gymnastic exercise, and defines its true subject, not as being or *ousia*, but as "all things that derive from the One". At 640–43, he asserts that Syrianus' explication of this theme required the postulation of deities or "henads". Isidorus was evidently more faithful to the master than Marinus, on whose shallowness see Damascius, *Isid.* 142–144.

13 This term is also applied to the dialogue in the anonymous sixth-century *Prolegomena to Plato*; the *Parmenides* appears here as the crowning work in a syllabus of ten.

14 I am not sure whether this phrase merely implies that he remembered Proclus' vision or that the dream came again to him. Damascius, *Isid.* 11–14 records that Isidorus was a regular recipient and interpreter of dreams. Such experiences, whether nocturnal or diurnal, are reported to have inspired the composition of Greek literature from the *Aitia* of Callimachus (third century B.C.) to the *Makrobioi* attributed to Lucian.

MARINUS OF NEAPOLIS:
PROCLUS, OR ON HAPPINESS[15]

Were I to contemplate the greatness of soul, or any of the other qualities, in Proclus, the philosopher of our time,[16] and again the preparation and facility in discourse possessed by those who ought to write his life, and then again to regard my own ineptitude in words, it would seem best to me to keep silence,[17] and not (as the saying is) to leap over the earthworks,[18] but to repel the danger that such discourse entails. But as it is, I do not measure my own worth by that standard, but reflect that even in temples those who approach the altars do not make their sacrifices from equal means, but some through bulls and goats and other creatures of this kind render themselves fit for communion[19] with the gods who possess the altars, and furthermore produce polished hymns, some in metre and some without metre;[20] others, by contrast, having nothing like this to offer, but consecrating, as it may be, a cake or handful of incense, and making their orison with some brief invocation, enjoy no less benign a hearing than the former.[21] I considered this, and was

---

15 The title resembles that of a panegyric (e.g. the *Evagoras* of Isocrates), but also of a Platonic dialogue. The titles of these dialogues (e.g. *Laches*) appear to have been original; the subtitles (e.g. *On Courage*) were added by such editors as Thrasyllus. Marinus makes it evident that the purpose of his biography (which he does not style a *bios*) is edification rather than entertainment.

16 Compare the opening sentence of Porphyry's *Plotinus,* which seems to have become a formula.

17 As philosophers do in the presence of the highest principle; cf. Proclus on the ascent to the One, *PTh* 2.11.

18 A metaphor for going to excess, which first appears at Plato, *Cratylus* 413a and is said by Simplicius, *Commentary on the Physics* 184.23 Diehl to be a proverb.

19 Neoplatonists held that one acquires a quality by participation in the paradigmatic bearer of that property; as a man grows in "likeness to god" (*Theaetetus* 176c, often cited below), he enters into communion with the gods and receives their favours. See Proclus, *DD* 1.20.10 on the providential bestowal of *metousia* in the Good in accordance with the worthiness of the recipient.

20 Examples of the latter would be the hymns of the Emperor Julian (r. 361–3) to Helios and to the Mother of the Gods. Proclus' own hymns were in hexameter verse.

21 Cf. Porphyry, *Abst.* 145–6 Nauck on the acceptability of a frugal sacrifice. At 146.10 these include libations (poured offerings) and the small cakes whose use is attested in the

moreover afraid lest, in the words of Ibycus,[22] I should receive honour from men while guilty of some sin not against the gods, as he phrases it, but against the wise man (for I was afraid that it might be impious for me alone of the company to be silent[23] and not to rehearse the truth about this man so far as in me lay, when indeed I had perhaps a greater duty to proclaim it than the others); and perhaps I shall not even receive honour from men, for they will not impute my neglect of the goal that lies before me[24] to any concern for avoiding ostentation, but rather to a certain idleness or even to some more severe debility in the soul. For all these reasons, I felt it incumbent on me to address myself to writing an account of some of the countless excellences in the life of this philosopher, and at any rate of the stories that have been truly told about him.[25]

2. Now I shall begin my account, not in the accustomed manner of writers, who plan the account sequentially by chapter headings; rather I believe that the happiness of the blessed man is the most suitable foundation that I can lay for my account.[26] For I believe that he was the happiest man of all those who have acquired renown in many a long age.[27] I am not speaking only of the happiness of the wise – though indeed he

---

classical age by e.g. Aristophanes, *Thesmophorians* 285. Such offerings were often given to heroes or daemons, or to gods as part of a larger ceremony. A more distinguished oblation would be the sacrifice of a whole beast.

22 A lyric poet of the sixth century B.C. In allusions to the classics, Platonists tended to follow the example of their master, who was fonder of lyric poetry than of tragedy or epic, quoting this line at *Phaedrus* 242d. Proclus in turn cites this at *Rep.* ii, 220 Kroll and alludes to it at *Crat.*47.26–7 Pasquali.

23 The memoirs of Proclus written by other disciples (if indeed they are not a rhetorical fiction of Marinus) have been lost.

24 A typical phrase for the principal subject of a Platonic dialogue. The identification of the goal or *skopos* was regarded as the first task of an exegete in the school of Proclus: see *Alc.* 6.6 (i, 4 Segonds).

25 Perhaps implying that some were false. See Festugière (1960) for examples of stock themes and occasional disclaimers in hagiography, esp. Eunapius, *Sophists* 459 Boissonade-Dübner on Iamblichus. Cf. also Isocrates, *Evagoras* 21, where he professes to have selected only the details that are generally agreed to be true.

26 Like Porphyry, Marinus sets out to illustrate the paradigmatic character of his subject. It is in fact not easy to find instances of the "typical" biography that Marinus describes: no doubt, then as now, there was a convention of unconventionality.

27 This explains the title of the work. Happiness was defined by Aristotle, from whom all later discussion originates, as an activity of the soul in accordance with perfect virtue.

possessed that in the most eminent degree – nor of the fact that his portion of virtue was sufficient for his well-being,[28] nor of that prosperity which is on the lips of many – though again fortune provided him with this as much as any man, as he was liberally endowed with all the so-called external goods[29] – no, the happiness that I want to speak of is perfect, without defect, and consisting in both kinds.[30]

3. First, let us divide the virtues into their kinds, the physical, the ethical and the political,[31] and again those which transcend these, the purificatory, the contemplative,[32] and those that are called theurgic,[33] while as to those that are higher even than these we shall keep silence, because they exceed the human condition.[34] We shall take the more natural ones as our starting-point. All those that dwell innately in

---

28 At Aristotle, *Nicomachean Ethics* 1098b, this term (*euzoia*) means living not merely pleasantly but admirably, and is almost a synonym for happiness. In Proclus' disciple Hierocles, *CA* 416 Mullach, likeness to god is said to consist in the recovery of one's proper *euzoia*.

29 While both health and pleasure are regarded as goods in Plato (*Republic* 357 etc.), he undertakes at *Republic* 361 to prove that justice is advantageous to its possessor even when its sole concomitants are pain and obloquy. For admirers such as Atticus, the belief that the internal goods are sufficient for happiness without the externals is one of the marks that distinguishes the school of Plato from that of Aristotle. The latter states that external goods are necessary to happiness at *Nicomachean Ethics* 1098b32–1099b8. The Stoics disagreed, and their position is eloquently defended in Book 5 of Cicero's *Tusculan Disputations*.

30 That is, of both internal and external goods.

31 Though Hadot (1978), 156 cites Damascius, *Phaed.* 3 Norvin as a parallel, this text divides virtues into contemplative, cathartic, political and ethical; the later expression "ethical and natural" in Damascius does not define two categories but adds an epexegetic term to the name of the fourth and lowest. A closer parallel would be the division of Plato's discoveries into physical, ethical, political and theological in the anonymous *Prolegomena* 5; there was evidently a fashion for such schemes, but no prevailing orthodoxy.

32 See Damascius, as in note above. The ascent to the higher virtues is recounted in detail in chapters 21 and 22, where the scheme follows Porphyry, *Sent.* 32 (24–26 Lamberz) or Plotinus, *Enn.* 1.2, often word for word. See the synopsis in Hadot (1978), 149–52.

33 Theurgy in Iamblichus and Proclus is the realisation of an innate capacity for union with the divine. Although Marinus indicates in chapter 28 that Proclus achieved this by the methods and precepts of the *Chaldaean Oracles*, Smith (1974) suggests that it is only the secondary, "providential" exercise of virtue that requires such instruments. The higher theurgy which both Iamblichus and Proclus appear to recognise – see also Sheppard (1982) – is the cultivation of the *anthos nou*, on which see n. 41.

34 The paradigmatic virtues, according to Porphyry, *Sent.* 32 (28–31 Lamberz) make a man not merely a god, but a father of gods.

their possessors from their birth were present by nature in this blessed man whom I am praising from the day when he was born. The vestiges of these were visible even in his final and shell-like covering.[35] First was outstanding keenness of sense, which they call indeed the wisdom of the body,[36] and especially of the more honourable senses, sight and hearing,[37] the ones that have been given for the purpose of philosophy and to produce good relations both with human beings and with the gods; this man retained them unimpaired throughout the whole of his life. Second was strength of body, impervious to extremes of cold and heat, not vitiated even by his mean and negligent diet[38] or the labours that he endured by night and day, prayerful even when he was meditating or writing down his doctrines, and also in the presence of his companions, each of whom he treated so attentively that he seemed to have no other business.[39] Power of this kind one might reasonably style the fortitude of the body. The third virtue of the body that pertained to him was that which corresponds to temperance; people think they discern this in bodily beauty, and with good reason. For just as temperance is discerned in the harmony and agreement of the soul's powers, so too the beauty in body is seen in a certain symmetry

---

35 On the mortal, "oyster-like" body which the soul receives as the covering of its "chthonic" or earthly body at the nadir of its descent from higher regions, see Proclus, *Tim.* iii, 298.16ff Diehl. Proclus contrasts this vehicle with a "connatural" and "uranian" body which is immortal, and another "naturalised" one which bears the soul from one "oyster-like" embodiment to another. The term "oyster-like" derives from *Republic* 611d. On the varieties of body in Neoplatonism see Dodds *On Proclus*, 313–21.

36 Each of the cardinal virtues (wisdom, fortitude, temperance, justice) is now related to a bodily attribute. Plato, *Symposium* 196–197 names these virtues in a different order in an encomium of Eros. The use of the cardinal virtues in such eulogies was evidently common: in Isocrates, *Evagoras* 22–24, bodily and inward virtues are mingled more promiscuously; *ibid.* 75 shows that praise of bodily attributes is expected in panegyric. In Iamblichus' *DVP* the virtues of Pythagoras and his followers are rehearsed in the order: wisdom (157), justice (167), temperance (187), fortitude (214). Proclus, *Alc.* 94 (77 Segonds) says that divining the powers of the soul from those of the body was a skill peculiar to the Pythagoreans.

37 This prejudice in favour of sight and hearing is as old as Heraclitus (Fr. 55 DK) and Hippocrates (*Regimen* 1.35). Metaphors for intellectual perception are predominantly visual in Plato and Aristotle.

38 Cf. Porphyry on Plotinus, chapter 9 and Iamblichus, *DVP* 16. On the attention paid to diet in the ancient world, see Foucault (1985), 95–140.

39 Contrast the intellectual abstraction of Plotinus, which is equally compatible with friendly association, but appears to involve no prayer. Affability is an admired characteristic even in the Cynics, as we see from Lucian, *Demonax* 5.

of its functioning parts.⁴⁰ He was lovely indeed to behold, for not only did he fully possess that symmetry, but also the force of his soul, blooming⁴¹ in his body like a living light, produced an astonishing radiance which it is scarcely possible to convey in words.⁴² So beautiful to behold was he that none of those who drew him could catch his likeness, and all the images of him that are current, beautiful though they are in themselves, fall none the less far short of the truth in their imitation of his form.⁴³ Fourthly, people are inclined to make health the analogue to justice in the soul, saying that the former too is a kind of justice in the body as the latter is in the soul. For the habit of exercising the parts of the soul with the least of discord is nothing else than justice,⁴⁴ while the sons of Asclepius⁴⁵ also give the name of health to that which produces orderly and agreeable co-operation in the disorderly elements of the body.⁴⁶ So beautifully fashioned in him was this from his infancy that he was able to say how often his body had

40 A position denied by Plotinus in *Enn.* 1.6.
41 Marinus may be thinking of the encomium of Eros, who lives among flowers at Plato, *Symposium* 196b; but also of the "bloom of the soul" (*anthos nou*), described by Proclus as the unitive element in intellectual activity, which brings us to the summit of the intellectual realm, but not to the One itself. See Beierwaltes (1963), Hierocles, *CA* 450 Mullach, and for the source of the metaphor Proclus' commentary on the *Chaldaean Oracles* (Fr. 1) in Des Places, *OC*, 209-210. It was already known to Plotinus: see *Enn.* 6.7.32 and Dillon (1992a) for other parallels to the *Oracles*.
42 The countenance of Isidorus, though not physically luminous, was equally diaphanous to wisdom: Damascius, *Isid.* 80 and 249. The radiance described here is more often associated with momentary transfiguration: Mark 9.2ff, Damascius, *ibid.* 211, *Hermetica* 13. In the last two cases it is a manifestation of the aethereal or astral body, which is particularly sensitive to divine communication (Iamblichus, *Mysteries* 3.14 etc.).
43 Marinus implies, like Porphyry (*Plotinus* 1) that words gave a better account of the philosopher than a picture – though Proclus was not so reluctant a sitter as Plotinus, and here it is the beauty, not the vileness, of his corporeal form that cheats the portrait-painter.
44 As Plato argues at length in the *Republic*. The parts of the soul are the rational, the "spirited" and the appetitive; true harmony consists in the voluntary subordination of the others to the first.
45 A name used for doctors, e.g. by Plato, *Phaedrus* 230a, because Asclepius, son of Apollo, was supposed to have been the first physician. But as chapters 19 and 29 show, Asclepius was more than a personification of medicine for this philosopher.
46 The soul performs the work of the Demiurge who brings the present world into being from its disorderly substrate in *Timaeus* 30. Plato, *Phaedrus* 252 had already made the soul a kind of artisan who perfects the inner being of the lover, and Plotinus, *Enn.* 1.6.8 had turned this into an image of self-fashioning. Neither had suggested that the body too is the object of the soul's workmanship, perhaps because (a) neither rates the body so highly as Proclus, and

succumbed to illness, a matter of only two or three times in a long life of fully seventy-five years.[47] A sufficient indication of this, to which I myself was a witness in his mortal illness,[48] is that he was quite unable to determine what kinds of suffering pertained to the body, as he himself had so little experience of them.

4. And even if these be only bodily assets, one might none the less call them harbingers of the several forms of perfect virtue. In any case, the prime attributes of soul were innate[49] in him, spontaneously and without instruction; and one can only marvel to see how these parts of virtue were identical with those that Plato proposes as the elements of the philosophic nature. For he had a good memory, learned easily, was noble and gracious, and showed a love and affinity for truth, justice, fortitude and temperance. For he never gave way willingly to mendacity, which he greatly abhorred, preferring guilelessness and truth. Indeed, one who means to apprehend the truth about reality must make this his goal from earliest infancy, since truth is the source of all good things for the gods and also for humanity. As proof of his superiority to pleasures of the body and his outstanding love of temperance I think it sufficient to mention only his intense predilection and zeal for mathematics[50] and

---

(b) neither wants to pursue a strict analogy between the soul and the Demiurge, who is properly its creator.

47 Probably an exaggeration (see chapter 35). Among Athenians noted for equal or greater longevity were Plato, Isocrates, Sophocles, Euripides and not least Arcesilaus, who is said to have received honour surpassing that of all other philosophers (Diogenes Laertius 4.44). Marinus reconciles this with a predicted figure of seventy in chapter 26. Neither here nor there, nor even in chapter 20, are the symptoms rehearsed in such detail as in Porphyry's *Plotinus* (chapter 2).

48 Thus Marinus can claim the intimacy with his dying teacher that had been denied to Plato, Aristotle and Porphyry. See *Plotinus*, chapter 2 and notes.

49 To render the Greek *sumphunta*, distinguished from being merely "naturalised" (*prosphuomena*) at Proclus, *Tim.* iii, 298 Diehl, commenting on the creation of the human body in Plato, *Timaeus* 42c–d.

50 For Plato, *Republic* 322c–331d this term covers arithmetic, geometry and astronomy. The Academy gave a high place to these sciences, as they gave access to pure and indefeasible knowledge. Neopythagoreans of the second century A.D. (particularly Nicomachus of Gerasa and Moderatus of Gades) derived all being from number, claiming the support of Plato's *Philebus* (in which Limit and the Unlimited are the sources of essence), *Parmenides* (which advances paradoxes of unity and multiplicity) and the so-called unwritten doctrines, which traced all things back to the Dyad and the One. Their doctrines were revived for the

everything of the kind. These pursuits do not allow creaturely and vulgar pleasure to arise even at the outset, but have the power to implant felicity in the essence of the soul.[51] As for avarice,[52] no words can say how foreign it was to him, since, notwithstanding the great wealth of his ancestors, he thought little of it even from his boyhood on account of his extreme love of philosophy. For this reason he was also a total stranger to parsimony and to what is known as meanness, since all and everything, divine and human, was his object. The nobility[53] engendered by this outlook made him think of human life as nothing, nor did he regard death as something terrible, as others do; he remained unterrified by everything that is dreadful in the eyes of others, simply because of this natural disposition, which it is not fitting to call by the name of any virtue other than fortitude. And from these facts it is surely already obvious, even to one who is not acquainted with the fine nature of this man, that from his earliest infancy he loved justice, being at once just and courteous, and was in no way a bad associate, a bad man to deal with or at all unjust. In fact, he showed us that he was by nature a well-regulated man,[54] no grasper and no miser, no imposter and no coward.

5.[55] As for the receptivity and fecundity of his soul, it might be excessive to give a minute account of it, and especially to those who have

---

Neoplatonists by Iamblichus, and Proclus, while he declared that mathematics fell short of knowledge of the Ideas (*Parm.* 653), is the author of a commentary on Euclid.

51 For the distinction between the mixed and transient pleasures of the senses and the pure and lasting ones of the soul see Plato, *Republic* 585c.

52 The same is said of his colleague Isidorus by Damascius, *Isid.* 18. Avarice is deprecated in the *Golden Verses* of Pythagoras: see Hierocles, *CA*, and by Proclus, *Alc.* 110 (i, 90–91 Segonds).

53 Making an inward quality of the *megaloprepeia* (commonly rendered "magnificence") which Aristotle praises at *NicEth* 1121a20, and which Veyne (1990), 14–18 treats as the foundation of "euergetism" (chapter 15).

54 Translating *kosmios*. Masullo notes an echo of Plato, *Republic* 486b. Damascius, *Isid.* 155–156 implies that Proclus' virtues were emulated by all his pupils, while Proclus, *Alc.* 24 (i, 19 Segonds) praises Socrates in like terms. Iamblichus, *DVP* 15 attributes the similar virtue of *eukosmia* to the young Pythagoras. Plato, *Republic* 500d seems to pun on the word *kosmos* when applying this adjective to God, and Proclus, *Tim.* 2e (i, 6.5 Diehl) expressly says that a man becomes *kosmios* by imitating the order of the cosmos. See further chapter 15.

55 Though Masullo divides the chapters differently here, I follow Boissonade's text, which is still more widely available in English-speaking countries.

seen and heard how much sublime learning teemed within him,[56] and how many thoughts he himself brought forth into the light[57] for the human race, so that this man alone seemed never to have drunk of the cup of forgetfulness.[58] Such was the power of his memory that he never grew weary, nor did he ever suffer what befalls the more forgetful, but retained the self-possession of one who constantly applied himself to learning and embraced only such activity as conduced to this end. His nature was entirely free from rudeness[59] or asperity, but he had an affinity for the higher qualities. And indeed, because of his urbanity and graciousness in common associations, as well as in his own sacred festivals and other such activities,[60] even while he lacked nothing in dignity, he drew his companions to him and sent them away with lighter hearts.[61]

6. Innately endowed as he was with all these and other natural blessings, the mother who gave birth to him was Marcella, the legal wife of Patricius.[62] Both of these were Lycians,[63] distinguished both in family and in

---

56 The human soul is female, and therefore is receptive to philosophy, in Plato, e.g. *Symposium* 209c.

57 The context suggests a metaphor for parturition; otherwise this is a trite Platonic phrase for the publication of a treatise which professed to divulge the wisdom of authoritative minds: see chapter 22.

58 Souls returning to the world were supposed to drink of the mythical river Lethe to efface the memory of their previous lives: see Plato, *Republic* 621. Most would also lose the knowledge that they had gained, at least until some skilful teacher restored it by provoking *anamnesis* or recollection: Plato, *Meno* 85–6.

59 *Amousos* again; see introduction. Proclus, noting the place that Plato gave to music in education, argues for an affinity between this pursuit and true philosophy, and claims that it has the power to induce good moral habits: *Rep.* i, 56–63 Kroll.

60 See chapter 36.

61 Much the same is said of Demonax, another Athenian philosopher, by Lucian, *Demonax* 6.

62 Proclus stresses this point perhaps (a) to indicate that the frugal Proclus had a right to the wealth of affluent parents, (b) to contrast him with Antisthenes, who took pride in being only half-Athenian (Diogenes Laertius 6.1), or (c) to mock the claims of divine paternity made on behalf of Christ and Apollonius of Tyana, whose mothers were therefore not the legitimate spouses of their fathers. In chapter 10 Marinus uses the concept of legitimate paternity to express the integrity of the Platonic school.

63 It was a rhetorical commonplace to praise a subject's antecedents, though as we see from Isocrates' *Evagoras* 12–18 and *Helen* 16–17 this motif would generally precede the enumeration of his personal merits and trace his genealogy further than his parents.

virtue. But his nurse[64] and midwife,[65] as it were, was the tutelary goddess of Byzantium,[66] who first became the cause of his existence at this time,[67] since he was born in her city,[68] and subsequently took care that he should turn out well when he came to boyhood and adolescence. For she, appearing to him in a dream, exhorted him to philosophy.[69] This, I think, is the reason for his strong association with the goddess, so that he celebrated her festivals particularly and observed her rites with great enthusiasm. But once he was born his parents took him to their own country Xanthus,[70] which is sacred to Apollo, and it was this that by a

---

64 Literally she "received him" (*hypodekhetai*); but, in view of the following note, Marinus seems to have in mind the receptacle of Plato's *Timaeus*, also called the nurse (52d), and later identified with matter. Cf. Proclus, *Tim.* iii, 141.18 Diehl on the true earth as receptacle of gods.

65 The verb *maieuesthai* (to be a midwife) is used by Plato, *Theaetetus* 150 as a figure for Socrates' custom of drawing out an answer from an interlocutor. Marinus implies that Rhea is the midwife of Proclus' embodied soul. For a similar interpretation of Rhea as mother of the gods and source of generation see Proclus, *Crat.* 52.9 and 81.2–15 Pasquali; *Tim.* iii, 194 and 248 Diehl, commenting on *Timaeus* 41a–d.

66 Modern Istanbul, then capital of the eastern (and wealthier) half of the Roman Empire. Chapter 8 explains why this was his birthplace. The goddess will be Rhea rather than Hecate, though both had famous cults in Byzantium according to Hesychius of Miletus, in Jacoby (1950), 168 and 170. Rhea's sanctuary was deemed to be the source of the city's fortune, and occupied the site of the later Basilica, but Hecate was the protector of Byzantium against the assaults of Philip of Macedon. Both goddesses are important in the *Proclus* (see chapters 15 and 28), as also are the Dioscuri (chapter 32) and Heracles (chapter 15), whom Hesychius includes among the deities of the old city.

67 The exact date is not known, but Évrard (1960a) argues that the evidence points either to 409/10 or 411/12. The horoscope in chapter 35 points to 8 February 412, though this would not allow Proclus to reach the age of 75 allotted to him by Marinus.

68 Rhea was a symbol of the generative principle for the Neoplatonists (see n. 65 and chapter 33). Byzantium had been refounded as Constantinople, with a dedication to a Christian martyr by the Christian Emperor Constantine in 330, and since then had contained no pagan temples; the allusions here and elsewhere to the goddess as the patron of the city and (almost) the parent of the philosopher may therefore be calculated to give offence to Christian readers, or at least reinforce the prejudice of pagans.

69 The importance of such foreshadowings is recognised in the lives of Plato. In the anonymous one, Socrates dreams of his future pupil as a singing swan; in that by Olympiodorus, after Apollo has mated with Plato's mother he instructs the father not to seek intercourse until the birth.

70 Standing on a river of the same name, this was the major city of Lycia in southwest Asia Minor, and is now most celebrated for its shrine to Leto, the mother of Apollo.

certain divine allotment[71] became his country. For it was, I think, necessary that one who was going to be a leader in every branch of knowledge should be nurtured and instructed by the leader of the Muses.[72] Hence, being trained in moral excellence, he acquired the moral virtues through being accustomed to love what ought to be done and spurn what ought not.

7. And at the same time it became apparent that he was naturally very dear to the gods. For once when his body was sick with fever and already in a state of incurable suffering, there stood by his bed a dazzling youth, extremely young and beautiful in looks; one could guess that he was Telesphorus[73] even before he spoke his name. When he none the less said who he was, uttered his name, and touched [Proclus'] head (for he stood there resting against the pillow), he immediately restored him from sickness to health, and thereupon became invisible to him. Thus the divine and his dearness to the gods were already present to him in adolescence.

8. After briefly attending lessons with a grammarian[74] in Lycia, he set out for Alexandria in Egypt, bringing with him already the traits of moral virtue, which also enabled him to choose his teachers there. For example, Leonas the sophist, an Isaurian[75] by race as I believe, who

71 The association with Apollo is felicitous because he is the god of prophecy and poetry, and shares a birthday with Plato (Olympiodorus, *VP*). Pythagoras too was his protégé, being known as the Hyperborean Apollo (Iamblichus, *DVP* 30, etc.).

72 Traditionally nine goddesses, who presided over the arts of epic, tragedy, comedy and pastoral, hymnody, lyric poetry, flute-playing, dance, astronomy and history. Plato, *Laws* 653c is the first prose writer to style Apollo the "leader of the Muses" *(Musêgêtês)*. Proclus, *Crat.* 103–4 Pasquali asserts that Apollo as Demiurge gives unity to the universe, while the Muses bring the perfection of the number nine and harmonise the energies of the soul. At *Tim.* 231c (ii, 294.32–3 Diehl) both the Musagetes and the Hermaic chain (chapter 28) proceed from the Demiurge. See Pausanias 1.31.1 on the shrine of the Muses in Athens and Plato, *Phaedrus* 237a–b for a famous prayer to them.

73 The cult of Telesphorus ("bringer of fulfilment") seems to have originated c. 100 A.D. among the Greeks of Asia Minor; by 250 A.D. he had been received in Athens as a son of Asclepius. There is (unsignalled) evidence in Sironen (1984), 49 that this deity was honoured by Plutarch of Athens.

74 This is a poor equivalent for *grammatikos*, which denotes a man who teaches the interpretation and criticism of literature. These studies were preliminary to rhetoric, the art of composition and delivery.

75 From Isauria in the centre of Asia Minor. On the rehabilitation of the term "sophist" see chapter 9 and Fowden (1982), 51.

enjoyed a high reputation among a host of fellow-practitioners in Alexandria, not only shared his studies with him, but saw fit to take him into his house, causing him to dine with his wife and children, as though Proclus too had become his own trueborn child.[76] He also introduced him to those who held the reins in Egypt, and they for their part, astonished by the natural acumen and moral integrity of the young man, came to treat him with particular affection. He also attended the school of the grammarian Orion, who was descended from the priestly caste in Egypt,[77] and, having a certain proficiency in the principles of his art, had gone so far as to compose small treatises of his own, which he left for the benefit of posterity. Furthermore, he attended the Latin schools and in a short while had also made great progress in their characteristic studies;[78] for at first he set out to follow the practice of his father, in which the latter had indeed acquired great renown when he engaged in litigation as part of his duty in the royal city.[79] At this young stage he seemed to take a particular pleasure in rhetoric, not yet having tasted philosophical discourse,[80] and he obtained a high reputation in it, making himself an object of great wonder to the companions who studied with him, and also to his teachers, on account of his skill in

---

76 Not so much a charitable measure as an alliance between distinguished families, as the following chapter will make clear.

77 Wilson (1967), 145 dates the acme of Orion to c. 425. On hereditary priesthood in Egypt see Thompson (1990), 100–101. Plato, *Timaeus* 22a and *Phaedrus* 274c–275c bequeathed to his followers a high esteem for the oral wisdom of Egypt. Plutarch, *Isis and Osiris* 352–5 believed that Pythagoras learned the use of symbols from this country. Smith (1974), 137n compares the transmission of knowledge by the Brahmins in Porphyry, *Abst.* 256 Nauck.

78 That is to say in forensic rhetoric, which was always a part of education for the wellborn Roman (see e.g. Lactantius, *Divine Institutes*, proem 10). Latin would be useful to any lawyer, as the laws were promulgated in that tongue, and it remained the official language of the courts.

79 Meaning Byzantium. We may infer that Proclus' father was engaged in official duties at the time of his birth. Jones (1940), 208–10 observes that by this date the chief magistrates were likely to be imperial appointees, perhaps from abroad, rather than members of the local aristocracy of wealth or "curial" class. Patricius (whose name is Roman) would probably have been of equestrian rank if, as his presence in the lawcourts indicates, he held the office of *procurator* or fiscal magistrate.

80 Marinus represents Proclus as following the *trivium* of grammar, rhetoric and philosophy, defined at about the same time by the Latin author Martianus Capella, *The Marriage of Hermes and Philology*, books 3–5. This is often regarded as an apology for pagan education against the Christians.

speech and his facility in learning, and moreover because he seemed to have the habits and pursuits of a teacher rather than a pupil.

9. While Proclus was still attending his school, Leonas the sophist[81] arranged for him to accompany him during his residence in Byzantium, which he undertook as a favour to his friend Theodorus, then prefect[82] of Byzantium, an urbane and noble man who was also a lover of philosophy. Young as he was, Proclus eagerly followed his teacher, in order not to be prevented from studying with him. But to speak more truly, it was some fortunate chance[83] that led him back to his original place of birth. For it was when he went there on that occasion that the goddess exhorted him to pursue philosophy and to visit the schools in Athens.[84] But before this he returned to Alexandria, and said farewell to the rhetoric and other arts of which he had lately been so fond; then he sought out the seminars of the philosophers there. And first he studied the doctrines of Aristotle with Olympiodorus, the widely-renowned philosopher;[85] and as for mathematics, he entrusted himself to Hero, a pious man who was extremely proficient in the techniques of education. These men were so struck by the character of the adolescent that Olympiodorus wished him to be engaged to a daughter of his whom he was also rearing in a philosophic manner;[86] while Hero imbued him with the whole of his own regime of piety, and made him the constant companion

---

81 As in Philostratus and Eunapius, this term signifies a professional orator or teacher of rhetoric. It does not carry the pejorative connotation which it possessed in the Athens of Plato (*Protagoras* 315c–e), as these itinerant speakers had become the standard-bearers of Greek culture throughout the Empire. Marinus, however, neglects no opportunity to assert the inferiority of rhetoric to philosophy.

82 The prefect in a major city administers the province on behalf of the Emperor. This post was the culmination of an equestrian career, and Leonas' friendship with Theodorus is an index of his own high social status.

83 Gifts of chance are disparaged by panegyrists (e.g. Isocrates, *Evagoras* 36), but chance is understood here, not as that which has no cause, but as that which could not be predicted from the motives and expectations of the human agent. Proclus, *DD* 8.51 etc. cites Plato, *Laws* 709b7–8 to show that chance and occasion are at the bidding of the gods.

84 A unique foundation c. 176 by the philosophical Emperor Marcus Aurelius: see Oliver (1981). There were chairs of Platonic, Peripatetic, Stoic and Epicurean philosophy, though there is no proof of unbroken succession either before or after 176.

85 Otherwise unknown, and not to be confused with the later Neoplatonist.

86 Gillian Clark points out to me that this need not mean that he taught her philosophy; the term *thugatrion* (a little daughter) implies that she would not have much say in her own affairs.

70 MARINUS

of his hearth.[87] Now Olympiodorus was a polished speaker, and few of his listeners were able to follow him on account of his cleverness and volubility. Proclus, however, when he left the seminar after hearing him, recited the entire proceedings, in the very same words, to his companions – and there was a great deal, as I have heard from one of his fellow-students, Ulpian of Gaza, another man whose philosophy is sufficiently apparent in his life.[88] And he very quickly mastered the logical treatises of Aristotle, simply by reading the works themselves, difficult though they are for those who attempt them.[89]

10. Having undergone schooling with these men in Alexandria, and having reaped as much from their seminars as they were able to offer, he thought one day, in the course of someone's lecture, that the interpretation being advanced was unworthy of the philosopher's intention. Thus, conceiving a contempt for these institutions, and remembering at the same time the divine vision and exhortation in Byzantium, he set off for Athens, escorted as it were by all the gods and good daemons[90] who are custodians of the oracles of philosophy.[91] For in order that the succession from Plato might be preserved without adulteration[92] or impurity, the gods were leading him towards [the city which is] the custodian of philosophy. This was proved conspicuously even by the events prior to his residence, and the truly god-sent omens that clearly foretold what he stood to

   87 As with Leonas there will have been more poverty than charity in this arrangement; the breadth of Proclus' education is sufficient proof of his family's affluence.
   88 It was generally assumed in late antiquity that philosophy is a mode of life, not merely a body of arguments: see e.g. Plato, *Theaetetus* 166–176.
   89 Aristotelian logic was conceived as an introduction to all philosophy, not merely that of the Peripatetic school, but it was customarily approached through a manual such as Porphyry's *Isagoge*; if the treatises of the *Organon* were read at all, a commentary would be employed. The claim to have read the *Categories* without a master seems to have been a conventional proof of native wit; cf. Augustine, *Confessions* 4.2.
   90 A daemon is a being intermediate between the divine and human: in Plato, Love or Eros is the most celebrated example (*Symposium* 202c–d). Platonists after Iamblichus distinguished good and evil ones, arguing that even the latter must be propitiated while the former ought to receive the devotion of those who were not yet worthy of the gods. In Egypt the name Agathodaemon ("good daemon") had been given from an early date to Hermes Trismegistus, the putative revealer of the cosmology and mystical theology contained in the *Hermetica* (first–fourth centuries A.D.).
   91 Meaning the *Chaldaean Oracles*: see chapter 28.
   92 Here and in the next sentence Marinus treats the legal right to inherit from one's father as an analogy to the inheritance of true doctrine from the master.

PROCLUS 71

gain[93] from his father and the succession to the school that was going to come to him above. For when he arrived at the Piraeus[94] and those in the city were informed of this, Nicolaus, who subsequently became illustrious as a sophist but was then a pupil with the teachers in Athens, went down to the harbour as though to an acquaintance, to welcome him and lead him to the city as his fellow-citizen; for Nicolaus was also a Lycian.[95] He led him therefore toward the city, but Proclus, feeling fatigue on the road because of the walk, and being close to the Socrateum[96] – though he had not yet learned or heard that honours were paid to Socrates[97] anywhere – begged Nicolaus to stop there awhile and sit, and at the same time also, if he could obtain water from anywhere, to bring it to him. For he was possessed, as he said, by a great thirst. Nicolaus readily complied, and caused[98] water to be brought from nowhere else, but from that sacred spot; for the spring from the statue of Socrates was not far off.[99] As he was drinking, Nicolaus noted the omen, which

93 The word *klêros* seems to refer here, not to a pecuniary inheritance, but to the reception that was due to him as the son of Patricius.

94 The harbour of Athens since the fifth century B.C. One could hardly come to Athens from Alexandria any other way, but it may be worth observing that in Proclus, *Rep.* i, 17.3–25 Kroll the journey up from the harbour to the city is construed as an image of progress in philosophy.

95 He appears at Damascius, *Isid.* 64 as a pupil of Plutarch and Proclus. Much of his prolific work survives.

96 This statue, standing in its own garden, seems to be a different monument from the one carved by Lysippus and set up by the Athenians in the Pompeium where Socrates was executed: Wycherley (1978), 47, 73. Lucian, *Demonax* 58 appears not to know of a statue of Socrates.

97 Socrates (470/69–399 B.C.) was the first philosopher to come from Athens. Though he left no writings, his students Plato and Xenophon have immortalised his ruthless interrogation of the beliefs of his fellow-citizens. Modern scholars tend to regard the "aporetic" dialogues of Plato, in which no conclusion is reached, as a truer portrait of his teacher than such works as the *Republic*, in which Socrates voices positive opinions. The ancients seldom recognised this distinction: thus Aristotle speaks of "Socrates" when he means his namesake in the dialogues. The so-called New Academy of the Hellenistic period made Plato as much a sceptic as his master, and Proclus avers that, even in an introductory dialogue, the character and philosophy of Socrates were an epitome of the whole Platonic corpus: *Alc.* 27 (i, 22 Segonds).

98 Here we learn for the first time that the fortunate pair were accompanied by a servant.

99 Statues over springs are attested in classical Greek literature, most famously perhaps at Plato's *Phaedrus* 264c–d; the setting of this dialogue in a watered glade near Athens was no doubt in Marinus' thoughts when he retailed this anecdote. We may contrast the importance attached to the statue here with the words of Plotinus in chapter 1 of his *Plotinus*.

he now perceived for the first time, that he was sitting in the Socrateum, and first drank the Attic water[100] from this place. Proclus for his part rose, made a sign of obeisance, and went on to the city. And as he was climbing up to the top,[101] he was met at the entrance by the doorman, who was already about to insert the keys – so much so that he said to him (I shall repeat the fellow's[102] very words), "Honestly, if you had not come, I was about to close up".[103] What omen, now, could have been more clear than this, which required no Polles or Melampus[104] or any such person for its interpretation?

11. Here too he completely disdained rhetorical studies, even though he became an object of competition among the rhetoricians, and, as if this were the one thing he had come for, the first person whose acquaintance he made was the philosopher Syrianus, son of Philoxenus.[105] Another person present at the seminar was Lachares, a man who was replete with philosophical discourse, and a colleague of the philosopher himself in these proceedings, yet had won as much admiration for himself in the sophist's art[106] as Homer in poetry. This man, then, was present, as I have

100 A metaphor for eloquence, as the greatest writers of the classic period (Plato, Xenophon, Demosthenes, Isocrates, Lysias) were all exemplars of the Attic dialect. At Damascius, *Isid.* 161 there is a reference to a spring of holy water, though it is not clear whether this is topographical or metaphorical.

101 The Academy was on rising ground to the north-west of the Dipylon gate, through which a road led to the market-place or Agora of the city.

102 Rendering *anthrôpiou*, a word chosen to emphasise the low status of the speaker.

103 An inadvertently pregnant phrase, unlike the words of Plotinus quoted in Porphyry's *Plotinus*. For other examples cf. the words of Caiaphas at John 11.49–51.

104 Melampus, first mentioned at *Odyssey* 11.281–97 and hero of the Melampodia attributed to Hesiod, was one of the most famous seers in legend; Polles, equally mythical, is a figure of whom only late antiquity seems to know. The *Suda* (s.v. Eudocia) credits him with a work on augury (divination from birds).

105 Often called his mentor or *kathêgemon* by Proclus, he succeeded Plutarch of Athens as master of the Platonic school in 431/2 A.D. Proclus makes it clear that he gave notable commentaries (whether written or oral) on the *Republic, Timaeus* and *Parmenides*; his contribution to Proclus' *Rep.* is studied in detail by Sheppard (1980), and Dillon (1987), xxx–xxxiv opines that a full investigation would prove that much of Proclus' other work derives from him.

106 Since Syrianus' few extant works include commentaries on the rhetorician Hermogenes as well as the *Metaphysics* of Aristotle, Marinus seems to be nursing a false dichotomy between rhetoric and philosophy. As for Lachares, though Damascius, *Isid.* 81 says that he owed more to training than to a natural bent for rhetoric, he adds that his works reveal nobility of character. Lachares had a son Metrophanes (*ibid.* 62). See Athanassiadi (1999b), 167n on an epigram praising him.

said, and it was the hour when visibility was failing. Even as they were talking, the sun sank low and the moon appeared for the first time in her new cycle.[107] Therefore they tried to send away the young man because he was a stranger, so they might have an opportunity to venerate the goddess by themselves. But he went on a little away, and then, seeing for himself the apparition of the moon in this quarter, he took off in that place what he was wearing on his feet,[108] and, as they watched, worshipped the goddess.[109] At this point, Lachares, struck by the boldness of the adolescent, addressed the philosopher Syrianus with this inspired utterance of Plato's about great natures: "Either this man will be a great good or the contrary".[110] And such, to mention only a few, were the signs that visited the philosopher from the gods as soon as he had begun to reside in Athens.

12. Syrianus took him along with him when he went to visit the great Plutarch,[111] son of Nestorius.[112] Seeing that he was a young man, barely

107 The *sunodos* is the point at which the moon occupies the same sign of the zodiac as the sun, and is therefore invisible by night. Worship of the moon was once regarded in Greece as a barbarism (Aristophanes, *Peace* 406), but the Platonic *Epinomis* (985d–e) upbraids the Greeks for their neglect. The moon was equated with Artemis (on whose day Socrates was born) and with Hecate, queen of the underworld and patroness of magic, who is the source of generation in the *Chaldaean Oracles* (see chapter 18). Proclus may also have been acquainted with the cult of the moon as Men in Asia Minor: Lane (1990).

108 Not a common feature of Greek prayer, but attested in Pythagorean sacrifice by Iamblichus, *DVP* 85, 105. Proclus may also have wished to imitate Socrates' notorious habit of going barefoot *(anupodêtos)*.

109 A clue to the significance of the act may be found in Proclus, *Rep.* i, 18–19 Kroll, where the moon is equated with the Thracian goddess Bendis, honoured by Socrates at the beginning of the *Republic*. Proclus, *loc. cit.* takes this worship as a symbol for the inception of the philosophic life.

110 Not in Plato or in Riginos (1976). In his edition of Proclus, Cousin (1864), 21 cites a similar saying about the philosopher from Plato, *Republic* 492a. Masullo seems to prefer *Lesser Hippias* 375e, a widely quoted text; but neither this nor her other suggestions (*Critias* 44d, *Gorgias* 521a) are a perfect match.

111 Known as Plutarch of Athens, Syrianus' predecessor as head of the school in that city. He appears to have rescued Athenian philosophy from a long eclipse, and Blumenthal (1978), 375–6 suggests that he may have used his private residence as a school. On his antecedents, see Évrard (1960b) and Castren (1994), 6–7. Since Proclus was 20 in 429/30 or 431/2, and Plutarch was then already an old man (perhaps about 70), the latter must have been born c. 360. Our only other biographical notice of him, in the *Suda*, is entirely dependent on Marinus, but he may be the Plutarch named in three inscriptions, discussed by Sironen (1984), 46–51. If so, he was a rich man, friend of archons, famous "sophist" and devotee of Telesphorus.

112 Proclus, *Rep.* ii, 64 Kroll speaks of another Nestorius, the grandfather of Plutarch. If this is the thaumaturge who is styled "the great Nestorius" at *Rep.* ii, 324–5 Kroll, the "great

in his twentieth year,[113] but hearing of his determination[114] and his great desire for the philosophic life, Plutrach was extremely taken with him, so that he readily let him join in his philosophical studies, even though his age was an impediment, as he was now extremely old. With him Proclus read Aristotle's *On the Soul* [115] and Plato's *Phaedo*.[116] The great man also exhorted him to write down what was said, making an instrument of his zeal, and saying that, when these notes were completed, there would be treatises on the *Phaedo* in Proclus' name.[117] He was also delighted in other respects by his experience of the young man's aptitude for liberal studies,[118] constantly calling him his son[119] and making him share his hearth. And when he perceived that he was stoutly committed to abstinence from live creatures[120], he enjoined him not to abstain from these completely, so that his body also might subserve the activities of his

---

Nestorius" of chapter 28 is also a different figure from the one in chapter 12. See Castren (1994), 7, n. 63, and on the identity of the man of this name at Zosimus, *New History* 2.18.11 see Taormina (1989), 148. Damascius, *Isid.* 88 notes that Proclus taught Plutarch's son Hierius. I am not sure why Athanassiadi (1999b), 173n suggests that Nestorius is another name for Plutarch and that his "grandfather" was in fact his parent.

113 Thus the date is either 420/30 or 431/2.

114 The word *hairesis* signifies the "choice" of a philosophy, hence a "sect", never a heresy in the Christian sense. Glucker (1978), 167–8 and n. 18 observes that the expression *hairesis biou* ("choice of life") is seldom met outside the Neoplatonists.

115 On Neoplatonic readings of the Aristotelian treatise (particularly prized because 3.5 appeared to affirm the existence of a separable and "active" or "making" intellect) see Blumenthal (1996), esp. 56–7 on this period. The edition of Plutarch's *Fragments* by Taormina (1989) shows that his commentary on this work by Aristotle was far more often consulted than his expositions of Platonic dialogues. Fr. 35 Taormina shows that he endorsed the "Platonic" view that the active reason operates independently of the lower functions of the soul.

116 Also often called *On the Soul*, because it argues for the immortality and separability of the soul. For three citations of Plutarch in Damascius' commentary on the *Phaedo* (early sixth century), see Taormina (1989), 137–8.

117 This work is lost. Though Blumenthal (1996), 57 implies that this was the commentary or lecture course on the *Phaedo* that was cited by Proclus' successors, he observes at 54 that *hypomnêmata* ("treatises" here) would more probably have taken the form of a series of essays.

118 Literally "the beautiful", i.e. Proclus is a *philokalos* or lover of beauty, as at *Phaedrus* 248. In this dialogue the love of beauty is presented as the initiation into philosophy.

119 Though Taormina (1989), 155 notes that "father" is a term used frequently of intellectual mentors among the late Neoplatonists, the use of "son" is not symmetrical with this, and here it seems that the issue is one of honour as much as of influence.

120 The proper habit of a Platonist, as we see from Porphyry's *Plotinus* and *Abst.*

PROCLUS

soul.[121] He also gave the same injunctions to the philosopher Syrianus concerning the young man's diet. But the latter replied to the old man, as that divine personage[122] related it to me, "let him learn what I wish, living abstemiously, and then, if he wishes, let him die".[123] Such on all occasions was his teachers' solicitude for him. Now the old man lived only two years more with Proclus as his lodger, and then when he died he entrusted the young man to his successor Syrianus, as he also did his grandson Archiadas.[124] And when Syrianus took him, he not only gave him more help with his scholarly pursuits, but made him his housemate from then on and a sharer in his philosophic life, finding in him the sort of hearer and successor that he had long desired to have,[125] as he was able to receive his manifold learning and divine teachings.

13. In less than two whole years, he read with him the entire works of Aristotle,[126] logical, ethical, political, physical and the science of theology which transcends these.[127] Once he had received sufficient

121 This passage does not substantiate the view of Évrard (1960b), 392–4 that Plutarch belonged to the tradition of Porphyry rather than Iamblichus, for Porphyry's *Abst.* condemns all eating of meat, whereas Iamblichus, *Myst.* justifies sacrifices. If, as Évrard surmises, Plutarch deprecated the theological interests of his pupil Syrianus, he would also have sighed over most of the works of Porphyry, who treats religious practices with no more reserve than any other Neoplatonist.

122 Literally "divine head", meaning Proclus.

123 Damascius, *Isid.* 126 reports that Proclus refused even in illness to relax his Pythagorean regime.

124 "Grandson" renders *eggonos*, which could mean child, but *Proclus* 28–9 implies that Plutarch's only child was his daughter Asclepigeneia. Taormina (1989) and Castren (1994), 6 show that the name was common in the family.

125 This "long desire" implies that Syrianus had been in charge of the school for some time already, just as the *Suda* indicates that Marinus succeeded Proclus before his death. Whereas Plotinus (*Plotinus* 3) sought out a teacher for himself, Proclus is sought by others as a pupil.

126 Saffrey (1987) maintains that, while Syrianus deemed the study of Aristotle indispensable to Platonists, he rated Plato above him and denied to Aristotle a true understanding of theology.

127 The logical works are the *Organon* (*Categories*, etc.), the next three species are all represented in the titles of famous works by Aristotle, the science of theology is contained in the *Metaphysics* and especially Book 12: Saffrey (1987), 136. The Platonists reconciled Aristotle with Plato by treating the non-theological writings as propaedeutic, much as they reconciled the "aporetic" dialogues of Plato with the more dogmatic ones. Since the edition of Andronicus certainly began with the *Organon* and placed the *Metaphysics* after the *Physics*, it is possible that the order of subjects here is of his devising. See further Gottschalk (1987), 1089–93.

direction in these, as in certain preliminary and lesser mysteries,[128] Syrianus directed him to the mystagogy[129] of Plato, in due sequence, and not, as the oracle says, "putting his foot across the threshold",[130] and caused him to behold[131] the truly divine rites in Plato's work, with the unclouded eyes of the soul[132] and the spotless vision of the mind.[133] Working day and night with tireless discipline and care, and writing down what was said in a comprehensive yet discriminating manner, Proclus made such progress in a short time that, when he was still in his twenty-eighth year, he wrote a great many treatises, which were elegant and teeming with knowledge, especially the one on the *Timaeus*.[134] In

---

128 Plato, *Symposium* 209e–210a distinguishes the lesser mysteries (that is, the works of poets and lawgivers) from the higher ones to which the true philosopher aspires. Analogies between philosophic wisdom and initiation into the secret cults called "mysteries" are legion both in Plato and in his followers, above all in those, like Proclus, who believed that theurgic practices conduced to the elevation of the mind. Thus at *Alc.* 6–7 (i, 5 Segonds) and 174 (ii, 236 Segonds) he compares the *Alcibiades* to a preliminary rite performed by those about to undergo initiation.

129 That is, initiation into mysteries. Though he disdained the ritualists of his day, Plato makes free use of the vocabulary of mystic rites, especially in the *Phaedrus* and *Symposium*, and his legacy matured in Middle Platonism, as Riedweg (1987) demonstrates. For Neoplatonists the reading of Plato himself was analogous to participation in mysteries in that (a) it required the discovery of latent meanings in a prolix narrative, and (b) it led to the illumination of the student. On (a) see Proclus, *Crat.* and Sheppard (1980); on (b) see the anonymous *Prolegomena* and Trouillard (1982), 1–32.

130 Hadot (1991), 188 n. 52 interprets this "Chaldaean" expression (*OC*, Fr. 176 Des Places) to mean that "the theurgist must not stray from the set order for the ritual", and gives parallels, including Damascius, *Isid.* Fr. 137 Zintzen.

131 The verb *epopteuein* was in regular use to denote the climactic vision which was imparted to initiates in the mysteries.

132 For this famous image see Plato, *Republic* 533d, echoed by Iamblichus, *Protr.* 21 and developed in the anonymous *Prolegomena*, 206 Hermann. Proclus, *Alc.* 194–5 (ii, 253 Segonds) maintains that the eye is first turned by instruction and dialectic.

133 The mind, for both Plato and Aristotle, is either the highest part of soul or a higher faculty altogether. The state of pure intellectual cognition is enjoyed by souls in the "supercelestial region" before they fall to earth (*Phaedrus* 247).

134 In this work the eponymous speaker offers a probable account of the creation of the universe by the Demiurge, with further pronouncements on human physiology and the providential government exercised by lesser gods. It was natural that Proclus should address himself to this "physical" dialogue before proceeding to such a theological work as the *Parmenides*: see *Tim.* 5a (i, 13 Diehl) on the difference between the two. The extant portion of his commentary, edited by H. Diehl, fills three thick volumes; the original must have been at least three times as long if it covered the whole of the dialogue at the same pace.

the course of these pursuits, his character also gained in beauty, acquiring the virtues along with knowledge.

14. And politics too he mastered from the political treatises of Aristotle and from the *Laws* and *Republic* of Plato.[135] Now he was debarred from political activity because his studies had been devoted to higher matters;[136] so that it might not seem that in these matters he confined himself to words and took no part in any affair, he urged Archiadas, the favourite of the gods, to this pursuit, simultaneously teaching him and training him in political virtues and methods, and, as one encourages people in a race, exhorting him to be at the very head of public affairs in his own city, and to be a private benefactor[137] to everyone according to every species of virtue, but especially in justice. And he did in fact excite a certain aspiration in him, teaching him to be liberal and munificent with regard to his wealth by giving to friends and relatives, to residents and strangers, and to demonstrate in every way his superiority to the possession of wealth. His own gifts to the public were not negligible either, and, dying after Archiadas, he left his possessions to the cities, both his native one[138] and Athens. The character of Archiadas as a lover of truth was so apparent, both in itself and through his friendship with Proclus, that whenever men of our time desired to make mention of him, no other commendation came to their lips than "the most pious Archiadas".[139]

---

135 The *Laws* is Plato's last and longest work, in which an Athenian stranger draws the plan of a hypothetical, but not unimaginable, commonwealth. The *Republic*, a more famous dialogue in which the principal speaker is Socrates, is a discussion of justice both in the soul and in the ideal state. Marinus here employs the plural form *Politeiôn* ("polities"), no doubt to indicate that the work is in ten books.

136 Meaning presumably that the true philosopher cannot be a Christian, or else that he did not choose to be a lawyer. See introduction on the legislation of Theodosius II.

137 The word *euergetein* is commonly used of bestowing ostentatious public benefits, and was applied in this period to civic magnates and above all to the Emperor: see Veyne (1990). Damascius, *Isid.* 18 ascribes the same liberality (and hence the same financial means) to his hero.

138 Literally "fatherland" (*patris*). Even in an Empire where every freeborn person was a citizen, a Greek would often consider himself primarily a citizen of the urban community from which he came – in this case Xanthus, rather than Proclus' birthplace Byzantium.

139 His piety is attested also by Damascius, *Isid.* 222.

15. And the philosopher himself sometimes took a hand in political deliberations, being present at public debates on the city's affairs,[140] offering shrewd advice and conferring with the magistrates[141] about matters of justice, not only exhorting them, but in a manner forcing them by his philosophic frankness[142] to give to each his due.[143] And again he publicly took an interest in the regular conduct[144] of scholars,[145] causing them to manage affairs with discretion,[146] not teaching by word alone but rather instructing them by his conduct throughout his life, and becoming as it were a prototype[147] of discretion to the rest. As for the species of fortitude that he displayed in politics, it was truly

---

140 As a metic, or resident alien, he would not have been allowed to participate in the Assembly in classical Athens, but such conventions could not survive when many of the magistrates appointed by the Roman government were from abroad: Jones (1940), 60, 76 etc.

141 In Athens these were called archons, as in the classical period. Sironen (1984) produces many inscriptions to prove that they were still active benefactors, and friends of a number of wealthy sophists. Lucian, *Demonax* 11 also stresses his hero's intimacy with those in power.

142 *Parrhesia* was regarded as the prerogative of philosophers. Socrates displayed it by his freedom of inquiry and his frank defence before the Athenian judges; then it was exemplified by Stoics in their defiance of imperial despotism and by Cynics in their unbridled mockery of Greek society and culture. Since the term can also denote the privileges enjoyed by a citizen of the ruling order, Proclus can be said to have abandoned his political rights to avail himself of philosophic liberty. At the same time, his inherited "freedom" will have done much to reduce the danger of his adopted "frankness". Lucian plays on the same ambiguity at *Demonax* 3 and 11.

143 Perhaps alluding to a concept of distributive justice formulated by Aristotle, *Nicomachean Ethics* 1130b.

144 The quality of *kosmiotês*, a combination of inward and outward order, is the one ascribed to Proclus himself at the end of chapter 4, and also the one induced by Demonax at Lucian, *Demonax* 6. According to Proclus, *Tim.* i, 6.5–6 Diehl it conduces to happiness (*eudaimonia*) and is acquired by being in harmony with the *kosmos* and with one's ideal destiny or "paradigm".

145 Literally "readers", a term used also by Plutarch, *Alexander* 1.

146 Translating *sôphronos*, relating to the virtue of *sôphrosunê*, which is often translated "temperance" when it occurs at *Republic* 432 etc., but there it is the specific virtue of the artisan class. In Plato's *Charmides* (161a), it is suggested that the essence of *sôphrosunê* is that each should do his own, which is all but identical with the definition of justice at *Republic* 433a–b.

147 Cf. Proclus, *Tim.* i, 16.8–10 Diehl on Plato's characters as types of what is proper to the disciple, and *Alc.* 42 (i, 34 Segonds) on the tutor's virtues as an inspiration to the pupil. Christians too liked this conceit: see e.g. George of Alexandria on Chrysostom as a type of monasticism in Photius, *Bibl.* 96 (79b Migne; 51 Henry).

Herculean.[148] For this man entered into the billowing tempest of affairs[149] at a time when monstrous[150] winds were blowing against the lawful way of life,[151] yet he carried on a sober and undaunted existence even amid the perils; and once when he was critically[152] harassed by certain giant birds of prey, he left Athens, just as he was, entrusting himself to the course of the world,[153] and made the passage to Asia with the greatest profit. For it was in order to prevent his being uninitiated into the more ancient rites still practised there[154] that his personal

---

148 The political virtues are being divided into four (see chapter 3 above). Heracles, the legendary son of Zeus and hero of the Twelve Labours, was a model of practical virtue for Stoics and Cynics (as Lucian hints with irony at *Peregrinus* 24); for Platonists (Plotinus, *Enn.* 1.1.12 etc.) Herculean virtue, though desirable, was inferior to that of a philosopher. Heracles had a cult in Athens (Pausanias 1.30.2), but Proclus, who speaks of him as an archetypal hero at *Crat.* 68.19 Pasquali may have encountered the mysteries in Byzantium: see Hesychius of Miletus, in Jacoby (1950), 168. See also *Crat.* 38–16–21 on giving the divine name to a man.

149 Saffrey (1975), 555–7 argues that the occasion was the conversion of the temple of Asclepius on the Acropolis into a Christian place of worship (see chapter 29 below). On the soul's exposure to tumults in the realm of generation cf. Proclus, *Alc.* 162 (ii, 225 Segonds).

150 Literally "Typhonian", with reference to a monster of Greek mythology, spawned by earth, who threatened to overthrow Zeus. The term *tuphôn* can also denote a whirlwind and an illness; it is also an alternative name for Seth, the Egyptian god who personifies the irrational forces leagued against the mind (Proclus, *Tim.* 24d = i, 77 Diehl). Plato, *Phaedrus* 230a alludes to Typhon as a proverbial monster, while Damascius, *Isid.* 5 makes him a paradigm of "earth-born" sensuality. See further Courcelle (1975).

151 Although since the late fourth century imperial legislation had favoured Christianity, Proclus speaks as though it were still unlawful (*paranomos*). Although it is not certain that Christianity was ever called officially a *religio non licita* (an illicit religion), the profession of it was a capital offence in the second and third centuries. Under pagan Emperors, Porphyry had written of the defection of Ammonius from the Church to a "way of life more in accordance with the laws" (Eusebius, *HE* 6.19). The burning of Porphyry's writings by order of Theodosius II in 448 (Justinian, *Digest* 1.1.3) will have both reinforced contempt and enjoined discretion among philosophers; Saffrey (1975), 558 is therefore probably right to see an allusion to the Christians in the charge of *paranomia* in Proclus, *Tim.* 252c (iii, 44.6 Diehl). By law or *nomos* Proclus understands a god-given order that cannot be dissolved by a change of government.

152 Translating here *en peristatei*, a cognate of which recurs in chapter 29 to enhance the tale of a miracle effected by Asclepius. This reinforces the conjecture of Saffrey (note above). *Peristasis* ("crisis") is a favourite term with Proclus' disciple Hierocles, *CA* 450 Mullach etc.

153 That is to the tutelage of unchanging providence, rather than to miraculous intervention.

154 Meaning in Lydia (see below).

daemon[155] contrived this pretext for his departure. For he himself acquired clear knowledge of their customs, and for their part, if through length of time they had neglected any of the practices, they learned from the philosopher's directions to serve the gods more perfectly.[156] And as he did all this and lived in this way, he escaped notice even more than the Pythagoreans, who preserve intact their master's injunction to "Live unknown".[157] Having spent only a year in Lydia,[158] he returned to Athens by the providence of the philosophic god.[159] Such then were the effects of his fortitude stemming both from his original nature and from habituation, and after that cemented by knowledge and an understanding of the principle.[160] And in another way he gave a practical demonstration of his skill in politics by his injunctions to those in power, by which he conferred benefits on whole cities.[161] The witnesses

155 The *daimonion* of Socrates, attested in his *Crito* and other writings, took the form of an inward voice forbidding wrongful or imprudent action. See *Plotinus* 10 on the guardian spirit in late antiquity.

156 The phrasing is deliberately obscure, as for example in Apuleius, *Metamorphoses* 10.23, because the mystic is bound to conceal the secrets of his initiation.

157 This saying of Epicurus (Fr. 551 Usener) is cited only for criticism by Plutarch, *On Whether it is a Good Precept to "Live Unknown"* 1128a. Siorvanes (1996), 45 n. 26 observes that it appears as a Pythagorean dictum at Philostratus, *Apollonius* 8.28.

158 Even the destination of his journey is temporarily concealed in Marinus' narrative. Lydia is on the west coast of Asia Minor, to the north of Proclus' native Lycia. The mysteries may have been those of the god Sandon, worshipped in the city of Sardes, who is supposed to have died on a pyre and was thus identified by Greeks with Heracles. Platonists will have seen this immolation as a symbol of the purging of the soul. If we follow the reconstruction of Fontenrose (1958), 107–113, Heracles' labours in Lydia will have included the slaying of a beast akin to Typhon. It is also possible that queen Omphale of Lydia, for whom Heracles worked in the guise of a woman, takes her name from Cybele, the mother goddess, on whose cult in Lydia see Burkert (1979), 102.

159 That is Apollo. Cf. *Alc.* 5.14 (i, 4 Segonds), where Proclus describes philosophy as a partaking of the providence of Apollo, which is denied to the uninitiate. For praise of one's subject as the favourite of providence cf. Isocrates, *Evagoras* 25.

160 The coupling of nature and discipline is commonplace (cf. Isocrates, *Against the Sophists* 14–18), but also Platonic. Socrates insists that understanding must be a part of courage (*Laches* 196d, etc.), as of every virtue, though at the same time it is admitted that a knowledge of what is fearful is not sufficient to banish cowardice. Protagoras at *Protagoras* 351a asserts that nature must make a contribution, and this issue is fundamental to the *Meno* (70a etc.). See also Proclus, *Alc.* 162 (ii, 225 Segonds) on the importance of nature in the choice of teaching method.

161 Civic legislation is attributed to a number of Greek philosophers, especially Pythagoras, who is said to have set up his own communities in Italy, as well as educating the famous lawgivers Zaleucus and Charondas (Diogenes Laertius 8.1.16). Both the

to my claim are his beneficiaries, some of whom are Athenians, some Andrians[162] and others of other peoples.

16. And beyond this he also promoted scholarly pursuits, both by directly sponsoring those who applied to him and by petitioning the magistrates to give subsidies[163] and other privileges to each according to his worth. And he did this neither uncritically nor with favour, but he forced the very people whom he was supporting to show intense concern for their personal disciplines, questioning and testing them about each of their studies; for he was himself a sufficient judge of all. And if he found anyone too slack in his calling, he rebuked him severely, so that he seemed rather hot-tempered[164] and too competitive, being at the same time willing and able to judge everything correctly. He was indeed competitive, but in him competitiveness was not a passion,[165] as in others. No, virtue and the good were the only objects of competition for him; and it may be that no great thing could occur among human beings without this sort of activity.[166] And he was indeed hot-tempered – that I do not deny[167] – but at the same time he

---

beneficence and the critical spirit of Proclus were imitated by Marinus' successor Isidorus: Damascius, *Isid.* 18.

162 Andros was an island in the Aegean with a capital of the same name. It fell under Athenian, then Macedonian, then Pergamene hegemony; Proclus may have felt that it had a claim on him as the mother-city of Aristotle's native Stagira.

163 *Sitêrêsia* is generally used before this of the wages paid to soldiers or the dole distributed by Roman patrons to their clients. Fowden (1982), 59 suspects that only in Athens could such a provision have been obtained for philosophers.

164 The "hot-tempered" (*thumoeidês*) man is one in whom the second of the three parts of the soul predominates. Plato, *Republic* 449–451 says that this part is the source of anger, shame and the love of humour; it is the natural ally of the reason in the suppression of the third, or appetitive, element, but once it takes command of the soul it leads to an unbalanced pursuit of honour at the expense of the genuine good (*Republic* 547–550). Cf. Aristotle, *Nicomachean Ethics* 1095b22. Damascius, *Isid.* 18 imputes the irascible nature of his hero to an excess of *thumos*.

165 A passion (*pathos*) is something suffered, as opposed to the "activity" (*energeia*) of the next sentence. In Neoplatonic thought, following Aristotle (*ibid.*, 1098a7 etc.), *energeia* is the fulfilment of a natural capacity, and thus a precondition of both happiness and virtue.

166 "Competitive" is my rendering of *philotimos* ("honour-loving") in this chapter. The ancient poet Hesiod (c. 700 B.C.) made a similar point at *Works and Days* 11–12, where he contrasts unhealthy emulation (*eris*) with the kind that stimulates virtue and achievement.

167 Such a confession is hard to parallel in accounts of teachers by their pupils.

was kindly,[168] for he was easily soothed and in the very statement of his verdict[169] he displayed a heart of wax.[170] For in that moment, so to speak, he melted, and his fellow-feeling[171] induced him both to benefit the men themselves and to appeal to the magistrates on their behalf.

17. And it is a good thing that his peculiar fellow-feeling has come into my thoughts, for I think that there has never been another man to whom so much has been attributed. For he had no experience of marriage or children, and this was by his personal choice, notwithstanding many proposals of marriage to persons eminent in birth or wealth; yet being, as I have said, free of all this, such was his care for his companions and friends, and for the children and wives that belonged to them, that he was a sort of common father and author of their being,[172] for he showed solicitude in every way even for each one's manner of life. And if any of his associates was afflicted by illness, first he strenuously appealed to the gods on his behalf with words and hymns,[173] then he attended the invalid solicitously, calling the doctors together and pressing them to exercise their skills without

---

168 Cf. Porphyry, *Plotinus* 9, Lucian, *Demonax* 9, Damascius, *Isid.* 18 and Hierocles, *CA* 445 Müllach, commenting on *Golden Verses* 18.

169 Literally, "in the turning of a potsherd (*ostrakon*)". In classical Athens, all citizens had the right to carve on a potsherd the name of a man whom they wished to expel ("ostracise") from the city. When the sherds were turned over in the counting of the vote, a man who had a sufficient number of votes against him would be banished without any further reason.

170 Anticipating the metaphor of melting that follows, and also punning on the terms *kêr* ("heart") and *kêrinon* ("wax"), as Socrates does in Plato, *Theaetetus* 194c–d. The "etymology" signifies that the heart (as seat of consciousness) should be impressionable, but at the same time pure and deep. At Damascius, *Isid.* 17 the word *kêrinon* signifies the "sensibility" of the senses.

171 *Sumpatheia* is a concept derived by Platonists from Plato's account of cosmic love at *Symposium* 186–7, with some assistance from the Stoics. It characterises the mutual attraction of similar elements or entities in the universe, and can thus account both for magic (Plotinus, *Enn.* 4.4.40 etc.) and for the unconscious understanding that exists between human beings. See Proclus, *Tim.* 12c (i, 36 Diehl) etc; at *Alc.* 130 (ii, 108 Segonds) he speaks of it as the divine love that enables the teacher to benefit his pupil.

172 Assimilating Proclus to Plato's Demiurge, who is called father at *Timaeus* 28c etc. Cf. Plato, *Sophist* 241d, where the Eleatic stranger pays the same compliment to Parmenides.

173 For the hymns of Proclus see now Saffrey (1994). This is the one kind of poetry (along with praises of good men) permitted by Plato at *Republic* 607a–b.

delay.[174] And in these circumstances he himself did something extra, and thus rescued many from the greatest perils. How humane[175] he was to the slaves who served him most, anyone who wishes can learn from the will[176] of the blessed man. Of all his associates he showed the greatest love for Archiadas[177] and those who were related to him by birth, first because he was by birth a descendant[178] of the philosopher Plutarch, then on account of Pythagorean friendship,[179] being at once his fellow-student and his teacher.[180] For of the two kinds of friendship seldom reported even among those before us,[181] the friendship of these men seemed the more profound; for Archiadas was nothing that Proclus was not also, nor was Proclus anything that Archiadas was not also.[182]

18. Having now put our own period to the summary of his political virtues, though it falls short of the truth, and having put the seal of

174 This most probably means that he paid their fees. Plato, *Republic* 406 observes that the poor cannot afford doctors.

175 Translating *philanthrôpos*. Philanthropy, or love of humankind, is generally shown by stronger beings to their inferiors, e.g. by gods to men or by kings to subjects: see chapter 31. The possession of slaves was not seen in antiquity as an outrage to human dignity, though the mistreatment of them was, at least by Stoics.

176 Diogenes Laertius, unlike Marinus, cites the texts of a number of wills made by philosophers. To judge by that of Aristotle (5.1.14–16), the provisions of a benign will would include the emancipation of certain domestics, perhaps with an endowment, and a stipulation that the rest should not be sold.

177 Probably the grandson of Plutarch of Athens: see chapter 12.

178 Literally "successor", *diadochos*, to indicate the parity between filial and pedagogic relations.

179 A famous trait of all Pythagoreans, stories of whose readiness to die for one another are recounted by e.g. Iamblichus, *DVP* 229–240. This is the first occasion in the life when Proclus is called a Pythagorean, and in the latter's writings admiration for the school is somewhat guarded. He believes that Timaeus was a Pythagorean at *Tim.*163c (ii, 79.6 Diehl), but in commentary on the more "theological" *Parmenides*, he treats as proponents of a mathematical method in philosophy (623d), and allows them only an inkling of the theory of Ideas (729d). The biographer, however, can adopt no higher model than Pythagoras, and must therefore discover Pythagorean qualities in his subject.

180 The relation being much like that of Plotinus and Amelius, as described by Longinus in Porphyry, *Plotinus* 19.

181 Marinus appears to mean the friendship of sympathy, which Proclus extended to many and the "Pythagorean" kind which he reserved for Archiadas.

182 Alluding to the notion that a friend is a second self, as in Aristotle, *ibid.*, 1170b6. Since Aristotle devotes two books to friendship in his treatise, which defines happiness (*eudaimonia*) as the highest good, it is natural that Marinus should recount his hero's friendships in a work whose second title is "On Happiness".

friendship on them,[183] let us now pass on to the purificatory virtues,[184] which are a different class beyond the political ones. For if the principal task[185] assigned to the latter is to purify the soul in some way, and to enable it to consider[186] human affairs without prejudice, so that it has that likeness to God[187] which is its highest end, nevertheless not all souls separate in the same way, but some more and some less.[188] The political virtues are indeed also purifications of a sort, which refine and ameliorate their possessors even while they remain in the present world,[189] giving bounds and measure to their temper and appetites,[190] and completely annihilating their passions and false opinions; but the purificatory virtues, superior to these, separate and liberate them from the truly

183 Both in the sense that friendship is the last and highest virtue to be enumerated, and that Marinus has testified to his own friendship; cf. *Theognis* 19, where a personal address is sealed with the author's name.

184 As Dillon (1983c), 92–96 observes, the distinction between political virtues, which merely restrain the appetites, and purificatory or cathartic virtues, which expel them from the soul altogether, is suggested by Plato, *Phaedo* 82a–c and expressed more systematically by Plotinus, *Enn.* 1.2 (see especially 1.2.2.14–17 for this passage), then by Porphyry, *Sent.* 32. Plato at least would not have recommended cultic practice as an instrument of purgation. Marinus' theory of virtue (which includes Stoic terminology on the passions) is the subject of a monograph by Schissel von Fleschenburg (1928); for a shorter account see Hadot (1978), 149–52.

185 The language of "task" and "end" in this sentence recalls the vocabulary of Aristotle's *Nicomachean Ethics*, though Aristotle's influence on later thought is too pervasive to justify the search for exact allusions.

186 On the *pronoia* (consideration) of the ruler, analogous to the providence of the gods, see Damascius, *Isid.* Fr. 364 Zintzen, and Proclus, *Alc.* 95 (i, 78 Segonds). On the doctrine of *pronoia* in Proclus see the *Tria Opuscula* (Westerink) and Beierwaltes (1977).

187 The goal of philosophy, according to Plato, *Theaetetus* 176c. Porphyry, *Sent.* 32 (25.9 Lamberz) states that this is achieved through the purificatory virtues. Plotinus, *Enn.* 1.2.4–6 implies that different states confer a likeness to different gods, and Hierocles, *CA* 483–4 distinguishes likeness to the Demiurge from likeness to the supreme divinity. See further chapter 21.

188 Proclus, *DD* 4.22 etc. explains how each person receives from providence according to his capacity. The separability of soul from body is a tenet maintained by the Platonists against the Aristotelians; the role of purification in effecting separation is explained later in this chapter.

189 Literally "here", making the contrast between the worlds "here" and "there" (i.e. in heaven) which is typical of Neoplatonism.

190 The two lower parts of the soul according to Plato's *Republic, Phaedrus*, etc., the "temper" (*thumos*) being responsible for the "hot-temperedness" mentioned in the preceding chapter.

leaden[191] world of generation, and produce an uncurbed flight[192] from the present world. And it was these that the philosopher pursued throughout the whole of his life, eloquently explaining in his discourses what they are and how one comes to possess these also, and living strictly in accordance with them, doing on all occasions the things that produce separation for the soul. Day and night he made use of apotropaic,[193] lustratory[194] and other purifications, sometimes the Orphic,[195] sometimes the Chaldaean,[196] going down to the sea without fear at the

---

191 A term from alchemy, which, since Zosimus of Panopolis (c. 300 A.D.), had been concerned not so much with the extraction of gold as with the deliverance of the soul from its "leaden" (*molubdinos*) environment of matter. Cf. the injunction not to blacken (*molunein*) the spirit at *Chaldaean Oracles*, 104 Des Places, cited in Proclus' *Extracts* at Des Places, *OC*, 208; also Hierocles, *CA* 432 Mullach and the use of *antitupos* ("reflective", hence "solid" like metal) at Damascius, *Isid.* 312.

192 See Plotinus, *Enn.* 1.6.8 and 6.99 for famous statements of this goal. The metaphor was already canonised in Plato's *Phaedrus*, where the soul is said to have lost its wings in a fall from heaven, and therefore to be (unconsciously) desirous of return.

193 These were required to drive away demons who would otherwise impede the rites of purification. Cf. Proclus, *On the Hieratic Art*, cited by Sheppard (1980), p. 145 n. 2.

194 That is, those that involved ritual ablutions, common to most mysteries of antiquity.

195 The large body of verse called Orphic claimed to be written by a legendary poet of Thrace, but the earliest documents probably date from the sixth century B.C. Proclus is one of our most valuable witnesses to the so-called "rhapsodic" theogony, which West (1983) regards as a late development. The principal elements are: a succession of divinities, beginning with the birth of Phanes (god of love and procreation) from a cosmic egg; serial atrocities, culminating in the victory of Zeus, as in the Hesiodic poems; the birth of Dionysus and his dismemberment by the Titans, leading to the creation of the human race from the ashes of the culprits. It is not clear how far Orphism was a cult with its own rites, distinct from those of Eleusis and the Dionysiac mysteries.

196 These theosophic verses, though alleged to have been composed in the second century by Julian the Chaldaean and his son, are not cited before the mid-third century: for their possible influence on Porphyry see Lewy (1956), 1–64. They were certainly an influence on Iamblichus and on Proclus, who found in them a divine revelation of the emergence of intelligible being from the ineffable monad through the medium of a dyad also known as power and life. They also taught that theurgy (the use of material instruments to control and commune with supernatural beings) was a legitimate instrument of theology. Lewy (1956) remains the most comprehensive study of this subject; for Proclus' use of the oracles see Saffrey (1981), and for the fragments of his commentary, Des Places, *OC*, 206–212. He derived from them such notions as the "noeric [intelligible] hymn" (Fr. 1), the "depth of the soul" (Fr. 2), the "flower of the mind" and the "silence" of the One (Fr. 3). Orphic and Chaldaean rites are recognised by Damascius, *Isid.* 126 as the ones most instructive to a philosopher.

beginning of every month,[197] and sometimes indeed twice or thrice in the same one; and this he did not only in the prime of his life, but even as he was approaching the evening of his life[198] he observed these customs unceasingly, as though they were mandatory.

19. As for the necessary pleasures[199] that arise from food and drink, he treated them as a way of avoiding illness, so that he would not be encumbered by them; for he gave them little attention.[200] For the most part he made it a rule to abstain from living creatures,[201] and if some pressing occasion called on him to eat them, he merely tasted them, and then only for the sake of piety.[202] Every month he celebrated the rites of the Great Mother of which the Romans, or rather the Phrygians before them, are devotees.[203] He was more careful in observing the unlucky days[204] of the Egyptians than they are themselves, and maintained a

---

197 Apuleius, *Metamorphoses* 11.1 describes this as a peculiarly Pythagorean practice, though Gwyn Griffiths (1975), 113–114 finds no evidence that it was so, and at Herodotus, *Histories* 2.37 it is Egyptian.

198 Apparently a common trope, which Longinus, *On the Sublime* 9.13 applies to Homer.

199 That is those without which one cannot live. Though the term is common enough, Marinus may have been thinking of Porphyry, *Sent.* 32 (33.1 Lamberz), which governs so much in his account of virtue.

200 Cf. again Porphyry, *Plotinus* 9 and Iamblichus, *DVP* 16.

201 Following the precepts of Syrianus rather than Plutarch in chapter 12.

202 That is, he participated in sacrifice, not sharing the contempt for cultic piety of Plotinus at Porphyry, *Plotinus* 10. For Christians (1Cor. 8.10 and 10.28) sacrifice was the one occasion on which the eating of meat was definitely forbidden. Karivieri (1994), 135–6 notes evidence of the sacrifice of pigs in the so-called House of Proclus.

203 The cult of the Phrygian goddess Cybele was brought to Rome in 205 B.C., and though, according to Dionysius of Halicarnassus, *Antiquities* 2.13, the rites were never observed by any trueborn Roman, they are described at length by Lucretius in *On the Nature of Things* 2, 601–43, and after Julian wrote his *Hymn to the Mother of the Gods* (c. 362), it appears to have been acceptable for an eminent Roman to be an initiate: Beard, North and Price (1998), ii, 386. Other names for the Mother in sacred poetry were Rhea and Demeter, and as early as the mid-second century a sect called the "Naassenes" had undertaken to conflate her mysteries with those of Egyptians, Greeks, Jews and even Christians (Hippolytus, *Ref.* 5.6–11). Karivieri (1994), 119 notes that she appears on a relief in the so-called "House of Proclus".

204 Borrowing the Athenian term *apophrades*, used also by Plato, *Laws* 800d to denote "unlucky" days when cultic business was suspended. See Lucian, *False Pedant* 12, an indignant polemic against those who deny the Attic pedigree of the term. According to Mikalson (1975), these should have fallen only (and not always) on the 27th, 28th and 29th of the

personal fast on certain days through revelation. For he went without food on every "old and new",[205] not even having dined the previous day, just as indeed he also performed conspicuous and holy rituals at the new moons.[206] One could almost say that he observed with the proper rituals the significant holidays of every people and the ancestral rites of each; and he did not, like others, make these an excuse for rest or for stuffing his body, but for supplications,[207] vigils,[208] prayers and the like. He left a body of hymns to prove this, which does not only embrace the subjects that are usually belauded among the Greeks, but also celebrates Marnas of Gaza,[209] Asclepius Leontuchos[210] of Ascalon,[211]

---

month; but John Lydus in his *On the Months* shows that Greeks of late antiquity respected the many unlucky days (*dies nefasti*) of the Roman calendar.

205 The Athenian name for the last day of the month: see Aristophanes, *Clouds* 1134 and 1222.

206 For libations to the new moon in classical Athens see Aristophanes, *Wasps* 96; Lucian, *Lexiphanes* 6 speaks of cocks dedicated to the new moon. Paul at Col. 2.16 alludes to the observance of the new moon at Colossae in Phrygia (to the north of Proclus' native Lycia). Porphyry, *Abst.* 146.7 Nauck describes the rustic garlanding of Hecate at the new moon.

207 *Entukhiai* are supplicatory prayers offered before the evocation of a divine helper: see Iamblichus, *Myst.* 3.13 (117 Des Places, with note) and Lewy (1956), 239.

208 The *Pythagorean Verses* 10 recommend frugality in sleep as in other bodily indulgences.

209 In his life of Bishop Porphyry of Gaza (395–420), Mark the Deacon tells us (64) that this god was the "Crete-born Zeus"; we may add that Zeus' cultic attendants, the "Idaean Dactyls", were associated with a Great Mother (Pausanias 8.31.3). Mark adds (65–69) that the temple in Gaza had been destroyed by Christians, so that Proclus' veneration of him can be seen as a commentary on such events (cf. chapter 29). Mussies (1990), 2415 suggests that Proclus' knowledge of the god was derived from Ulpian of Gaza (chapter 19), or from the Samaritan Marinus. Gaza, at the crossroads of Palestine and Egypt, was an important Christian centre, but also one where Proclus may have had friends, as it tolerated a circle of Christian Platonists even in the following century: see Stroumsa (1999), 124–6 and Athanassiadi (1999b), 352–3.

210 This title means "lion-headed"; such figures are common in the ancient Near East, and under the Empire lion-headed serpents represent the malevolent Ahriman in Mithraic shrines and the purblind Demiurge in Gnostic literature. Neoplatonists may have thought that they saw a Chaldaean symbol: Psellus, *Exegesis* 1133 (Des Places, *OC*, 171). Porphyry, *Abst.* 241–2 Nauck defends the representation of gods in the form of non-human creatures, on the grounds that divinity permeates all things.

211 Since Ascalon is in Phoenicia, this may be the same Asclepius whom Damascius, *Isid.* 302 identifies with the god Eshmoun. He is said to have been a handsome youth, beloved by the Great Mother, but killed like Adonis in the course of a hunt. He was made

another Theandrites,[212] a god much honoured among the Arabs, Isis who is still honoured in Philae,[213] and in a word all the rest. For one maxim that this most godfearing[214] philosopher had always at hand and was always uttering was that a philosopher ought not to worship in the manner of a single city or the country of a few people, but should be the common priest of the entire world.[215] And thus he practised self-denial with a purity befitting holy things.[216]

20. As for ailments he shunned them, or if they fell on him he bore them meekly, and made them less because the best part of him did not share

---

a god by the insufflation of "divine heat", which is allegedly the meaning of his Phoenician name. Marinus the Samaritan will have known that Gaza and Ascalon are cities of the Philistines (Judges 6.4; 2 Sam. 1.20), just as he let his colleagues know (Damascius, *Isid*. 141) that his native town of Flavia Neapolis or Shechem was a sacred site to Abraham's descendants.

212 Damascius, *Isid*. 198 asserts that this was "a god of masculine aspect who inspired in his devotees a life that was not effeminate". Saffrey (1966), 98 notes that John of Scythopolis (c. 532) alludes to this deity in a scholium on Ps.-Dionysius Areopagita, Letter 4.

213 This Egyptian goddess, treated in Plutarch's *Isis and Osiris* as an emblem of the soul, was best remembered for her wanderings in search of her dead and dismembered brother Osiris, whose remains were interred in Egypt. In Roman times she was widely venerated as the power who averts misfortune, and had subsumed the attributes of many female deities. See Apuleius, *Metamorphoses* 11, the *Kore Kosmou* in the Hermetic corpus; Witt (1971); Gwyn Griffiths (1975). Porphyry, *Plotinus* 10 reveals that the cult of Isis did not impress.

214 The term *theosebês* ("god-fearing") occurs in Porphyry, *Abst*. 85.7 Nauck; but could Proclus be unaware that this term was often applied to Gentiles who had adopted the exclusive monotheism of the Jews? See Mitchell (1999), 115-121 on their cult of the "Highest (*Hypsistos*) God".

215 A variation on the notion that a philosopher should be a "cosmopolitan" or citizen of the world, which is ascribed to Diogenes, founder of the Cynics (Diogenes Laertius 6.63). The aspiration to belong to every fatherland by religion may be compared with that of the second-century *Epistle to Diognetus* 6, that Christians are at home in every country so far as manners go, though their faith remains unique.

216 In contrast, no doubt, to the fasts and holidays of Christians, which aimed to supersede all other cults. Even in the *Apology* of Apuleius we see that Platonising thinkers boasted of initiation into many cults. Since Porphyry (*On the Return of the Soul*, in Augustine, *City of God* 10.32 etc.) it had been a Neoplatonic commonplace that there is no one universal way of salvation, and this premiss was shared by ordinary Romans like the senator Aurelius Symmachus in his *Relation* of 384 A.D., which pleaded for the restoration of a pagan altar.

the suffering.[217] The resistance of his soul to these was also sufficiently proved by his mortal illness. For oppressed by this as he was, and gripped by pangs, he tried to cast off the ailment. He therefore urged us to chant hymns on each occasion, and as the hymns were chanted there followed total relief and quiescence[218] of his sufferings; and, what is more remarkable still than this, he retained a memory for what was said, even though he forgot almost all human things as the paralysis advanced.[219] For as we were chanting, he completed the hymns and the greater part of the Orphic verses, for we sometimes read these out in his presence.[220] And he maintained this impassibility not only toward the sufferings of his body, but even more toward external accidents that beset him, and happenings that seemed contrary to reason. Thus his response on each of these occasions was "Things are as they are, things are as ever".[221] This dictum seems to me worthy of remembrance and a sufficient index of the greatness of the philosopher's soul.[222] And he chastened his temper,[223] so far as he was able, so that either it was not aroused at all, or else the rational soul had no part in his wrath and the involuntary motion belonged to the other part, and even then was slight and

---

217 That is, his rational element, which, according to Platonic teaching, ought to remain inviolable while it restrains (without extinguishing) the motions of the two lower parts of the soul. Porphyry, *Sent.* 32 (33.4 Lamberz) affords a parallel to this passage, as does Plotinus, *Enn.* 1.2.5.9–10.

218 The term *ataraxia* ("undisturbedness') represents the goal of Stoic and Epicurean ethics; but here it indicates only relief from pain. As Dillon (1983b) notes, many Platonists inaccurately credited Stoics with a belief that all passions are vicious. Plato had censured those who mistook absence of pain for pleasure (*Republic* 585a); felicity is obtained by the proper direction, not the extinction, of the erotic impulse.

219 This, the one circumstantial detail, suggests a wasting illness. Otherwise we know only that Proclus' physician was called Jacobus: Damascius, *Isid.* 126.

220 The style of Proclus' own hymns shows that the Orphics, along with Homer, were his model. This passage implies that the students used a book rather than reciting from memory.

221 Fortitude in illness was a customary virtue in philosophers, as we see from Porphyry, *Plotinus* 2. Proclus was fortified by his own arguments at *DD* 6.32–38 that (a) the wise man receives real, but not apparent goods from providence; (b) evil circumstances bring to light virtues that would otherwise be hidden; (c) if virtue were always rewarded it would be practised for the wrong reasons; (d) no goods are allotted only to members of a single class.

222 *Megalopsuchia*, the highest of the Aristotelian virtues, implying a sense of worth without presumption. In late antiquity it often has the sense of "generosity" (e.g. Constantine, *Oration to the Saints* 8).

223 Translating *thumos* again.

weak.[224] As for the physical pleasures of love,[225] I think he went so far as to partake of them in imagination, and even this was superficial.[226]

21. And thus the soul of the blessed man, collecting itself from every side and gathering itself within itself,[227] all but departed from the body, even while it seemed to be still detained by it.[228] For its thinking was not the political kind that consists in acting well with regard to matters that could be otherwise, but knowing in itself, pure and simple, a reversion to itself[229] without any share in the impressions of the body.[230] As for its

224 The word is *aproairetos*, modifying Aristotle's contrast between actions performed with choice (*proairesis*) and those done ignorantly or under duress. The closing words of the sentence echo Porphyry, *Sent.* 32 (34.3 Lamberz) and Plotinus, *Enn.* 1.2.5.14 (which adds that one who has not suppressed the involuntary is only half a god). At *DD* 5.28–31 Proclus argues that the movements of the irrational soul are natural, but become preternatural if they compromise the hegemony of reason.

225 It was a commonplace that philosophers would resist these. At Plato, *Symposium* 182a–b the sexual pleasures belong to the lesser Aphrodite, and at *Republic* 429 b–c Sophocles is glad to be rid of them. Marinus' passage has a parallel at Porphyry, *Sent.* 32 (33.8 Lamberz) and Plotinus, *Enn.* 1.2.5.17–21.

226 So Guthrie (1925) in Oikonomides (1977), 67; but it may mean "uncontrollable" (and therefore venial). Porphyry, *loc. cit* implies that the experience would be limited to dreams, on which see Damascius, *Isid.* 219. The term translated as "imagination" is *phantasia*, which in Proclus denotes the capacity to form internal images, which presides over our non-rational perceptions: *Tim* 327a–b (iii, 286 Diehl). It can also signify the anticipation of something understood but not yet experienced: *Tim.* 344a (iii, 342 Diehl). Apart from Iamblichus, *Myst.* 3.2, Watson (1988), 117–26 offers no parallels to the usage of the term to denote a "fantasy" with no origin in perception or desire.

227 A simple (i.e. immaterial and hence indivisible) substance in itself, the soul experiences dispersion as it participates in the fragmentary perceptions of the body; abstraction from the body restores its unity.

228 Philosophy is thus for Proclus not just a preparation for death, but the actual separation of soul and body.

229 Cf. Porphyry, *Plotinus* 8 and notes. Marinus is alluding to the contrast between the *nous pathêtikos* ("passive mind"), which receives impressions and thereby undergoes constant change of form, and the higher one whose objects are eternal. Cf. Proclus, *Tim.* 327c–d (iii, 287 Diehl) which distinguishes between perceptions that are generic and common (the highest), those that are common but "passive" (governed by *doxa*) and those that are partial and "empathic" (governed by *phantasia*). The thread that connects these doctrines to the Aristotelian concept of the "active reason" (*On the Soul* 3.4–5) is long and tenuous.

230 The term *sundoxazein* (taken here from Porphyry, *Sent.* 32, at 24.9–15 Lamberz; cf. Plotinus, *Enn.* 1.2.3) implies participation in *doxa* or opinion, which for Plato, *Republic* 510a–b is a lower cognitive state than genuine knowledge. For Proclus it is the ruling faculty of the rational life: *Tim.* 327 (iii, 286 Diehl). Its objects, however, being merely sensory, are particular contingents: *Rep.* i, 262–4 Kroll.

temperance,[231] it consisted in not associating with the lower part, not even feeling in moderation, but absolutely and in every way devoid of feeling.[232] Its fortitude consisted in not being afraid when departing from the body. And, as mind and reason were his guides, the inferior faculties offering no resistance to purificatory justice,[233] the whole of his life was perfectly regulated.

22. Having virtues of this kind,[234] he advanced painlessly and smoothly, and as it were by the steps of initiation,[235] and ascended to those that are greater and above these, being led on by a natural rectitude and skilful pedagogy.[236] For having already been purified and mastering generation,[237] and looking down on the aspirants[238] within it, he became an adept in the foremost things, and became a personal witness of the truly blessed sights in that place,[239] no longer gaining knowledge of them by discursive and demonstrative reasonings,[240] but as if by vision beholding

231 Translating *sôphrosunê*. Marinus is now attributing to the soul of Proclus the four Platonic virtues that in chapter 3 he allotted to his body.

232 Platonists often professed to aim at *metriopatheia,* or moderate feeling, rather than the chimerical *apatheia,* or insensibility, of the Stoics: cf. Plutarch, *Consolation to Apollonius* 102d and Dillon (1983b), 511–512. Proclus achieves the purificatory virtue of *apatheia* in his soul, the political one of *metriopatheia* in his body, as Porphyry prescribes at *Sent.* 32 (25.7-9 Lamberz).

233 Justice consists in the harmonisation of the three other virtues, in the soul as in the city: Plato, *Republic* 432-3. The whole clause echoes Porphyry, *Sent.* 32 (25.5-6 Lamberz).

234 The word *idea* is here used as the equivalent to *eidos*, in the sense of "kind" or "species".

235 Cf. *Phaedrus* 248d for this meaning of *telestikon*.

236 Cf. Proclus, *Alc.* 225 (ii, 276-7 Segonds) on the confluence of rectitude, discipline and dialectic in the purification of the soul.

237 A possible reference to the natal daemon, who, according to Porphyry, *Nymphs* 80. 15ff Nauck must be propitiated by sacrifice and self-denial. Proclus yielded less to his natal daemon than either Socrates, who wrote poetry (*Phaedo* 61a) or Porphyry, who married (*Marc.* 24.6 Nauck).

238 Literally "wand-bearers" (*narthêkophoroi*), with an allusion to the Orphic/Dionysiac maxim that "there are many wand-bearers, but few Bacchoi", quoted by Plato at *Phaedo* 69c (= *Orphica* Fr. 5 Kern). The word translated "became an adept" here is *ebakkheuse*, referring to the achievement of the highest grade in the cult of Dionysus.

239 Literally "there" (*ekei*), i.e. in the supercelestial realm from which our souls originate. The vision of this is here conceived as the *epopteia* of a mystery.

240 Literally "syllogisms", an Aristotelian form of argument which involves a major premiss (stating a general law), a minor (relating an actual case to that law), and a consequential inference. Though Marinus seems to be using the term more generally, Proclus

92   MARINUS

the paradigms in the divine mind[241] by simple strokes[242] of intellectual
energy. To this he added virtue, to which one could not properly give the
name of practical reason, but will rather style wisdom, or else by some
more dignified appellation.[243] Acting in accord with this the philosopher
easily penetrated the whole theology of Greeks and of barbarians,[244]
clouded as it was by mythical fictions, and brought it to light[245] for those
who were willing and able to follow it, expounding everything in an
inspired manner[246] and bringing it into harmony. He went through all

---

often supports his exegesis of Plato by appeal to the *Organon* of Aristotle. For the notion
that knowledge of transcendent truths is non-discursive, cf. Plotinus and the discussion in
Sorabji (1983), 157–74.

241 The doctrine that the Ideas of Plato are thoughts in the mind of God has several
roots: (a) the *Timaeus*, in which the Demiurge creates the world in accordance with the
"paradigm" containing the ideas of natural kinds; (b) Aristotle, *Metaphysics* 12, where
God is said to be the thought of thoughts, with no object of reflection but himself; (c) the
Aristotelian concept of the active reason (*On the Soul* 3.4–5), which as pure mind does not
depend upon contingent knowledge, though it makes all thinking possible. Alexander of
Aphrodisias (*Mantissa*) appears to have equated (c) with (b), while Plotinus (*Enn.* 5.5) repudiated any interpretation of (a) which left the "intelligibles" outside the intellect. Proclus,
PTh 5 distinguishes at length between the higher "noeric" aspect and the lower "noetic"
aspect of the demiurgic intellect. The former begets the activity, the latter the object of
thought; the first is father, the second creator. See further Armstrong (1960), Rich (1954).

242 For *epibolê* as intuitive comprehension cf. Proclus, *PTh* 2.5 (ii, 37 Saffrey and Westerink), with Rist (1967), 49–52. For "simple strokes" cf. Proclus, *Alc.* 246.21 (ii, 294
Segonds). See also *Plotinus*, n. 241.

243 *Phronêsis* (practical wisdom) is the chief principle of virtue in the *Nicomachean
Ethics* of Aristotle and remains a fundamental term of moral philosophy after him;
wisdom or *sophia* ("theoretical wisdom" to Aristotle) is the root of all other virtues in the
Protagoras of Plato.

244 "Barbarian" means a person who does not speak Greek, not (as it often does in
Latin) one who lives outside the Roman Empire. Chapters 18 and 19 above reveal the catholicity of Proclus' investigations; above all the *Chaldaean Oracles* may be intended by
Marinus.

245 The claim to be rescuing wisdom from arcane sources is conventional. Cf. Porphyry,
Nymphs 81.5, Nauck defending the mythical *plasma* of the Homeric poems; the whole of
Porphyry's treatise is an exercise in bringing veiled philosophy to light, as is Marinus'
Proclus: cf. chapters 5 and 31.

246 The word is *enthusiastikôteron*. Cf. *Phaedrus* 249d and Porphyry, *Plotinus* 15,
though in both cases the word is applied to poetry, not to philosophical exposition. Sheppard (1980), 175–80 shows that Proclus allotted different types of inspiration to the exegete
and the poet, and allowed enthusiasm to intervene at an earlier stage in the philosopher's
education than Plotinus did (*Enn.* 6.9.11.13–15).

the treatises of his predecessors, and if anything in them was sound he made critical use of it, but if he found anything worthless, he rejected this entirely as an absurdity, and if anything was contrary to good principles, he refuted it polemically with severe examination.[247] In his seminars also he dealt with each point ably and clearly, and wrote everything down in treatises. So immense was his love of labour[248] that he expounded five topics, sometimes even more, in the course of a day, and generally wrote about seven hundred lines. He also conferred with the other philosophers, taking the initiative, and in the evening held further seminars that were not written up. And all this after that nocturnal and unsleeping worship of his,[249] after his obeisance to the rising, midday and setting sun.[250]

23. And he himself became the father[251] of many doctrines, physical, intellectual and those that are even more divine.[252] For this man was the first to teach that there is a kind of souls that are able to see many forms at once, which he quite reasonably assigned to a middle place between the mind which simultaneously and in one stroke considers everything[253]

247 True enough, especially in the commentary on the *Timaeus*, which is our capital source for many teachings of the Middle Platonists, as well as of Amelius, Porphyry and Iamblichus.

248 *Philoponia*, a quality admired in Athenian prose (e.g. Isocrates, *To Nicocles* 45), was predicated also of the Christian Origen and of Marinus' contemporary John Philoponus, a Christian theologian of Alexandria and a leading commentator on Aristotle. Damascius, *Isid.* bestows it (not without disparagement) on Proclus' pupils Hermias (74), Ammonius (79) and Marinus himself (142). At Proclus, *Tim.* iii, 247.12 Diehl, it is applied disparagingly to Atticus.

249 See chapter 19 on his vigils.

250 Socrates already prays to the sun at dawn: Plato, *Symposium* 220d. A regular cult spread through the Roman Empire under the auspices of the emperor Aurelian (270–275). It was commended to philosophers in a hymn by the Emperor Julian, which treats it as the physical symbol of ineffable light. Proclus' first hymn in Saffrey (1994) is addressed to the sun.

251 Cf. Plato, *Sophist* 241d on Parmenides, the "father" of a philosophy that strongly impressed Plato; also Proclus, *Tim.* i, 9.16–18 Diehl, where the "father" of words (i.e. philosopher) is said to bear a likeness to the "Father of works" (i.e. the Demiurge). Marinus cannot, of course, congratulate Proclus on his human children, in the manner of Isocrates at *Evagoras* 72.

252 Physical doctrines are those of e.g. the *Timaeus*; intellectual doctrines pertain to the Ideas, beyond which lies the ineffable, the subject of theology. See the *Suda* (above) on Marinus and the *Philebus*.

253 The middle state to which Marinus alludes here is perhaps the one described by Proclus at *Rep.* ii, 187 Kroll, which maintains that the soul is able to see the whole of generation when released from the present body. A doctrine of three types of soul is suggested in Proclus, *ET* 184–5.

and the souls that make a progress from one form to another.[254] And one who wishes can encounter the rest of his offspring by approaching his works (which in the present case I have declined to do, so as not to prolong my account by enumerating everything).[255] And one who encounters them will know that the whole of the foregoing narrative concerning him is true, and all the more so if anyone has seen him and enjoyed the spectacle of him,[256] hearing his exposition and his delivery of the most exquisite discourses, as year by year he celebrated the festivals of Plato and Socrates.[257] For it seemed that he spoke under divine inspiration, and that the words truly fell like snow[258] from that wise man's[259] mouth. For his eyes seemed to be filled with a sort of brilliance, and the rest of his visage had a share of divine illumination. Once in the course of his exposition, a man called Rufinus, one of the most conspicuous figures[260] in politics, a truthful person and otherwise worthy of respect, saw a light playing round his head. And when he reached the end of his exposition, Rufinus stood up, made an obeisance and testified on oath to the divine vision. It was this Rufinus too who sent him a large amount of gold at the time when the crisis had passed and he had returned from Asia.[261] This gift, however, Proclus regarded with disdain and would on no account consent to accept it.

24. But let us return to our original design. Now that we have already recounted, even if not at adequate length, the facts about his contemplative wisdom, the next thing to be spoken of is the justice commensurate with virtues of this kind. For this no longer exists in a number of parts, as the ones preceding it do, nor in the consent of one with another, but

---

254 I do not know whether Marinus also has in mind the myth of *Phaedrus* 247-8, in which each soul assumes the mode of life on earth that corresponds to the Form which it pursued in heaven. At *Rep.* i, 108 Kroll he says that myths depict the gods as overseers of our specific (*kat' eidos*) choice of life.

255 Could he be intending to contrast his reticence with the duplicated list of Plotinus' works in Porphyry?

256 See the description in chapter 3.

257 Cf. Porphyry, *Plotinus* 2.

258 Gillian Clark reminds me (and Masullo notes) that this simile is anticipated at *Iliad* 3.222.

259 See Sheppard (1980), 176 n. 42 for a fuller exposition of the meaning of this word.

260 Translating *epiphanês*, which carries a connotation of light.

261 See chapters 15 and 29.

none the less this too is defined in itself as doing one's own[262] and is peculiar to the rational soul. Now what is peculiar to it is nothing else than to work in accord with mind and god,[263] which the philosopher also did in an eminent degree. For he scarcely took a break from his daily labours, and if occasionally he did resign his body to sleep, perhaps even then he did not refrain from thinking.[264] Nevertheless there were times when he quickly cast this off as a sort of idleness of the soul, and since the night was not far gone and the hour of prayer did not yet beckon, being by himself on his bed he either composed hymns or examined doctrines and found [solutions], then rose at day and wrote them up.

25. In addition he possessed the temperance that corresponds to these. This is the inward reversion of the soul to the mind, a state in which it cannot be impinged on or distracted by anything else. To these he added in perfection the concomitant fortitude, desiring the impassibility of that which he beheld – this being itself impassible by nature[265] – and living entirely, as Plotinus says, not the human life of the good man, which political virtue thinks proper to live, but leaving this behind and exchanging it for another, which is that of the gods.[266] For it was their likeness,[267] not that of good men, that he was attaining.

262 Again the definition of justice at Plato, *Republic* 434c8, but in this treatise justice is the harmony of the three parts of the soul or the three classes of citizen when each displays its own virtue. Porphyry uses the term *oikeiopragia* ("doing one's own") three times in *Sent.* 32: first (23.11 Lamberz) of the harmonisation of the parts of the soul in political virtue, then (28.1) of the subordination of soul to mind in the third stage of virtue, and finally (29.5) of an operation peculiar (*oikeion*) to mind itself in the fourth or paradigmatic stage. He is refining a discussion in Plotinus, *Enn.* 1.2.1.20ff.

263 It is not clear which is higher, or whether Marinus identifies the two. For Porphyry, *Sent.* 31 (21 Lamberz) god appears to rank above mind in the progress of the soul, though likeness to god is only the reward of purificatory virtue (25.9 Lamberz), obedience to mind is only the third stage (28.1), while in the fourth the man himself is a father of gods (31.8).

264 Thus he excels Plotinus, who did at least relax his contemplation in sleep, uncommon though this was: Porphyry, *Plotinus* 8. Restraint of sleep is enjoined in the Pythagorean *Golden Verses* 10.

265 Referring now to the Good, the One, the First, (the) God/god or whatever one calls it, which, being immaterial, ineffable and simple, is not affected by anything, or even participated by any lower entity.

266 Porphyry, *Sent.* 32 (25.8–9 Lamberz) contrasts the life of the good man, which is according to nature, with the *apatheia* (impassibility) of one who achieves the likeness of god. Cf. Plotinus, *Enn.* 1.2. Anne Sheppard points out to me that the notion of "exchange" has a parallel at Iamblichus, *Myst.* 3.1–2 and 3.4.

267 *Theaetetus* 176c again.

26. And these were the virtues that marked his life while he was still a student with Syrianus and working through the compositions of the older writers.[268] As for the Orphic and Chaldaean theology, he received certain rudiments and as it were seeds of them from his master,[269] not having managed to engage him in verbal discussion of them. The reason was that Syrianus set before him and Domninus the Syrian philosopher who was also a successor[270] the task of expounding one of these, either the works of Orpheus or the *Oracles*,[271] and left it open to them to choose the alternative. But they did not concur, and did not both choose the same things, Domninus choosing the works of Orpheus, while our philosopher chose the Oracles. The [exposition of] this, moreover, was prevented by the fact that the great Syrianus did not survive very long. He thus, as I said, received his first instruction from the master, and in his wake carefully studied his commentaries on Orpheus, together with the voluminous works of Porphyry[272] and Iamblichus[273] on the *Oracles* and on the concomitant writings of the Chaldaeans.[274] Nourished also by the divine oracles, he ascended rapidly to the heights of virtue in relation to the human soul, which the inspired Iamblichus styled, in his

---

268 Meaning Plotinus, Porphyry, Iamblichus etc. Much of our information on the authors who belonged to this canon comes from Proclus' works. See chapter 22.

269 *Stoicheia* ("rudiments") is a term often used for letters, and the comparison of letters to seeds is at least as old as Plato, *Phaedrus* 276.

270 According to the *Suda* (= Damascius, *Isid*. Fr. 227 Zintzen), he was from Laodicea in Syria. Having understood the teaching of Plato in too low a sense, he composed a recantation when Proclus convinced him of his errors.

271 Proclus also cites them in this laconic manner, e.g. at *Tim*. 267f (iii, 103.10 Diehl).

272 Our best testimony to Porphyry's use of the *Oracles* is Augustine, *City of God* 10, which appears to quote a work called *On the Return of the Soul*. This ascribed to the *Oracles* only the power of purifying the irrational soul, and has often been assumed to represent a later, less superstitious phase of Porphyry's writing than such credulous compilations as his *Philosophy from Oracles*. O'Meara (1959) shows how little philological evidence can be found for such distinctions, while Lewy (1956), 1–60 and Hadot (1967) both attempt to show that Porphyry's use of the *Oracles* was more pervasive.

273 See introduction on Iamblichus. According to Damascius, *First Principles* 43, he composed a 28-book commentary on the *Oracles*.

274 It seems that Marinus makes a distinction between the oracles themselves, which are the utterance of gods, and the commentaries produced by the Chaldaeans, meaning no doubt the "hyphegetic" works of Julian the Theurgist to which Proclus alludes at *Tim*. 277d (iii, 124.33 Diehl) and the "books of the theurgists and theologians" mentioned at *ibid*. 279f (iii, 132.1–2 Diehl).

sublime manner, the theurgic ones.[275] And bringing together the exegeses of previous philosophers, he worked on them with due discrimination, and collated the other Chaldaean treatises and the chief commentaries with the god-given oracles,[276] taking five whole years to complete this task. In connection with this he saw the following vision: it seemed to him that the great Plutarch was telling him in a dream that the number of years he would live was going to be equal to the number of tetrads that he had composed on the Oracles. Now when he counted them, he found that there were seventy[277] of them. That this was indeed a divine dream was apparent from what occurred near the end of his life. For he lived, as I have said above, seventy years and a further five,[278] but during the five was no longer in good health. For that intolerably harsh diet of his,[279] together with his frequent ablutions and other such austerities, had fatigued his body, despite its natural advantages, and it began to fail after his seventieth year, becoming debilitated in all its activities. For though even in this condition he prayed, composed hymns and wrote a few things, as well as associating with his companions, he did all these things more weakly. Therefore he recalled his dream with astonishment, and kept on saying that he had lived only seventy years. When he was in this weak condition, his passion for exegesis was stirred above all by the young Hegias,[280] a man who from his adolescence was a brilliant

---

275 Attributing to him the same *enthousiasmos* that is asserted of Proclus in chapter 22. For theurgy in Iamblichus see *Myst.* passim, esp. 1.2 and 2.11, with Smith (1974), 83–99, and now Shaw (1995). On his use of coercive magic see Eunapius, *Sophists* 5.2.1–7. Cremer (1969) shows that his *On the Mysteries* is steeped in Chaldaean lore.

276 Proclus believed so firmly in their divine provenance that the fourth hymn in Saffrey (1994) is dedicated to the gods of the *Chaldaean Oracles*. Athanassiadi (1999a), 164–77 contrasts his interpretation, which has dominated scholarship on the *Oracles*, with the less practical and more reticent exposition of Damascius.

277 A significant number, as the product of seven and ten. Proclus, *Tim.* 46e (i, 151 Diehl) asserts that seven, being prime, is a fitting image of Athena because it derives from the father (i.e. the monad) alone. At *Tim.* 168c (ii, 95 Diehl), he adds that seven is the light according to mind where the monad is mind itself. At *Rep.* ii, 169 Kroll he says that the Decad is an image of the perfected cosmos latent in the monad. Neither statement is original, as Kern, *Orphica* 314–315 makes clear.

278 Dying in 485 A.D. as proved in chapter 36.

279 Hierocles, another disciple of Plutarch, urges that Pythagoras counselled moderation in fasting at *CA* 455–9 Mullach.

280 Presumably the scholarch of whom Damascius, *Isid.* 221 says that he was head of the school at a time when philosophy in Athens suffered unprecedented neglect. We also hear that he was praised by Isidorus for his attempt to rescue philosophy (*ibid.* 230) and that the

pattern of all his ancestors' virtues and of the golden chain[281] of descent that led back to Solon.[282] He attended Proclus solicitously in [his exposition of] Platonic and other theologies.[283] And the old man kept handing his writings to him, and was filled with joy when he saw the youth progressing step by step[284] in each of the studies. And this is a superficial account of his lucubrations on the Chaldaean writings.

27. When I was reading the works of Orpheus in his presence,[285] and hearing in his exegeses not only the thoughts of Iamblichus[286] and Syrianus,[287] but at the same time many others more germane to theology,

---

latter shared his faith in the divinity of the "hieratic art" (i.e. theurgy: 227). Castren (1994), 6–7 surmises that he was the son of Plutarch's daughter Asclepigeneia and Theagenes (a descendant of Plato), and was head of the school c. 500.
281 A metaphor which at Damascius, *Isid.* 151 refers to the succession at the Academy. Lévêque (1959) shows that it can be traced to Homer, *Iliad* 8.19. For an Orphic version of Homer's lines see Kern (1922), Fr. 166 (Proclus, *Tim.* ii, 24.23 Diehl). At *Sophists* 9–10 Boissonade-Dübner Eunapius styles Porphyry a "Hermetic chain".
282 Solon (fl. 600 B.C.) was remembered as the founder of democracy, and also of the tradition of personal poetry, in Athens. Lovers of Plato knew him as the first Greek to learn the story of Atlantis, which he then told to his kinsman Dropides (*Timaeus* 20e), from whom it passed down the generations to his descendant and Plato's uncle Critias (22a). Proclus, *Tim.* 26b (i, 83.10–11 Diehl) speaks of Solon as one who stood at the head of Plato's genealogy and shared a common life with him. At *Alc.* 24 (i, 20 Segonds) he notes an instance of Socrates' habit of calling his interlocutors by their fathers' names, arguing that where the father is noble, the patronymic acts as a call to self-examination.
283 *Platonic Theology* is the title of a work in six books in which Proclus presents his theology systematically, using the *Parmenides* of Plato as his template.
284 In Greek *kata pêchun*, cubit by cubit. The term which originally designated the length from elbow to fingertip is now used generically of small quantities. Could this have a bearing on Matt. 6.27 ("who can add a cubit to his stature?")?
285 See chapter 20.
286 Though Orpheus appears five times in *DVP* (62, 145, 146, 151, 243), no exposition of his work is extant in the writings of Iamblichus, and even the cursory references in the *Theology of Arithmetic* (311, 314, 315), falsely attributed to that author, contain little interpretation. At *DVP* 145 he says that Pythagoras derived his numerology from Orpheus, though at 146 he suspects that writings ascribed to Orpheus may be rather the work of one Telauges. The works to which Marinus alludes must therefore have been lost.
287 Kern (1922) contains seventeen citations from Syrianus' commentary on the *Metaphysics* of Aristotle. This collocation of authors seems less strange when we recall that one of the longest Orphic fragments (21a Kern) is found in the pseudo-Aristotelian treatise *On the World*. The *Suda* speaks of treatises by Syrianus *On the Theology of Orpheus* and *On the Agreement of Orpheus, Pythagoras and Plato*. Brisson (1987b), 48–5 suggests that Proclus,

I begged the philosopher not to leave such inspired poetry uninterpreted, but to write a more perfect commentary on this also. His reply was that he had often been eager to write, but had been categorically forbidden by certain visions. For he said that he had seen his own master restraining him with threats. Meditating another stratagem, therefore, I besought him to make a note of what he commended in his master's books. Such was his good nature that he complied, and when he had made his notes on the margin of the commentaries, we made a single collation of them all, and the result was that there were many lines of notes and comments by him on Orpheus, even if in the event he did not do this on the whole of the divine myth or on all the rhapsodies.[288]

28. Now as I have said, the result of his instruction in such matters was that he attained theurgic virtue in a higher and more perfect degree.[289] Consequently he did not live according to only one of the modes that characterise divinity,[290] that of pure thought and aspiration to the better,[291] but he also displayed a more divine consideration[292] of

---

to whom these works are falsely credited elsewhere in the *Suda*, left copious marginalia in the commentaries of Syrianus.

288 The Orphic myth known to Proclus is often called the *Rhapsodic Theogony*, because it consisted of 24 books "stitched together". The number may be intended to equal the sum of books in the *Iliad* and the *Odyssey*, which were supposed to have been preserved by "rhapsodes". See further West (1983), 227–8.

289 Sheppard (1982), 221 cites Proclus, *Crat.* 32.18 and 65.16 Pasquali to show that he conceived a higher mode of philosophy than practical theurgy. Both passages state that there are gods that cannot be named (and hence cannot be compelled or approached) by "theologians", though 66.17–19 Pasquali admits the possibility of analogy.

290 It had always been a problem for the Platonists to explain how gods could have knowledge of the second order, i.e. of things inferior to themselves, since this appeared to entail that the objects of their knowledge were imperfect and transitory, and therefore that the gods themselves were subject to imperfect and transitory affections. At *DD* 3.12–16 Proclus explains that the knowledge of gods is always definite (i.e of the kind that grasps the ideal form) even when the object of this knowledge is indefinite (i.e. a contingent particular in the material universe). At *Parm.* 951–2 Cousin he argues that in their intelligible (noetic) aspect, gods have knowledge only of the ideal forms, but in their intellectual (noeric) one they have knowledge of things below them.

291 Combining Aristotle's conclusion that God thinks only of himself (*Metaphysics* 1074b25–34) with the myth of Plato's *Phaedrus* (247–52), where each god pursues the Form proper to him.

292 *Pronoia* is often rendered "providence", at least when used of gods, but in chapter 18 (on political virtues), the verb *pronoein* was translated "consider". Marinus alludes to that

things in the second rank, not merely in the political way recorded earlier. For he made use of the conjunctions[293] and supplications of the Chaldaeans, together with their divine and ineffable revolutions.[294] These he acquired for himself, and from Asclepigeneia, the daughter of Plutarch,[295] he learned the invocations and the rest of the apparatus.[296] For she alone preserved the rituals, and the whole process of theurgy, handed on to her from the great Nestorius by her father.[297] But before these the philosopher was purified in due order by the Chaldaean purifications,[298] and experienced the fiery apparitions of Hecate[299] with his own eyes, as he himself records in one of his own

---

chapter here; cf. also 23. Proclus, *Alc.* 20.19 (i, 26 Segonds) maintains that the souls of good men exercise a *pronoia* over their inferiors, analogous to that of the gods.

293 The word is cited once in Des Places, *OC*, 114, as Fr. 208, and his note (p. 150) says that it means the conjunction of the magician with his god.

294 The Byzantine polymath Michael Psellus, *Exegesis* 1133 (cited by Des Places, *OC*, 179–80), speaks of a bullroarer, consisting of a golden sphere enclosing a sapphire, decorated throughout with symbols and whirled on an oxhide thong. He adds that such an instrument is called a *iunx* (hence "jinx"), but as for the significance says only that it is ineffable and that the ritual is sacred to Hecate.

295 See Castren (1994), 6, 7 and 13. The daughter of Plutarch, she became the mother of Archiadas, whose daughter, Asclepigeneia the younger, married the wealthy archon Theagenes and became the mother of the scholarch Hegias. See chapters 12, 14, 17 and 29. The name attests the family cult of Asclepius.

296 Mechanical ploys of the sort that Plotinus derides in his "Gnostics" at *Enn.* 2.9.13. A close relation between some Gnostic writings and the *Oracles* is indicated by Majercik (1992).

297 On Nestorius see chapter 12. Plutarch, priest as he was, was clearly more religious than Évrard (1960b) is disposed to admit.

298 See Porphyry, *On the Return of the Soul*, in Augustine, *City of God*, 10.9 on the purgation of the irrational souls from sins, a process which (10.27) enables it to rise to the ethereal regions, but not to the father or eternal life. This is reserved for the intellectual soul, which is purified by continence rather than by coercive rituals (10.27).

299 On the role of Hecate, as mistress of magic, source of souls, etc. see Johnson (1990). Psellus, *Chaldaean Exposition* says that the highest triad in the system consists of the "Once Transcendent", Hecate and the "Twice Transcendent". Below it are the intellectual triad, then one comprising the empyrean, the aether and the material universe; hence fire is the medium of Hecate's appearances. For this reason, Des Places, *ibid.*, 171 n. 3 refers the term *phasma* ("apparition") to Aristotle, *Meteorology* 338b2 etc. Proclus may have known of the lamp-bearing Hecate in his own Byzantium: see Hesychius of Miletus, in Jacoby (1950), 170. At *Crat.* 105.26-8 Pasquali he asserts that the virginity of Hecate represents the stable centre of the life-giving or zoogonic triad, which imparts to the intellect what it receives from the unparticipated gods.

writings.[300] He actually caused rains by an apposite use of a *iunx*,[301] releasing Attica[302] from a baneful drought. He also laid down defences against earthquakes, and tested the power of the prophetic tripod,[303] and produced verses on its decline.[304] For when he was in his fortieth year,[305] he seemed in a dream to utter the following words:[306]

> There hovers the supercelestial and immortal radiance,
> Leaping forth from the roaring fire that congregates[307]
>   at the source.

And at the beginning of his forty-second year, he seemed to utter the following in a loud voice:[308]

---

300 See Des Places, *OC*, 206–212 for the remaining fragments of Proclus' commentary on the oracles, which do not contain this episode.

301 Cremer (1969), 71–72 and n. 278 lists appearances of the *iunx* in literature, beginning with its birth as a bird from Pan and Echo. Though Johnson (1990), 80 notes that rainmaking was more characteristic of ordinary magic than of Chaldaean theurgy, the claim to control the elements already appears, c. 500 B.C. in Empedocles Fr. 111.3 DK.

302 The region of Greece whose capital was Athens.

303 That is, at Delphi, where the Sibyl is said to have sat on a three-legged stool in order to receive inspiration from the vapours. Parke and Wormell (1956), I, 340–4 note that Delphi had associations with Heracles, Orpheus and Asclepius.

304 This is noted even in the late first century in Plutarch's *On the Decline of the Oracles*. Here in his *On the Pythian Oracles*, Plutarch argues that supernatural communications are no longer required in an age when the mind itself has become attuned to the promptings of divinity. Julian, however, had attempted to revive the oracle; Iamblichus in his *Mysteries* had defended oracles at less famous sites, and therefore it would have been interesting to know what sort of explanation Proclus would have offered.

305 That is in 444/5 A.D.

306 The diction is Chaldaean. Cf. Fr. 44 Des Places, where the soul is a fiery spark, and Fr. 42 (Proclus, *Parm.* 769 Cousin), in which the love of the soul, fire entwined with fire, leaps forth from mind, where the "flower" of fire mixes cups at the source (*pêgaious*). In Proclus' lines the congregation at the source is the first, ineffable triad.

307 Literally "from the fiery-roaring congregation". The word *purismaragos* ("roaring like fire") belongs to the precious Hellenistic style of verse that we call Alexandrian (Theocritus, *Syrinx* 8), while *thiaseia* ("[Bacchic] congregation") is rare, though Anne Sheppard has pointed out to me that it is attested also in Proclus, Hymn 1.21. Alexandrian poetry was admired by the Neoplatonists, not only because it was difficult, but because it was prone to a hieratic manner, and, being composed outside the classical boundaries of Greece, was thick with references to obscure traditions and exotic cults.

308 More typical Chaldaean imagery (Fr. 61 Des Places etc.). The cycles will be the revolutions mentioned above, and the lines describe the purification of the soul which prepares the mind for illumination. The aether is the eternal element that surrounds the

> My soul has come, breathing the might of fire,
> And, opening the mind, to the aether in a fiery whirl[309]
> It rises, and clamours immortally[310] for the starry[311] orbits.

And in addition to what I have said, he clearly beheld that he was of the Hermaic chain[312] and believed because of a dream that he had the soul of Nicomachus the Pythagorean.[313]

29. And if one wished to make a long story, one could say a great deal in relating the theurgic practices of the happy man.[314] But I shall recall just one of a myriad, for it is marvellous even to hear. Once Asclepigeneia, the daughter of Archiadas and Plutarche, and the wife of Theagenes our benefactor,[315] while she was still a maid and being reared by her parents,

---

planetary system and nourishes the stars. On the ethereal body which the soul possesses after physical death see Proclus, *Tim.* 43f (i, 142 Diehl) etc.

309 Translating *pursoeliktos*, a word found only here.

310 This seems to be a unique appearance of the word *athanates* ("immortal"), while *bremei* ("clamours") as a transitive verb is also unusual. The diction remains equally unusual if the line means "the starry orbits clamour for [the soul] in its immortality", as Masullo suggests.

311 The adjective *poluteirês* has this sense in the "Alexandrian" poet Aratus, *Phenomena* 604.

312 See chapter 26, and especially Eunapius, *Sophists* 9 Boissonade-Dübner on Porphyry. This chain represents the succession of true scholarchs. At Proclus, *Alc.* 196.21 (ii, 255 Segonds) we are told that all learning hangs on the Hermaic chain; it has been explained at 187–8 (ii, 248 Segonds) that Hermes is the patron of learning as son of Maia (Socrates' method of drawing out the knowledge of the soul is called "maieutic"), and of discovery as messenger of the omniscient Zeus. Cf. Proclus, *Crat.* 9. 23 Pasquali.

313 A Neopythagorean, whose *Life of Pythagoras* was quarried by both Porphyry and Iamblichus: Rohde (1871–2). His mathematical writings, which derived all being from number, had a great influence on the Neoplatonists: Dillon (1977), 352–61. Dillon (1969) calculates a date of 196 for his death, which puts him a generation later than most scholars now suggest. Morrow, in an appendix to Proclus, *Eucl.*, 344 cites Taran (1969) on the commentary on Nicomachus by Asclepius, a pupil of Proclus. The ability to remember previous incarnations was a proof of enlightenment (see Iamblichus, *DVP* 63 on Pythagoras' recollection of Euphorbus), and doubly so, no doubt, if the precursor was himself a great philosopher.

314 Even if Marinus did not know John 21.25, which asserts that the world could not contain all the stories of Jesus, he may have wished this miracle to be compared with those of Christ.

315 On the mother and granddaughter of this name see chapter 28. Theagenes' benefactions to the Academy will have been conducive to the installation of his son Hegias as

was gripped by a severe illness which the doctors were unable to cure.[316] Archiadas, whose hope of offspring rested entirely in her, was distraught and full of grief, as one would expect. When the doctors gave up, he went as his custom was to the philosopher who was his final anchor,[317] or rather his benevolent saviour,[318] and earnestly begged him to come quickly and make his own prayers on behalf of the daughter. Taking with him the great Pericles from Lydia,[319] a man who was himself no mean philosopher, Proclus visited the shrine of Asclepius to pray to the god on behalf of the invalid. For at that time the city still enjoyed the use of this and retained intact the temple of the Saviour. And while he was praying in the ancient manner,[320] a sudden change was seen in the maiden and a sudden recovery occurred, for the Saviour, being a god, healed her easily.[321] And when the sacred acts were done, he went to Asclepigeneia and found that she had just been released from the critical[322] sufferings

---

scholarch c. 500. Since he gave this name to his son, he may have been related to the archon Hegias, sponsor of civic festivals, who is commemorated by civic inscriptions: Sironen (1994), 26–8. This conjecture is strengthened by an inscription to the "sophist" Plutarch (Sironen, *ibid.* 46–8), who also supported festivals and may be the great philosopher. The fact that the philosopher Hegias spoke of the virtues required in an archon (Damascius, *Isid.* Fr. 364 Zintzen) suggests that his family was accustomed to government.

316 A typical case demanding the intervention of Asclepius, whose name of course she bore. Could a deliberate contrast be intended with Mark 5.26, which follows hard on a verse (5.22) where Jesus is asked to cure the daughter of the ruler of the synagogue?

317 A common Christian metaphor: see Clement of Alexandria, *Stromateis* 4.23.152.

318 Allotting to Proclus a title of Asclepius, as well as of Christ. On the rivalry between them see Edelstein (1945), 132–138. We should note that Proclus, unlike Christ, does not perform the miracle himself: to heal without prayer, magic or any physical intermediary is almost the unique prerogative of the Christian saviour, as Arnobius (*Against the Nations* 1.49) had already noted c. 300 A.D.

319 Beutler (1940) collects the little that is known of him. More a colleague than a pupil of Proclus, he ascribed to Plato and Aristotle the teaching that prime matter is a body devoid of qualities. He is a dedicatee of Proclus, *Parm.* and the author of a conjecture at *Parm.* 832 Cousin.

320 In contrast to the novel orisons introduced by Christians, who had no ancestral faith.

321 Jesus (Mark 5.41–2) raises Jairus' daughter by touch and a word, but shows the capacity to heal without contact at e.g. Mark 7.29, Luke 7.10. Proclus sees his patient when the healing is complete; whenever Jesus heals at a distance the beneficiary is a gentile whom he never sees at all.

322 See chapter 15, where a similar term is applied to the dangers incurred by Proclus as a votary of Asclepius.

of her body and was in a healthy condition. Such was the act he performed, yet in this as in every other case he evaded the notice of the mob,[323] and offered no pretext to those who wished to plot against him. The house in which he dwelt was in this respect of great assistance to him.[324] For in addition to the rest of his good fortune, his dwelling too was extremely congenial to him, being also the one inhabited by his father Syrianus and by Plutarch, whom he himself styled his forefather.[325] It was a neighbour to the shrine of Asclepius[326] celebrated by Sophocles,[327] and of that of Dionysus by the theatre,[328] seen, or if not it became visible,[329] from the acropolis of Athena.[330]

30. How dear he himself was to the philosopher-goddess is sufficiently established by his choice of the philosophical life, which was such as my account reveals; but the goddess herself also indicated it plainly when her statue, which at that time was situated in the Parthenon,[331] was

323 For different (and debated) reasons, Jesus commanded secrecy after the raising of Jairus' daughter: Mark 5.43. For Marinus the mob consisted of Christians who flourished under the Emperor's protection, and who were soon to destroy the shrine of Asclepius.

324 On the excavation of a house on the south side of the Acropolis see Karivieri (1994).

325 The terms denote a sequence of teachers rather than biological descent. See chapter 12.

326 On the south side of the Acropolis; see Travlos (1980), 127–38 on the remains, which were rediscovered in 1876. There may be a depiction of Asclepius in the so-called "House of Proclus": Karivieri (1994), 119.

327 For his paean see Edelstein (1945), i, 325–326.

328 Also on the south side of the Acropolis; see Travlos (1980), 537–551. On the Metroon, or House of the Mother, that it contained, see *ibid*. 352 and Pausanias 1.3.5; this was replaced by a Christian building in the fourth century. Pickard-Cambridge (1946), 247–71 says that there is nothing to report about the use of the theatre in the fifth century, even though the stage was restored by the archon Phaedrus, perhaps c. 400: see further Sironen (1994), 43–45. Platonists would be less interested in performance than in Dionysus himself, a god associated both with Delphi and with Apollo, according to Plutarch, *Isis and Osiris* 365a.

329 I take this to mean that it became visible after the shrine of Asclepius was destroyed. Karivieri (1994), 116–117 and n. 11 cites two interpretations and hints at a third. The clearest is that of Castren (1991), 475: "Marinus wanted to stress that the House of Proclus was visible from the Acropolis and also otherwise somehow manifest, obviously because of the considerable bulk of the construction immediately below the eyes of the spectator".

330 Athena is the addressee of Proclus' seventh hymn, which alludes to her dwelling on the Acropolis: Saffrey (1994), 48. At *Crat.* 106.6 he construes her virginity in the same way as that of Hecate (chapter 28).

331 The temple of Athena as virgin goddess, decorated with sculptures by the great Phidias (fifth century B.C.), and goal of the great procession in which the robe of Athena was carried; see Plato, *Euthyphro* 6b–c.

displaced by those who move even the immovable.[332] For it seemed to the philosopher in a dream that he was approached by a woman of fair aspect, who announced that he must prepare his house as quickly as possible. "For the mistress of Athens," she said, "desires to live with you."[333] As for his affinity with Asclepius, that was indicated first by the act just mentioned, but we were also persuaded by the epiphany of the god in his final illness.[334] For when he was halfway between sleep and dreaming, he saw a serpent crawling about his head,[335] from which moment the illness began to subside, and thus through the epiphany he enjoyed some remission of the illness. Indeed, had not his great and eager desire for death prevented it, and had he deigned to give the appropriate care to his body, I believe that perfect health would have returned.[336]

31. And when he recalled these memorable events, it was not without sympathetic tears. For he feared, as his age increased, that the arthritic illness of his father, which for the most part is apt and likely to pass to children from their fathers,[337] should in this way come to him also. And his fears were not, I think, in vain.[338] For even before this, as I had to

332 Referring of course to the new-fangled ways of the Christians. Trombley (1993), 311 n. 12 points out that Marinus is quoting Herodotus, *Histories* 6.134, though a slightly different locution at Porphyry, *Abst.* 87.16 Nauck suggests that we may be dealing with a proverb.

333 The word translated "mistress" is the feminine of *Kurios* (Lord); cf. Mark 14.14. The most famous precedent for such a translation was the reception of Asclepius into the house of the great tragedian Sophocles. On the (late) reports of this and his other acts of piety see Mikalson (1991), 218.

334 Cf. the more discreet appearance (according to my interpretation) in Porphyry, *Plotinus* 2; also the epiphany of Telesphorus during another illness in chapter 7 above. Proclus speaks of visions of Asclepius at *Alc.* 166 (ii, 228–9 Segonds).

335 For Asclepius as serpent see Ovid, *Metamorphoses* 15.670; Lucian, *Alexander* 14 etc. Edelstein (1945), ii, 214–231 suggests that he was more frequently represented as a human figure accompanied by a serpent. The serpent is also the image of the Good Daemon (*agathos daemon*) in Hermetic literature and popular magic.

336 Whereas Plotinus accepted death as the remedy for the ills of life, Proclus chose it himself as a superior nostrum to that offered by the god.

337 I do not know if arthritis is said elsewhere to be hereditary; it certainly requires an explanation here, as Porphyry, *Abst.* 127.15–20 Nauck avers that a long affliction of the joints can be relieved by abstinence from meat. On the difficulty of defining the disease see Grmek (1989), 83 and 378, n. 122.

338 A play on *edediei* ("feared") and *adees* ("needless"), which is not worth reproducing in English.

recount above, he was conscious of an ailment of this kind – on which occasion, indeed, another wonderful thing happened to him.[339] For on the advice of certain people, he applied to his ailing foot the so-called liniment,[340] and as he was lying on his bed a bird[341] swooped down suddenly and snatched away the liniment. This was therefore a divine symbol[342] and truly Paeonian,[343] sufficient to give him confidence in the future. And yet, as I have said, he was none the less preoccupied by fear of the illness at a later time. So he supplicated the god about this, entreating him to give some clear message, and in his sleep he saw – for bold though it is even to think of this, one must nevertheless be bold to bring the truth to light[344] without shrinking – he saw, as it seemed, someone coming from Epidaurus[345] and leaning over his leg. So humane[346] was he that he did not even refuse to kiss the knees. From this time on, therefore, as he went through the rest of his life he was confident about this,

---

339 For the first such instance see chapter 7 on the apparition of Telesphorus.

340 In contrast to Porphyry, *Plotinus* 2, the details of the illness remain obscure but the remedies, both human and divine, are commemorated. The word *ptugmation* ("liniment" here), found only in late antiquity, is a diminutive of *ptugma*, a lint bandage. Marinus seems to apologise for a term that falls below the usual dignity of his prose.

341 See Damascius, *Isid*. Fr. 200 Zintzen for the use of the *strouthos* in Chaldaean rites.

342 The apophthegms of Pythagoras were called *sumbola* by disciples who believed that they concealed a deeper meaning. Dillon (1975), 251 cites Proclus, *Rep*. i, 73 Kroll to show that a *sumbolon* was allowed to bear less resemblance than the *eikon* to the thing that it signified. It was therefore an apter medium for the representation of the supersensory and ineffable, which cannot resemble anything. At the same time, as Sheppard (1980), 151–6 observes, the link between the symbol and its counterpart was supposed to be natural rather than conventional, as in *Chaldaean Oracles* Fr. 108 Des Places. *Crat*. 35.17–28 Pasquali defines the symbol as a radiation from the gods, midway between the utterable and the unutterable, which reveals the power of the gods in a manner appropriate to each recipient. Symbols are higher than names, and are unified in higher levels, manifold in the lower. Rangos (1999), 262–3 cites the definition of the related word *sunthêma* at Proclus, *Rep*. 242 Kroll – "a visible manifestation of invisible powers" – and argues that, unlike modern thinkers, Neoplatonists did not demand that symbols function in a system.

343 Paeon being a title of Apollo and Asclepius as healers, or sometimes the name of another divine physician. According to Callimachus, *Hymn 2* 103 it was bestowed on Apollo after his slaying of the serpent Python at Delphi; thus it is a name of special import for a patron of the shrine.

344 See chapters 5 and 22 for this metaphor.

345 In western Greece, the most famous shrine of Asclepius, from which, for example, he came to Rome: Ovid, *Metamorphoses* 15.723. See Edelstein (1945), ii, 238–242.

346 *Philanthrôpia* again, as in chapter 17, but this time used of a god.

and reached a great old age[347] with no further experience of such suffering.

32. Moreover the god in Adratta[348] clearly revealed his affinity with this man who was dear to the gods. For when Proclus visited his sanctuary he received him graciously with manifestations. Proclus was in perplexity, and prayed to learn what god or gods frequented the place and were honoured there, since different tales prevailed among the locals.[349] Some opined that the temple belonged to Asclepius and had many signs to confirm this: thus they said that voices were actually heard somewhere in the place, that there was a certain table dedicated to the god, that oracles that brought healing were constantly being given, and that those who came there were saved from the greatest jeopardy. But others believed that the Dioscuri[350] frequented the place. For some time ago, certain people had also seen, in a waking vision as it seemed to them,[351] two youths on the road to Adratta, extremely fair of aspect, riding horses and saying that they were hurrying to the temple. From their look they took them to be men, but were instantly persuaded that the apparition was of a more daemonic kind.[352] For when the men arrived at the sanctuary, they were told

---

347 Literally a "deep old age", recalling Plato's tribute to the depth of the aged Parmenides at *Theaetetus* 183e.

348 A place in Lydia. This event must therefore have occurred during the visit recorded in chapter 15.

349 A common question, as was the equivocal answer: cf. Sophocles, *Oedipus at Colonus* 39–43.

350 Literally "sons of Zeus", but it was generally believed that Polydeuces was the one true son of Zeus, while his twin Castor, though also a child of Leda, was the son of her human mate Tyndareus. Immortalised as the constellation Gemini, they were venerated in many Greek states: Farnell (1921), 175–233. On their cult in Byzantium, the birthplace of Proclus, see Hesychius of Miletus, in Jacoby (1950), 168.

351 The word *hupar* is used to distinguish waking or veridical perceptions from illusions, e.g. by Plato, *Republic* 520, *Statesman* 277d. Maximus of Tyre claims to have seen the Dioscuri by a temple in such a vision: *Philosophumena* 9.7a Hobein. As his list of acquaintances includes Heracles and Asclepius, and might have included Hector and Achilles, it seems that heroes, rather than gods, are visible in this manner.

352 See Cremer (1969), 68–86 on the origin and currency of the Neoplatonic commonplace that the invisible divine is revealed to us only through the visible daemonic. The priest in Porphyry, *Plotinus* 10 was therefore justified in expecting a daemon rather than a god. See Proclus, *Tim.* 314d (iii, 245–246 Diehl) on the ability of divine energies to assume daemonic, heroic or human rank; cf. *Rep.* i, 110–111 Kroll.

even without asking that the pair had been seen by the men who wait on the temple, but in the sight of the latter had suddenly become invisible.[353] For this reason then, as has been said, the philosopher was perplexed, unable to disbelieve the story; and as he begged the gods of the place to disclose their identity to him, it seemed to him that the god visited him in a dream and gave him this clear prompting: "What is this? Have you not heard Iamblichus saying who the two are, and making hymns to Machaon and Podalirius?"[354] And apart from this, the god thought the happy man worthy of such grace that he also appeared and, in the way that one pronounces an encomium of someone in the theatre,[355] he said in an actor's tone,[356] with his hand extended in a gesture[357] – I shall declare the very words of the god – "Proclus is the glory[358] of the city". Now what greater testimony could there be than this that the man who was happy in everything was also dear to the gods? Yet on account of his great fellow-feeling with the divine, he was always moved to tears if ever he told us his

---

353 A typical sign of divinity: Virgil, *Aeneid* 1.423 etc.

354 Whatever Iamblichus said, the two Homeric physicians were honoured throughout the Empire as sons of Asclepius: see Edelstein (1945), I, 78–95 on Machaon and 95–104 on Podalirius. Philosophers remembered that Aristotle was descended from Machaon (Diogenes Laertius 5.1), and the mock-wedding between Podalirius and the mother of the charlatan Alexander of Abonutichus suggests that the heroes had their own mysteries (Lucian, *Alexander* 39).

355 On the conventions of encomia, or speeches of praise, a popular species of showpiece oratory in late antiquity, see Russell and Winterbottom (1981), xxiv–xxxiv. Theatres, being little used for drama, were a frequent venue for sophistic displays, as we see from both Philostratus, *Sophists* and Eunapius, *Sophists*. Isidorus at least attended them and was noted for his discriminating praise: Damascius, *Isid.* 276 Zintzen.

356 The term *hypokrisis* implies dramatic simulation, but not deceit. Platonists, none the less, had once maintained that direct communication from the gods had been rendered obsolete by the advance of reason: cf. Plutarch, *Pythian Oracles* 404b, where we are told that the god does not speak through the Sibyl as the author of a play (or perhaps an actor) speaks through a mask or *prosopon*.

357 Though Sheppard (1980), 111–13 rightly observes that Proclus follows Plato in disparaging dramatic performances at *Rep.* 198.9–11 Kroll etc., he is happy to liken Socrates to a *deus ex machina*, whether on stage or in the mysteries, at *Alc.* 142 (i, 118 Segonds). Porphyry, *Gaurum* 48 Kalbfleisch is another Neoplatonist who was not ashamed to attend the theatre.

358 The word is *kosmos*, which denotes beauty of dress, character etc. and is thus often used to praise the order of the universe. In this translation, I have rendered *kosmios* as "regular".

memories of the things that he had seen, and the divine encomium that had been spoken to him.[359]

33. But if in this manner I opted to run through everything, to tell of his friendship with Pan the son of Hermes[360] and the great grace and salvation that he received from the god in Athens, or to divulge the magnitude of the good fortune that was allotted to him by the Mother of the Gods,[361] which gave him cause for extreme boasting and jubilation, I might seem to my readers to be babbling, and even to some to be saying things unworthy of belief. For many and extraordinary were the things that the goddess did or said for his benefit every day, and because they were so numerous and unforeseen I now possess no connected memory of them that I could write down. But if anyone desires to see what an adept he was in this, let him take in his hands Proclus' book on the rites of the Mother.[362] There he will see that it was not without divine possession[363] that he expounded the whole theology pertaining to the goddess, and in a philosophical manner disclosed the other things that are mythically[364] related of her and Attis,[365] so that the ear is no longer troubled

---

359 Contrast the reticence of the hero in Porphyry, *Plotinus* 3.

360 Called Pan ("all"), according to *Homeric Hymn* 19, because he received his name from all the gods. Despite his reputation as an unsuccessful gallant, he was also invoked as a Saviour (Longus, *Daphnis and Chloe* 2.26–28). Because of the famous "panic" that he inspired, he was regarded as a mystagogic deity, e.g. by Iamblichus, *Myst.* 3.10. On his association with the Mother and other goddesses see Bourgeaud (1988), 147–57.

361 See chapter 19.

362 Now lost. However, it will no doubt have followed Sallustius (*On the Gods and the World* 4) and the Emperor Julian (*Oration* 5, 161 and 166–9) in equating the Mother with the force of generation, and Attis with the creator who spills his generative powers into the lower world, and then castrates himself to return to union with his source.

363 *Katochê* denotes a temporary seizure by a benign force rather than permanent occupation by a malignant one: see Iamblichus, *Myst.* 3.10 (111 Des Places) and Plotinus, *Enn.* 5.3.14.

364 In defending the myths of Plato against Colotes the Epicurean, Proclus, *Rep.* ii, 105–9 Kroll asserts that this "phantastic" mode of expression must accompany philosophy so long as the soul itself retains its sensuous element, which he equates with the potential intellect of Aristotle. He adds that myth's two modes of representing the ineffable are metaphor and analogy.

365 The minion or offspring of the Great Mother, who castrated himself to avoid the effects of love (Arnobius, *Against the Nations* 5.5–8 etc.). In the so-called Naassene Sermon, a "key to all mythologies of the second century" (Hippolytus, *Ref.* 5.6–11), he is the archetypal man, and he also appears in a vision in Damascius, *Isid.* 131.

by the inarticulate lamentations[366] and the other things that are secretly[367] communicated there.

34. But now, as I am running through the operations and blessings that arose from his theurgic virtue, and have shown throughout my narrative that the man was equally furnished with all the virtues to a degree that men have never seen in a long time, let us now put an end to our account of him. My beginning has proved to be not only a beginning, not even as the proverb has it "half of the whole",[368] but actually the whole thing in its entirety. For I began with his happiness, and passing through that as an intermediary we have returned to it again, having presented in our account the goods vouchsafed to the righteous man from the gods and from providence[369] as a whole, describing auditory and visual manifestations, together with healings and all their other acts of guardianship, and also what fate and good fortune dispensed to him, namely his fatherland, parents and natural soundness[370] of body, congenial teachers and all his other assets. My presentation has shown that both in magnitude and in brilliance these surpassed those found in others, and furthermore I have enumerated the excellences that sprang from his own volition and not from any external factor (for such were the attainments of his soul in keeping with his comprehensive virtue). In a word, I have demonstrated that the activity of his soul proceeded according to perfect virtue,[371]

---

366 Described e.g. by the indignant Firmicus Maternus, *RP* 22, a work which, as it petitioned the Christian Emperors for the abolition of pagan sacrifices (c. 340), will have been even more objectionable to Neoplatonists than the gloating over Plotinus in his *Mathesis*. Apart from Christians, Romans took offence at the castrations performed by the Galli or priests of Cybele, and Catullus 63.90–92 prays to be delivered from her power.

367 On this term see Hadot (1968), i, 301. Proclus, *Alc.* 188.2 (ii, 248 Segonds) associates secrecy above all with Hermes (see chapter 28), the most cunning of the gods. At *Crat.* 332.22 Pasquali the properties that are secret in the gods are revealed by symbols to lower orders. It was a commonplace of Neoplatonic thought that solemn mysteries cannot be exposed to vulgar eyes. In justification of allegory they argued that the ancients had been forced to conceal such doctrines under a gaudy, lewd or profane exterior.

368 See Leutsch (1851), ii, 13: "the beginning is half the whole", with several instances; Plato, *Laws* 753e or Iamblichus, *DVP* 162 may be in Marinus' mind.

369 Translating *pronoia* again; cf. chapters 18, 23 and 28.

370 That is *euphuia*, on which see notes to Porphyry, *Plotinus* 1, together with Damascius, *Isid*. Frs 127, 148, 209, 284, 324 Zintzen. As these passages show, it is more often a property of soul than of body, though no guarantee of proficiency in virtue.

371 The Aristotelian definition of happiness at *Nicomachean Ethics* 1102 a5.

sufficiently furnished as it was with all the other goods, both human and divine, and in a completed span of life.[372]

35. But so that the more erudite[373] may be able to conjecture, from the configuration of stars under which he was born, that the choice dispensed to him did not fall among the last, nor even among any in the middle, but among the first,[374] I have set out their positions as they were at his birth.[375]

Sign	Degrees	Minutes
Sun in Aries	16	26
Moon in Gemini	17	29
Saturn in Taurus	24	23
Jupiter in Taurus	24	41
Mars in Sagittarius	29	50
Venus in Pisces	23[376]	
Mercury in Aquarius	4	42
Horoscope in Aries	8	19

372 A condition suggested by Aristotle at *ibid.*, 1101a10–13. The maxim that we should not call anyone happy until he is dead was conventionally attributed to Solon (Herodotus, *Histories* 1.33).

373 Applying the term *philokalos* ("lover of beauty": *Phaedrus* 248d; cf. Proclus, *Alc.* 202, ii 262 Segonds) to a study that Plato himself did not encourage. The word had come to signify the pursuit of liberal studies other than philosophy. In late antiquity astrology was regarded as a science; what we now call astronomy, the empirical observation of stellar motions, had been vigorously pursued in Plato's school, but had made little progress anywhere since Claudius Ptolemaeus (first century A.D.).

374 Alluding to Plato, *Republic* 619–620, where souls released from one embodiment choose their lot in the next according to a determined sequence, the choice of Odysseus being the last of all. Proclus, *Rep.* ii, 418 Kroll explains that the order of choices is related to the temper of the soul. The result is sanctioned by the fates and thus becomes indefeasible: according to Proclus, *Rep.* ii, 342.22–23 it includes not only the kind of life (occupation, rank etc.) but also adventitious circumstances apportioned to us by the universe. All Platonists assumed that the will retains a certain liberty after allowances are made for station in life and natural temperament.

375 Not having mastered the principles of astrology, I have followed the translation of Neugebauer and Van Hoesen (1959), 135–6, accepting the emendations to the manuscript which are common to them and other editors. In Marinus' favour it should be noted that Proclus, *Rep.* ii, 318 Kroll appeals to "barbarous spheres of the Egyptians and Chaldaeans" to prove that signs of the zodiac are appointed to govern different lots in life.

376 Neugebauer and Van Hoesen (1959), 135 n. 6 suggest that a figure for minutes has dropped out.

Mid-heaven in Capricorn	4	42
Ascendant node in Scorpio	24	33
Preceding conjunction in Aquarius	8	51[377]

36. He died in the 124th year since the reign of the Emperor Julian,[378] when Nicagoras the younger was archon of Athens,[379] on the 17th of the Athenian month of Munichion,[380] which was also the 17th of the Roman April.[381] And his body was judged worthy of rites according to the ancestral custom of the Athenians[382] and as he himself had prescribed while still alive. For to this blessed man, if to anyone, belonged knowledge and solicitude concerning what is done for the departed. For there was no occasion on which he neglected their customary rites, but every year on certain appointed days he visited the places of the Attic heroes,[383] the tombs of the philosophers[384] and of others who had become his own friends or acquaintances, paying the customary honours not through an intermediary but in his own person.[385] And after he performed the rites for each, he returned to the Academy and in a certain place he severally propitiated the souls of his

377 Neugebauer and Van Hoesen (1959), 135–6 endorse previous reckonings which set the date of birth at 8 February 412, even though this is not compatible with the age of 75 at death (see next note).

378 If Julian assumed the throne in December 361, and the year is dated from midsummer according to Attic practice, his first year commences in July 361, his 124th in July 484, and Proclus will thus have died in April 485. See Neugebauer and Van Hoesen (1959), 135 and Freudenthal (1888). I cannot see any alternative to Freudenthal's surmise (p. 493) that Marinus made an error in reckoning. The question then arises: did he know the right date and give the wrong horoscope or give the right horoscope and know the wrong date?

379 From classical times one of the nine elected archons had given his name to the year, which began after the first summer solstice (June/July). See Hansen (1991), 44 and 135.

380 The tenth month of the Athenian year, which started in July. Parke (1977), 137 notes that it was sacred to Artemis.

381 Now the fourth month of the Roman year.

382 According to Garland (1985), 102–20 these included offerings and even sacrifice in archaic times, though Solon greatly curtailed the ceremonies.

383 Heroes were men who, because of their divine parentage, their manner of death or their great works, were believed to deserve a cult. See Farnell (1921), and on the Pythagorean duty of honouring gods, daemons and heroes see Hierocles, *CA* 417–26 Müllach.

384 The locations have not been recorded in most cases, but Diogenes Laertius 3.41 relates that Plato himself was buried in the Academy. At 2.43 he asserts that a statue of Socrates was erected in the Pompeium after his death.

385 The practice of conveying perfunctory offerings to the dead through a third party is attested as early as the mid-fifth century B.C.: Aeschylus, *Libation-Bearers* 89–90.

ancestors and other kindred ones.[386] And again in another part he made a common libation to the souls of all past philosophers. And after all that, this paragon of holiness marked out a third place, where he made offerings to the souls of all the departed.[387] As has been said, his body was dressed according to his own precept, and, borne by his companions, was interred in the eastern suburbs of the city by Lycabettus,[388] where the body of his mentor[389] Syrianus also lies. For this is what Syrianus enjoined upon him while still alive, and for that reason he had the depository of the tomb made double. There were times after his death when Proclus, in his outstanding piety, was concerned that this might be improper; then he seemed to see the same dream threatening him, simply on account of this one thought. On the tomb is inscribed the following four-line epigram,[390] which he himself wrote for himself:

> Proclus I was, by race a man of Lycia, whom Syrianus
> Fostered here to become the successor[391] to his own school.
> This is the common tomb which received the bodies of both men;
> Oh may a single Place[392] be a portion of both their souls.

37. Before the year of his death there were portents such as an eclipse of the sun, so conspicuous that it became night by day. For a deep darkness

---

386 Moved, no doubt by the Pythagorean verses which commend honouring of parents: Hierocles, *CA* 426-8 Mullach. See also Farnell (1921), 343-60 on the veneration of ancestors.

387 There seems to be an ascending order from prayers through libations to other offerings, though we may safely assume that no animals were sacrificed even in the third category.

388 A large hill to the north of Athens, which, according to Plato, *Critias* 112a, was one extremity of the city in its forgotten age of glory.

389 The word *kathêgemon* is frequently applied to Syrianus in Proclus' writings: *Rep.* i, 270.5, ii, 113.11 Kroll, etc. Sheppard (1980), 39-48 discusses the extent of Proclus' indebtedness to his teacher.

390 Composed as usual in the elegiac metre (hexameter alternating with pentameter), which I have tried to reproduce in translation. See Gelzer (1966) for other epigrams of Proclus.

391 Gelzer (1966), 9 notes that this term (applied to the Lycians in Homer's *Iliad*) may also imply that Proclus' achievements were the repayment of Syrianus' labours.

392 Gelzer (1966), 11-13 sees here an allusion to the *apokatastasis* or restoration of the soul to heaven.

descended and the stars appeared.[393] This took place in Capricorn on its eastern centre.[394] The observers of days have also noted another, to occur after the completion of the first year.[395] When commotions such as this are seen to occur in heaven, they are said to be significant of occurrences on earth,[396] and we take them as portents of the deprivation and as it were the eclipse of the light of philosophy.

38. So now let this narrative of mine suffice concerning the philosopher. Anyone who wishes may also write the truth about the companions who associated with him. For he had many visitors from many parts, some coming simply to hear him, while others were disciples and studied with him for the sake of philosophy.[397] As for his writings, let a more industrious[398] person enumerate their titles. What I have been led to write here is for the sake of my own conscience and in order to pay my devoirs to his divine soul and the good daemon to which he was allotted.[399] Of his writings I will say only this, that he always preferred his commentary on the *Timaeus* to all the rest, though he was also very pleased with that

---

393 Compare the eclipse that coincides with the death of Jesus at Luke 23.44–5. As Origen indicates at *Against Celsus* 2.33, this portent had been questioned by the pagans as early as the second century, and authenticated by an appeal to dubious authorities.

394 Neugebauer and Van Hoesen (1959), 136 say that this occurred on 14 January 484. According to Porphyry, *Nymphs* 71.17–20 Nauck (commenting on Plato, *Republic* 615d), Capricorn, as the sign in which the sun is furthest from our latitude, is the gate through which souls ascend to the upper world.

395 I take this to mean that Marinus wrote this work within months of Proclus' death, unlike Porphyry, who waited thirty years to record the life of his master. The eclipse, according to Neugebauer and Van Hoesen (1959), 136 occurred on 19 May 486, thirteen months after Proclus' death.

396 At *Tim.* 34a–b (i, 109.24–30) Proclus ascribes to Porphyry (following Aristotle, *Meteorology* 1.7) the doctrine that comets portend extremes of climate, according to the quarter of the sky in which they appear. Seneca, *Natural Questions* 7.17 and 21 records appearances of comets at the deaths of Roman Emperors, though at 7.30–32 he hesitates to affirm that they are special revelations from the gods.

397 Making a clear distinction between hearers and disciples; cf. Porphyry, *Plotinus* 7.

398 See chapter 22 on *philoponia*. Marinus may wish to imply that Proclus' works were more numerous than those of Plotinus, or else that Porphyry wasted his time by drawing up a catalogue of the latter.

399 Echoing Porphyry, *Plotinus* 10 and Plotinus, *Enn.* 3.4., but adding the epithet "good" to the daemon. The phrase had a religious connotation in this period, denoting a heavenly patron and revealer, and was conferred as a title on both Asclepius and Hermes Trismegistus.

on the *Theaetetus*.[400] It was a frequent habit of his to say this also: "If I had the power, of all the books of the ancients I would have only the *Oracles* and the *Timaeus* survive, and all the rest I would conceal from the men of the present, since they have even caused harm to some of those who approached them in a casual and uncritical manner".[401]

---

400 This is lost, but it would always have been evident that this dialogue, one of Plato's longest meditations on the nature of knowledge, made an excellent introduction to his philosophy. It establishes the motive for philosophy (the irreducible presence of evil in the world), the purpose of philosophy (likeness to god according to one's capacity) and the method of philosophy (the midwifery which Socrates inherits from his mother Phaenarete).

401 Abrupt conclusions are typical of Greek and Latin literature in all periods. This one conveys the essence of Proclus' thought by naming his favourite books, and explains why his times were in need of such a philosopher, and hence of such a biographer as Marinus.

APPENDIX: THE CHRONOLOGY OF PORPHYRY'S *LIFE OF PLOTINUS*

Porphyry shows more than usual care in attaching dates to events in his own life and his master's; for all that, and despite his reputation as a chronicler,[1] some of his dates are difficult to reconcile with any mode of reckoning that was current in late antiquity. He counts by the regnal years of Roman Emperors; but at least four different ways of marking the year were open to him:[2]

(a) In the Egyptian calendar, the year begins on 29 August.[3] The first year of a monarch comes to an end, and the next begins, on the 29 August that immediately follows his accession.
(b) The same principle is adopted in the Macedonian calendar, except that its New Year's Day is 1 October.[4]
(c) In the Roman calendar the consular year begins on 1 January, and again the same rule of computation holds.
(d) If one reckons from the day of the Emperor's accession, his *dies imperii*, his first year terminates exactly twelve months later, and every ruler's years therefore commence on a date peculiar to his reign.[5]

1 Though the existence of a separate *Chronicle* is doubted by Croke (1983).

2 The question was first addressed at length by Oppermann (1929), who, while he prefers the Egyptian calendar, says at 40, n. 3 that there are no conclusive grounds for rejecting the Macedonian system.

3 Samuel (1972), 147 states that regnal years in Egypt began on Thoth 1 under the Ptolemies (323–30 B.C.), and at 177 n. 1 he adds that when the Egyptian and Julian calendars were synchronised in 30 B.C. Thoth 1 coincided with 29 August.

4 So Barnes (1976), though Boyd (1937), 243 n. 23 was not so certain of the *termini* of the Macedonian year. McCown (1933) offers this as a probable date for the start of the year, though it may be only approximate, and 23 August (Augustus' birthday) is also possible. Samuel (1972), 174 notes that this was the New Year's Day decreed by Rome for the cities of Asia, but the same decree ordained that this would henceforth be the first day of the Macedonian month that corresponded to October. According to *ibid.*, 147 Macedonian regnal years had originally commenced with the anniversary of each king's accession – method (d).

5 The choice of Boyd (1937), though his discussion at 250–257 reveals that the method is both unusual and difficult to apply.

118   APPENDIX

Two of Porphyry's calculations suffice to eliminate (c) and (d), if not (b) also:

1. Plotinus died in the second year of Claudius Gothicus, and Porphyry in chapter 2 infers from the information that he was sixty-six years old and that he was born in the thirteenth year of Septimius Severus. According to (c) the 13th year of Severus, who acceded early in 193, would begin on 1 January 205; the second year of Claudius, who acceded in late summer 268, would begin on 1 January 269. According to (d) the thirteenth year of Severus would begin early in 205, the second year of Claudius late in 269. On neither reckoning could Plotinus even have been as old as sixty-five at the time of death.[6] If we say, on the other hand, that the second year of Severus began on 29 August or 1 October in 193, the beginning of his thirteenth would be the same date in 204. Since Claudius came to the throne late in the year, his second year would not commence before 29 August in 269, perhaps not even before 1 October. This allows Plotinus to be over sixty-five at his death; if we assume that Porphyry meant only that he was "in his sixty-sixth year",[7] it will be possible to reconcile his arithmetic with method (a) or (b). If, as seems probable, Claudius took the throne between 29 August and 1 October,[8] his second year by the Macedonian reckoning (b) would begin in 268 and end on 1 October 269. In that case method (a) is the only one that would give Plotinus a span of more than sixty-five years.

2. Amelius is said to have spent "twenty-four whole years" in the school of Plotinus, from the third of Philip the Arab to the first of Claudius.[9] Philip's tenure was certain by the middle of 244; his third year would thus begin on 29 August 245 by method (a), on 1 October 245 by method (b), on 1 January 246 by method (c) and

---

6 So also Barnes (1976), 66; cf. Boyd (1937), 243–4.

7 See Goulet (1982c), against Igal (1982), 32, who thought this an impossible solecism.

8 Rea (1972), 19. Nothing is to be gained at any point by speculation on the delays that might impede the diffusion of news of a ruler's death. As Boyd (1937), 247 observes against Oppermann (1929), 37, Porphyry had three decades to correct inaccuracies in his chronography.

9 *Plotinus* 3.41. At 3.19 "eleven whole years" is the interval from the twenty-eighth to the thirty-ninth year of Plotinus. He clearly rounds up a fraction at *Plotinus* 5.5, where he says that his acquaintance with Plotinus, extending from the tenth to the fifteenth year of Gallienus, lasted six years, though here at least he refrains from saying "whole years". See Boyd (1937), 243–5.

later in 246 by method (d). The first year of Claudius ends on 29 August 269 by method (a), at latest on 1 October 269 by method (b), on 1 January 269 by method (c) and late in 269 by method (d). By (a) the maximum interval from the third of Philip to the first of Claudius is 24 years, by (b) the same, by (c) 23 years, by (d) a little over 23. Unless Amelius came to Rome on the day of Philip's accession, and left at the turn of Claudius' second year, none of these calendars will allow a full twenty-four years for his studies, but it is clear that (a) and (b) will yield the closest approximation to that figure. Once again, if Claudius became Emperor before 1 October in 268, only (a) can stand.

The following table of dates therefore assumes method (a), the Egyptian reckoning:

Autumn 204 (13th Severus)	Birth of Plotinus (*Plotinus* 2.37).
231–2[10]	Studies with Ammonius commence (3.6).
234[11]	Birth of Porphyry.
242–3	Plotinus leaves Egypt (3.19–20).[12]
Early 244 (death of Gordian)	Plotinus flees to Antioch (3.21–2).
Summer 244 (1st Philip)	Plotinus in Rome (3.23).
Autumn 245 (3rd Philip)	Amelius in Rome (3.40).
Summer 254 (1st Gallienus)[13]	Plotinus starts to write (3.35).
Summer 262	Porphyry first in Rome (5.1–3).[14]
Summer 263 (10th Gallienus)[15]	Porphyry in Rome (4.1).
Late summer 268 (15th Gallienus)	Porphyry leaves for Sicily (6.2).
Late summer 269 (1st Claudius)	Amelius departs (3.41).
Summer 270 (2nd Claudius)	Death of Plotinus (2.31).

10 Plotinus was in his twenty-eighth year, therefore not yet 28.
11 At 5.9 he gives his age as thirty when he arrived in Rome.
12 Plotinus was in his thirty-ninth year, therefore not yet 39.
13 Gallienus' father Valerian acceded in autumn 253, appointing Gallienus as co-regent. I give summer as the date because Porphyry (3.35) asserts that Plotinus had been ten years in Rome.
14 The "six years" of 5.5 do not include this sojourn during Plotinus' summer vacation, which is said to have occurred "shortly before the six-year period".
15 Porphyry adds that Plotinus was about 59 years old and that Amelius had been with him 18 years.

BIBLIOGRAPHY

A. TEXTS CITED BY ABBREVIATION AND/OR NAME OF EDITOR

Note: this is not an index of most recent editions, nor of all texts cited in the commentary. It is intended to elucidate rather than supplement the notes, and includes those works for which an abbreviation, or an editor's pagination, has been employed.

ALBINUS, *Isagoge in Platonem*, ed. C.F. Hermann, *Plato*, vol. 6 (Leipzig 1874), 141–6.
ALCINOUS (*Isagoge*), *Isagoge in Platonem*, ed. C.F. Hermann, Plato, vol. 6 (Leipzig 1874), 147–89.
ATTICUS, *Fragments*, ed. J. Baudry (Paris 1931).
CHALDAEAN ORACLES (*OC*), *Oracles Chaldaïques*, ed. E. Des Places (Paris 1971).
DAMASCIUS (*Isid.*), *Vitae Isidori Reliquiae*, ed. C. Zintzen (Hildesheim 1967).
—— (*Phaed.*), [Olympiodorus] *In Phaedonem*, ed. W. Norvin (Leipzig 1913).
EUNAPIUS (*Sophists*), *Vitae Sophistarum*, ed. J.P. Boissonade, revised F. Dübner (Paris 1849).
EUSEBIUS OF CAESAREA (*HE*), *Ecclesiasticae Historiae*, ed. E. Schwartz, 3 vols (Leipzig 1903–9).
—— (*PE*), *Praeparatio Evangelica*, ed. E.H. Gifford, 5 vols (Oxford 1903).
—— (*VC*), *Vita Constanini*, ed. I. Heikel (Leipzig 1902), rev. F. Winkelman (1975).
FIRMICUS MATERNUS (*Math.*), *Mathesis,* ed. W. Kroll and F. Skutsch (Leipzig 1897).
—— (*RP*), *De l'Erreur des religions païennes*, ed. R. Turcan (Paris 1982).
HERMETICA, ed. A.D. Nock and A.-J. Festugière, 2 vols (Paris 1945).
HIEROCLES (*CA*), *Commentarium in Carmen Aureum*, ed. O. Müllach, *Fragmenta Philosophorum Graecorum* (Paris 1860), 408–84.
HIPPOLYTUS (*Ref.*), *Refutatio Omnium Haeresium*, ed. M. Marcovich (Berlin 1986).

IAMBLICHUS, *Commentariorum in Platonis Dialogos Fragmenta*, ed. J.M. Dillon (Leiden 1973).
—— *De Anima*, in Stobaeus, *Anthologia*, ed. C. Wachsmuth (Berlin 1884), 362–458.
—— (*DCMS*), *De Communi Mathematicorum Scientia*, ed. N. Festa (Leipzig 1975).
—— (*DVP*), *De Vita Pythagorica*, ed. F. Dübner (Leipzig 1957).
—— (*Myst.*), *Les Mystères d'Égypte*, ed. E. Des Places (Paris 1966).
—— (*Protr.*), *Protreptique,* ed. E. Des Places (Paris 1989).
LYDUS, J. (*Mens.*), *De Mensibus*, ed. R. Wünsch (Leipzig 1898).
MARINUS (*Proclus*), *Vita Procli*, ed. J.P. Boissonade (Paris 1850).
—— (*Proclus*), *Vita di Proclo*, ed. R. Masullo (Naples 1985).
MAXIMUS OF TYRE, *Philosophumena,* ed. H. Hobein (Leipzig 1910).
NUMENIUS, *Fragments*, ed. E. Des Places (Paris 1973).
OLYMPIODORUS (*VP*), *Vita Platonis*, ed. A. Westermann (Leipzig 1881).
ORIGEN (*Hom. Cant., Cant.*), *Homilien, Kommentar im Hohenliede*, ed. W.F. Baehrens (Leipzig 1925).
PHILOSTRATUS (*Apollonius*), *Life of Apollonius*, ed. and trans. F.C. Conybeare (London/New York 1912).
—— (*Sophists*), *Vitae Sophistarum*, ed. A. Westermann, rev. F. Dübner (Paris 1849).
PHOTIUS (*Bibl.*), *Bibliothèque*, ed. R. Henry, vol. 2 (Paris 1960).
PLOTINUS (*Enn.*), *Ennéades*, ed. P. Henry and H.-R. Schwyzer, 3 vols (Oxford 1964).
—— (*Enn.*), ed. with trans. A.H. Armstrong, 7 vols (London and New York 1966–85).
PORPHYRY (*Pyth., Nymphs, Abst., Marc.*), *Vita Pythagorae, De Antro Nympharum, De Abstinentia, Ad Marcellam*, in *Porphyrii Opuscula*, ed. A. Nauck (Leipzig 1886).
—— (*Anebo*) *Lettera ad Anebo*, ed. A. Sodano (Naples 1958).
—— *Fragmenta*, ed. A. Smith (Leipzig 1993).
—— (*Gaurum*) *Ad Gaurum*, ed. K. Kalbfleisch (Berlin 1895).
—— (*Oracles*) *De Philosophia ex Oraculis Haurienda*, ed. G. Wolff (Berlin 1856).
—— (*Plotinus*), *De Vita Plotini et Ordine Librorum eius*, ed. A.H. Armstrong, *Plotinus*, vol. 1 (London and New York 1966).
—— (*Plotinus*) other editions of the *Life* sometimes cited are those of

A. Westermann (Leipzig 1881), E. Bréhier (Paris 1924) and P. Kalligas (1991). See also Brisson, L. (1982, 1992).
—— (*Regr.*), *De Regressu Animae* appears as appendix 2 to Bidez (1913).
—— (*Sent.*), *Sententiae ad Intelligibilia Ducentes*, ed. E. Lamberz (Leipzig 1975).
—— (*Statues*), *De Statuis*, appears as appendix 1 to Bidez (1913).
PROCLUS *Opera Inedita*, ed. V. Cousin (Paris 1864).
—— (*Alc.*), *Sur le premier Alcibiade de Platon*, ed. A.Ph. Segonds, 2 vols (Paris 1985–6).
—— (*Crat.*), *In Platonis Cratylum*, ed. A. Pasquali (Leipzig 1908); F. Romano (Catania/Rome 1989).
—— (*DD, Prov.*), *De Decem Dubitationibus circa Providentiam* and *De Providentia et Fato*, in *Tria Opuscula*, ed. H. Boese (Berlin 1960).
—— (*ET*), *Elements of Theology*, ed. E.R. Dodds (Oxford 1933).
—— (*Parm.*), *Commentarius in Platonis Parmenidem*, ed. V. Cousin (Paris 1864).
—— (*PTh*), *Théologie Platonicienne*, ed. H. Saffrey and L.G. Westerink, 6 vols (Paris 1968–94).
—— (*Rep.*), *In Platonis Rem Publicam Commentarii*, ed. W. Kroll, 2 vols (Leipzig 1899, 1901).
—— (*Tim.*), *In Platonis Timaeum Commentarius*, ed. E. Diehl, 3 vols (Leipzig 1903–6).
PROLEGOMENA IN PLATONEM, ed. C.F. Hermann, *Plato*, vol. 6 (Leipzig 1874), 196–222.
VITA PLATONIS, ed. A. Westermann (Leipzig 1881).
ZOSIMUS OF PANOPOLIS, selections in Scott, vol. 4 (1936), 104–53.

B. SECONDARY LITERATURE, TRANSLATIONS AND COMMENTARIES, CITED BY AUTHOR AND DATE

ALLEN, M. (1984), *The Platonism of Marsilio Ficino* (Berkeley).
—— (1989), *Icastes: Marsilo Ficino's Interpretation of Plato's Sophist* (Berkeley).
ALLT, P. and ALSPRACH, R.K., eds (1989), *W.B. Yeats: Poems. Variorum Edition* (London).
ALT, K. (1993), *Weltflücht und Weltbehajung. Zur Frage des Dualismus bei Plutarch, Numenios, Plotin* (Stuttgart).
ANDERSON, G. (1986), *Philostratus* (Beckenham).
ANDRÉ, J. and FILLIOZAT, J. (1986), *L'Inde vue de Rome* (Paris).

ARMSTRONG, A.H. (1936), "Plotinus and India", *Classical Quarterly* 30, 22–8.
—— (1955–6), "Was Plotinus a Magician?", *Phronesis* 1, 73–9.
—— (1960), "The Background of the Doctrine that the Intelligibles are not outside the Intellect", *Entretiens Hardt 5: Les Sources de Plotin* (Geneva), 391–425.
—— (1991), "Aristotle in Plotinus: The Continuity and Discontinuity of Psyche and Nous", *Oxford Studies in Ancient Philosophy*, supplement, 117–28.
ARMSTRONG, A.H., ed. (1967), *The Cambridge History of Later Greek and Early Mediaeval Philosophy* (Cambridge).
ATHANASSIADI, P. (1981), *Julian and Hellenism* (London), reprinted as *Julian: An Intellectual Biography* (London 1992).
—— (1999a), "The Chaldean Oracles: Theology and Theurgy", in P. Athanassiadi and M. Frede (eds), *Pagan Monotheism in Late Antiquity* (Oxford), 149–84.
—— (1999b), *Damascius. The Philosophical History* (Athens).
AUSTIN, J.L. (1967), "*Agathon* and *Eudaimonia* in Aristotle", in J. Moravcsik (ed.), *Aristotle: A Collection of Critical Essays* (New York).
BALDWIN, A. and HUTTON, S., eds (1994), *Platonism and the English Imagination* (Cambridge).
BARNES, J. (1989), "Antiochus of Ascalon", in M. Griffin and J. Barnes (eds), *Philosophia Togata* (Oxford), 51–96.
—— (1995), "Life and Work", in J. Barnes (ed.), *The Cambridge Companion to Aristotle* (Cambridge), 1–27.
BARNES, T.D. (1973), "Porphyry against the Christians: Date and Attribution of the Fragments", *Journal of Theological Studies* 24, 424–42.
—— (1976), "The Chronology of Plotinus' Life", *Greek, Roman and Byzantine Studies* 17, 65–70.
BEARD, M., with S.R.F. PRICE and J. NORTH (1998), *Religions of Rome*, 2 vols (Cambridge).
BEATRICE, P. (1989), "*Quosdam libros Platonicos*: The Platonic Readings of Augustine in Milan", *Vigiliae Christianae* 43, 248–81.
—— (1991), "Le Traité de Porphyre contre les chrétiens: l'état de la question", *Kernos* 4, 119–38.
BEIERWALTES, W. (1963), "Der Begriff des 'unum in nobis' bei Proklos", *Miscellanea Mediaevalia* 2 (Berlin), 255–66.

—— (1977), "Pronoia und Freiheit in der Philosophie des Proklos", *Freiburg Zeitschrift für Philosophie und Theologie* 24, 88–111.
BEUTLER, R. (1940), "Perikles (8)", in G. Wissowa et al. (eds), *Paulys Realencyclopädie der classischen Altertumswissenchaft*, supplement 7, 899.
BIDEZ, J. (1913), *Vie de Porphyre le philosophe néoplatonicien* (Ghent).
BIDEZ, J. and CUMONT, F. (1938), *Les Mages hellenisés*, 2 vols (Paris).
BLUMENTHAL, H.J. (1966), "Did Plotinus Believe in Ideas of Individuals?", *Phronesis* 11, 61–80.
—— (1978), "529 and its Sequel: What Happened to the Academy?", *Byzantion* 48, 369–85.
—— (1984), "Marinus' *Life of Proclus*: Neoplatonist Biography", *Byzantion* 54, 469–94.
—— (1991), "*Nous Pathêtikos* in Later Greek Philosophy", *Oxford Studies in Ancient Philosophy*, supplement, 191–206.
—— (1996), *Aristotle and Neoplatonism in Late Antiquity: Interpretations of the De Anima* (London).
BORGEAUD, P. (1988), *The Cult of Pan in Ancient Greece* (Chicago).
BOWERSOCK, G. (1969), *Greek Sophists in the Roman Empire* (Oxford).
—— (1990), *Hellenism in Late Antiquity* (Oxford).
BOWIE, E.L. (1978), "Apollonius of Tyana: Legend and Reality", *Aufstieg und Niedergang der Römischen Welt* 2.16.2, 1652–99.
BOYD, M. (1937), "The Chronology of Porphyry's *Vita Plotini*", *Classical Philology* 32, 241–57.
—— (1957), "Longinus, the Philological Discourses and the Essay 'On the Sublime'", *Classical Quarterly* 7, 39–46.
BREGMAN, J. (1982), *Synesius of Cyrene: Philosopher and Bishop* (Berkeley).
BRENK, F.E. (1977), *In Mist Apparelled: Religious Themes in Plutarch's Moralia and Lives*, *Mnemosyne* supplement 48 (Leiden).
—— (1992), "The Origin and Return of the Soul in Plutarch", in M.G. Valdes (ed.), *Acta del III Simposio International sobre Plutarco* (Oviedo), 1–24.
—— (1996), "Time as Structure in the Daimonion of Socrates", in L. Van der Streckt (ed.), *Plutarchea Louvaniensia* (Louvain), 59–81.
—— (1998), "Genuine Greek Demons, 'In Mist Apparelled'. Hesiod and Plutarch", in his *Relighting the Souls. Studies in Plutarch,*

Greek Literature, Religion and Philosophy and in the New Testament Background (Stuttgart), no. 10.
BRISSON, L. (1982), "Notice sur les noms propres", in Brisson (ed.), Vie de Plotin, 49–140.
—— (1987a), "Amélius: sa vie, son oeuvre, sa doctrine, sa style", Aufstieg und Niedergang der Römischen Welt 3.36.2, 793–860.
—— (1987b), "Proclus et l'Orphisme", in Proclus. Lecteur et interprète des anciens. Colloques internationaux du C.N.R.S. (Paris), 43–103.
—— (1990), "L'Oracle d'Apollon dans la Vie de Plotin par Porphyre", Kernos 3, 77–88.
—— (1992), "Platon et la magie", in Brisson (ed.), Vie de Plotin, 465–75.
BRISSON, L., ed. (1982, 1992), La Vie de Plotin, 2 vols (Paris).
BRISSON, L. and FLAMAND, J.-M. (1992), "Structure, contenu et intention de l'Oracle d'Apollon", in Brisson (ed.), Vie de Plotin, 565–617.
BROWN, P. (1978), The Making of Late Antiquity (Cambridge, Mass.).
BURKERT, W. (1972), Lore and Science in Ancient Pythagoreanism (Cambridge, Mass.).
—— (1979), Structure and History in Greek Ritual and Myth (Berkeley).
BUTLER, A.J. (1978), The Arab Conquest of Egypt and the Last Thirty Years of the Roman Dominion, ed. P.M. Fraser (Oxford).
BURY, R. G. (1897), The Philebus of Plato (Cambridge).
CAMERON, A. (1968), "The Date of Iamblichus' Birth", Hermes 96, 374–6.
—— (1969), "The Last Days of the Academy at Athens", Proceedings of the Cambridge Philological Society, 7–29.
CAMERON, A. and HALL, S.G. (1999) (trans.), Eusebius: Life of Constantine (Oxford).
CARLIER, J. (1998), "L'Après-mort selon Porphyre", in A. Charles-Saget (ed.), Retour, repentir et constitution de soi (Paris), 133ff.
CASEY, P.M. (1976), "Porphyry and the Origin of the Book of Daniel", Journal of Theological Studies 27, 15–33.
CASTREN, P. (1991), review of A. Frantz, Late Antiquity 267–700, in Gnomon 63, 474–6.
—— (1994), "General Aspects of Life in Post-Herulian Athens", in P. Castren (ed.), Post-Herulian Athens (Helsinki), 1–14.
CHERNISS, H. (1944), Aristotle's Criticism of Plato and the Academy (Baltimore).

CHROUST, A.-H. (1973), *Aristotle. New Light on his Life and Some of his Lost Works*, vol. 1 (London).
CILENTO, V. (1971), *Paideia Antignostica* (Florence).
CLARK, E.G. (1989), *Iamblichus: On the Pythagorean Life* (Liverpool).
CLARKE, G.W. (1973), "Two Measures in the Persecution of Decius? Two Recent Views", *Bulletin of the Institute of Classical Studies* 20, 118–23.
COPENHAVER, B. (1992), *Hermetica* (Cambridge).
CORRIGAN, K. (1985), "Body's Approach to Soul: An Examination of a Recurrent Theme in the *Enneads*", *Dionysius* 9, 37–52.
—— (1986), "Is there more than one Generation of Matter in the *Enneads*?", *Phronesis* 31, 167–81.
—— (1987), "Amelius, Plotinus and Porphyry on Being, Intellect and the One. A Reappraisal", *Aufstieg und Niedergang der Römischen Welt* 2.36.2, 975–93.
COURCELLE, P. (1975), "Le Typhus, maladie de l'âme d'après Philon et d'après Saint Augustin", *Corona Gratiarum: Miscellanea E. Dekkers* 1 (Bruges), 245–88.
COX, P. (1983), *Biography in Late Antiquity: A Quest for the Holy Man* (Berkeley).
CREMER, F.W. (1969), *Die Chaldäischen Orakel und Jamblich, De Mysteriis* (Meisenheim am Glan).
CROKE, B. (1983), "Porphyry's Anti-Christian Chronology", *Journal of Theological Studies* 34, 168–85.
CROMBIE, I.M. (1963), *An Examination of Plato's Doctrines*, vol. 2 (London).
CUMONT, F. (1919), "Comment Plotin détourna Porphyre de suicide", *Revue des Études Grecques* 32, 113–20.
DE BLOIS, L. (1976), *The Policy of the Emperor Gallienus* (Leiden).
—— (1989), "Plotinus and Gallienus", *Instrumenta Patristica* 19, 69–82.
DECK, A.N. (1967), *Nature, Contemplation and the One* (Toronto).
DES PLACES, E. (1984), "Les Oracles chaldaïques", *Aufstieg und Niedergang der Römischen Welt* 2.17.4, 2299–2335.
DEUSE, W. (1983), *Untersuchungen zur mittelplatonischen und neuplatonischen Seelenlehre* (Wiesbaden).
DIELS, H. (*DK*), *Fragmente der Vorsokratiker*, revised by F. Kranz, 3 vols (Berlin 1951).
DILLON, J. (1969), "A Date for the Death of Nicomachus of Gerasa?", *Classical Review* 19, 274–5.

—— (1972), "Iamblichus and the Origin of the Doctrine of Henads", *Phronesis* 17, 102–6.
—— (1975), "Image, Symbol and Analogy: Three basic Concepts of Neoplatonic Exegesis", in R. Baine Harris (ed.), *The Significance of Neoplatonism* (Norfolk, Va.), 247–62.
—— (1977), *The Middle Platonists* (London).
—— (1979), "The Academy in the Middle Platonic Period", *Dionysius* 3, 63–77.
—— (1983a), "What Happened to Plato's Garden?", *Hermathena* 133, 51–9.
—— (1983b), "*Metriopatheia* and *Apatheia*: Some Reflections on a Controversy in Greek Ethics", in J.P. Anton and A. Preuss (eds), *Essays in Ancient Greek Philosophy* II (New York), 508–17.
—— (1983c), "Plotinus, Philo and Origen on the Grades of Virtue", in H.-D. Blume and F. Mann (eds), *Platonismus und Christentum. Festschrift für Heinrich Dörrie* (Munster), 92–105.
—— (1986), "Plotinus and the Transcendental Imagination", in J.P. Mackey (ed.), *Religious Imagination* (Edinburgh), 58–64.
—— (1987), "Iamblichus of Chalcis (c. 240–325 A.D.)", *Aufstieg und Niedergang der Römischen Welt* 2.36.2, 862–909.
—— (1989), "Solomon Ibn Gabirol's Doctrine of Intelligible Matter", *Irish Philosophical Journal* 6, 59–81.
—— (1992a), "Plotinus and the *Chaldaean Oracles*", in S. Gersh and C. Kannengiesser (eds), *Platonism in Late Antiquity* (Notre Dame), 31–40.
—— (1992b), "Porphyry's Doctrine of the One", in M. Goulet-Caze and D. O'Brien (eds), *Sophies Maietores* (Paris 1992), 356–66.
—— (1992c), "The Roots of Reason in John Scotus Eriugena", *Philosophical Studies* 33, 25–8.
—— (1993), *Alcinous. The Handbook of Platonism* (Oxford).
—— (1994), "Singing without an Instrument: Plotinus on Suicide", *Illinois Classical Studies* 19, 231–8.
—— (1999), "Monotheism in Gnostic Thought", in P. Athanassiadi and M. Frede (eds), *Pagan Monotheism in Late Antiquity* (Oxford), 69–79.
DILLON, J. and MORROW, G. (1970), *Proclus' Commentary on the Parmenides of Plato* (Ithaca, NY).
DODDS, E.R. (1928), "The *Parmenides* of Plato and the Neoplatonic One', *Classical Quarterly* 22, 129–45.

—— (1947), "Theurgy and its Relation to Neoplatonism", *Journal of Roman Studies* 37, 55–69.
—— (1960), "Numenius and Ammonius", *Entretiens Hardt* 5: *Les Sources de Plotin* (Geneva), 3–61.
—— (1965), *Pagan and Christian in an Age of Anxiety* (Cambridge).
DORESSE, J. (1950), "Les Apocalypses de Zoroastre, Zostrien et Nicothée", in *Studies in Honour of Walter Ewing Crum* (Constantinople).
DÖRRIE, H. (1955), "Ammonios, der Lehrer Plotins", *Hermes* 83, 439–77.
EADIE, J. (1996), "One Hundred Years of Rebellion: the Eastern Army in Politics", in D.L. Kennedy (ed.), *Journal of Roman Archaeology, Supplement 18: The Roman Army in the East* (Ann Arbor), 135–51.
EBBESEN, S. (1990a), "Porphyry's Contribution to Logic: A Reconstruction", in R. Sorabji (ed.), *Aristotle Transformed* (London), 141–71.
—— (1990b), "Boethius as an Aristotelian Commentator", *ibid.*, 373–92.
EDELSTEIN, L. (1945), *Asclepius*, 2 vols (Baltimore).
EDWARDS, M.J. (1988), "Scenes from the Later Wanderings of Odysseus", *Classical Quarterly* 38, 509–21.
—— (1989), "*Aidos* in Plotinus: *Enneads* 2.9.10", *Classical Quarterly* 83, 228–32.
—— (1990a), "Neglected Texts in the Study of Gnosticism", *Journal of Theological Studies* 41, 26–50.
—— (1990b), "A Late Use of Empedocles: The *Oracle on Plotinus*", *Mnemosyne* 43, 151–5.
—— (1990c), "Porphyry and the Intelligible Triad", *Journal of Hellenic Studies* 110, 91–100.
—— (1991), "Two Episodes from Porphyry's *Life of Plotinus*", *Historia* 40, 456–64.
—— (1993a), "Ammonius, Teacher of Origen", *Journal of Ecclesiastical History* 44, 1–13.
—— (1993b), "A Portrait of Plotinus", *Classical Quarterly* 43, 480–90.
—— (1994), "Plotinus and the Emperors", *Symbolae Osloenses* 74, 137–47.
—— (1996), "Porphyry's *Cave of the Nymphs* and the Gnostic Controversy", *Hermes* 124, 88–100.

—— (1997), "Biography and the Biographic", epilogue to M.J. Edwards and S.C.R. Swain (eds), *Portraits* (Oxford), 227–34.
—— (2000), "Birth, Death and Divinity in Porphyry's *Life of Plotinus*", in T. Hägg and P. Rousseau (eds), *Biography and Panegyric in Late Antiquity* (Berkeley).
EITREM, S. (1942), "La Théurgie chez les néoplatoniciens et dans les papyrus magiques", *Symbolae Osloenses* 22, 48–79.
ELSAS, G. (1975), *Neuplatonische und Gnostische Weltablehnung in der Schule Plotins* (Amsterdam).
ÉVRARD, E. (1960a), "La Date de la naissance de Proclus le néoplatonicien", *L'Antiquité Classique* 29, 137–141.
—— (1960b), "Le Maitre de Plutarque d'Athenes et les origines du néoplatonisme athénien', *L'Antiquité Classique* 29, 108–13 and 391–406.
FALKNER, J.M. (1895), *The Lost Stradivarius*, ed. E. Wilson (Oxford 1954).
FARNELL, L.R. (1921), *Greek Hero Cults and the Idea of Immortality* (Oxford).
FESTUGIÈRE, A.-J. (1936), "Une Source hermétique de Porphyre", *Revue des Études Grecques* 49, 586–95.
—— (1950–4), *La Révélation d'Hermès Trismégiste*, 4 vols (Paris).
—— (1954), *Personal Religion among the Greeks and Romans* (Berkeley).
—— (1960), "Lieux communs littéraires et thèmes de folklore dans l'hagiographie primitive", *Wiener Studien* 83, 123–52.
FINAMORE, J. (1985), *Iamblichus and the Theory of the Vehicle of the Soul* (Chico, California).
FINE, G. (1993), *On Ideas. Aristotle's Criticism of Plato's Theory of Forms* (Oxford).
—— (1996), "Immanence", *Oxford Studies in Ancient Philosophy* 4, 71–98.
FLASHAR, H. (1977), "The Critique of Plato's Theory of Ideas in Aristotle's *Ethics*", trans. and expanded by M. Schofield in J. Barnes, M.F. Burnyeat and R. Sorabji (eds), *Articles on Aristotle 2: Ethics and Politics* (London), 1–16.
FLINTERMAN, J.-J. (1995), *Power, Paideia and Pythagoreanism: Greek Identity, Conceptions of the Relationship between Philosophers and Monarchs and Political Ideas in Philostratus' Life of Apollonius*, trans. P. Mason (Amsterdam).
—— (1996), The Ubiquitous Divine Man", *Numen* 43, 82–96.

FONTENROSE, J. (1958), *Python* (University of California).
FOUCAULT, M. (1985), *History of Sexuality*, vol. 2: *The Use of Pleasure* (Harmondsworth).
FOWDEN, G. (1982), "The Pagan Holy Man in Late Antique Society", *Journal of Hellenic Studies* 102, 33–59.
—— (1986), *The Egyptian Hermes* (Cambridge).
—— (1990), "The Athenian Agora and the Progress of Christianity", *Journal of Roman Archaeology* 3, 494–501.
FRANCIS, J. (1995), *Subversive Virtue. Asceticism and Authority in the Second-Century Roman World* (Pennsylvania).
FREDE, D. (1992), "Disintegration and Restoration: Pleasure and Pain in Plato's *Philebus*", in R. Kraut (ed.), *The Cambridge Companion to Plato* (Cambridge), 425–63.
FREDE, M. (1987), "Numenius", *Aufstieg und Niedergang der Römischen Welt* 2.36.2, 1034–75.
—— (1999), "Eusebius' Apologetic Writings", in M.J. Edwards, M.D. Goodman and S.R.F. Price (eds), *Apologetics in the Roman Empire* (Oxford), 223–50.
FREUDENTHAL, J. (1888), "Über die Lebenszeit der Neuplatoniker Proklus", *Rheinisches Museum* 43, 486–93.
GARLAND, R. (1985), *The Greek Way of Death* (London).
GEFFCKEN, J. (1978), *The Last Days of Greco-Roman Paganism*, trans. S. MacCormack (Amsterdam).
GELZER, T. (1966), "Die Epigramme der Neuplatoniker Proklos", *Museum Helveticum* 23, 1–36.
GERSON, L. (1994), *Plotinus* (London).
GLUCKER, J. (1978), *Antiochus of Ascalon and the Late Academy* (Göttingen).
GOTTSCHALK, H.B. (1987), "Aristotelian Philosophy in the Roman World from the Time of Cicero to the End of the Second Century", *Aufstieg und Niedergang der Römischen Welt* 2.36.2, 1079–1174.
GOULET, R. (1977), "Porphyre, Ammonius, les Deux Origènes et les Autres", *Revue de l'Histoire de Philosophie et Religion* 57, 471–96.
—— (1982a), "Variations romanesques sur la mélancolie de Porphyre", *Hermes* 110, 443–57.
—— (1982b), "L'Oracle d'Apollon dans la *Vie de Plotin*", in Brisson (ed.), *Vie de Plotin*, 369–410.

—— (1982c), "Le Système chronologique de la Vie de Plotin", in Brisson (ed.), *Vie de Plotin*, 187–227.
GOULET-CAZÉ, M.-O. (1982), "L'Édition porphyrienne des *Ennéades*", in Brisson (ed.), *Vie de Plotin*, 280–94.
GRAESER, A. (1972), *Plotinus and the Stoics* (Leiden).
GRAHAM, D. (1987), *Aristotle's Two Systems* (Oxford).
GRMEK, M.D. (1989), *Diseases in the Ancient Greek World* (Baltimore).
—— (1992), "Les Maladies et la mort de Plotin", in Brisson (ed.), *Vie de Plotin*, 335–54.
GWYN GRIFFITHS, J. (1965), *Plutarch: De Iside et Osiride* (Oxford).
—— (1975), *Apuleius of Madauros. The Isis Book* (Leiden).
HADOT, I. (1978), *Le Problème du néoplatonisme alexandrin. Hierocles et Simplicius* (Paris).
—— (1991), "The Role of the Commentaries on Aristotle in the Teaching of Platonism according to the Prefaces of the Neoplatonic Commentators on the *Categories*", *Oxford Studies in Ancient Philosophy*, supplement, 175–90.
HADOT, P. (1960), "Être, vie, pensée chez Plotin et avant Plotin", in *Entretiens Hardt 5: Les Sources de Plotin* (Geneva), 107–37.
—— (1961), "Fragments d'un commentaire de Porphyre sur le *Parménide*", *Revue des Études Grecques* 74, 410–38.
—— (1967), "La Métaphysique de Porphyre", in *Entretiens Hardt 12: Porphyre* (Geneva), 123–62.
—— (1968), *Porphyre et Victorinus* (Paris).
—— (1990), "The Harmony of Plotinus and Aristotle According to Porphyry", in R. Sorabji (ed.), *Aristotle Transformed* (London), 125–40.
HAHN, J. (1990), "Quellen und Konzeption Eunaps im Proömium der *Vitae Sophistarum*", *Hermes* 118, 476–97.
HALFWASSEN, J. (1992), *Die Aufstieg zum Einen: Untersuchungen zu Platon und Plotin* (Stuttgart).
HALLSTROM, G. (1994), "The Closing of the Neoplatonic School in A.D. 529: An Additional Aspect", in P. Castren (ed.), *Post-Herulian Athens* (Helsinki), 141–60.
HANKINS, J. (1990), *Plato in the Italian Renaissance* (Leiden).
HANSEN, M.H. (1991), *The Athenian Democracy in the Age of Demosthenes* (Oxford).
HARDER, R. (1936), "Eine neue Schrift Plotins", *Hermes* 64, 1–10.

—— (1960), "Zur Biographie Plotins", in *Kleine Schriften* (Munich), 277–82.
HEATH, M. (1999), "Longinus, *On Sublimity*", *Proceedings of the Cambridge Philological Society* 45, 43–74.
HEATH, T.L. (1913), *Aristarchus of Samos, the Ancient Copernicus* (Oxford).
HELLEMAN-ELGERSMA, W. (1980), *Soul-Sisters. A Commentary on Enneads IV.3 [27], 1–8 of Plotinus* (Amsterdam).
HENRY, P. (1934), *Plotin et l'occident* (Louvain).
—— (1938), *Les États du texte de Plotin* (Brussels).
—— (1953), "La Dernière parole de Plotin", *Studi Classici e Orientali* 2, 116–117.
HIRSCHLE, M. (1979), *Sprachphilosophie und Namenmagie im Neuplatonismus* (Meisenheim).
HOLFORD-STREVENS, L. (1988), *Aulus Gellius* (London).
HIJMANS, B.J. (1987), "Apuleius, Philosophus Platonicus", *Aufstieg und Niedergang der Römischen Welt* 2.36.1, 395–475.
HUNTER, W.B. (1959), "Milton's Arianism Reconsidered", *Harvard Theological Review* 52, 9–35.
IGAL, J. (1981), "The Gnostics and the Ancient Philosophy in Plotinus", in H.J. Blumenthal and R.A. Markus (eds), *Neoplatonism and Early Christian Thought* (London), 138–49.
—— (1982), *La Cronologia de la Vida de Plotino de Porfirio* (Deusto).
—— (1984), "El Enigma del oraculo de Apolo sobre Plotino", *Emerità* 52, 83–115.
INGE, W.R. (1911–12), *The Philosophy of Plotinus* (London).
JACKSON, H.M. (1990), "The Seer Nicotheus and his Lost Apocalypse", *Novum Testamentum* 32, 250–77.
JACOBY, F. (1950), *Die Fragmente der Griechischen Historiker*, vol. IIIB (Leiden).
JAEGER, W. (1948), *Aristotle: Fundamentals of the History of his Development*, trans. R. Robinson (Oxford).
JOHNSON, S.I. (1990), *Hekate Soteira* (Atlanta).
JONES, A.H.M. (1940), *The Greek City from Alexander to Justinian* (Oxford).
KAHN, C. (1992), "Aristotle on Thinking", in M. Nussbaum and A.O. Rorty (eds), *Essays on Aristotle's De Anima* (Oxford), 359–80.
KALLIGAS, P. (1991), ΠΟΡΦΥΡΙΟΥ ΠΕΡΙ ΤΟΥ ΒΙΟΥ ΤΟΥ

ΠΛΩΤΙΝΟΥ ΚΑΙ ΠΕΡΙ ΤΗΣ ΤΑΞΕΩΣ ΤΩΝ ΒΙΒΛΙΩΝ ΑΥΤΟΥ (Athens).
KARIVIERI, A. (1994), "The House of Proclus on the Southern Slopes of the Acropolis: A Contribution", in P. Castren (ed.), *Post-Herulian Athens* (Helsinki), 115–40.
KEAVENEY, A. and MADDEN, J.A. (1982), "Phthiriasis and its Victims", *Symbolae Osloenses* 57, 87–100.
KELLY, J.N.D. (1975), *Jerome* (London).
KENNY, A. (1966), "Aristotle on Happiness", *Proceedings of the Aristotelian Society* 66, 93–102.
KERN, O. (1922), *Orphicorum Fragmenta* (Berlin).
KINGSLEY, P. (1990), "The Greek Origin of the Sixth-Century Dating of Zoroaster", *Bulletin of the School of Oriental and African Studies* 53, 245–65.
KOSMAN, L.A. (1992), "What Does the Maker Mind Make?", in M. Nussbaum and A.O. Rorty (eds), *Essays on Aristotle's De Anima* (Oxford), 343–58.
LAMBERTON, R. (1986), *Homer the Theologian: Neoplatonist Allegorical Reading and the Growth of the Epic Tradition* (Berkeley).
LANE, E.N. (1990), "Men: A Neglected Cult of Roman Asia Minor", *Aufstieg und Niedergang der Römischen Welt* 2.18.3 (1990), 1161–74.
LANE FOX, R. (1986), *Pagans and Christians* (Harmondsworth).
LANGERBECK, H. (1957), "The Philosophy of Ammonius Saccas", *Journal of Hellenic Studies* 77, 67–74.
LARSEN, H. (1972), *Jamblique de Chalcis* (Aarhus).
LEOPARDI, G. (1932), *Pensieri,* etc., ed. A. Donati (Bari).
—— , trans. (1982), *Porphyrii De Vita Plotini et Ordine Librorum eius*, ed. C. Moreschini (Florence).
LEUTSCH, E.L. (1851), *Paroemiographi Graeci*, 2 vols (Göttingen).
LÉVÊQUE, P. (1959), *Catena Aurea Homeri* (Paris).
LÉVY, I. (1926), *Recherches sur les sources de la legende de Pythagore* (Paris).
LEWIS, D.M. (1957), "The First Greek Jew", *Journal of Semitic Studies* 2, 264–6.
LEWY, H. (1956), *The Chaldaean Oracles and Theurgy* (Cairo).
LIM, R. (1993), "The Auditor Thaumasius in the *Vita Plotini*", *Journal of Hellenic Studies* 113, 157–60.
LLOYD, A.C. (1987), "Plotinus on the Genesis of Thought and Existence", *Oxford Studies in Ancient Philosophy* 5, 155–86.

L'ORANGE, P. (1951), "The Portrait of Plotinus", *Cahiers Archéologiques* 5, 15–30.
McCOWN, C.C. (1933), "The Calendar and Era of Gerasa", *Transactions and Proceedings of the American Philological Association* 44, 81–8.
MACKENNA, S. (1928), *Plotinus: The Enneads* (London).
MAIJER, P.A. (1992), *Plotinus on the Good or the One (Enneads VI.9)* (Amsterdam).
MAJERCIK, R. (1992), "The Existence-Life-Intellect Triad in Gnosticism and Neoplatonism", *Classical Quarterly* 42, 475–88.
MARKS, C.L. (1966), "Thomas Traherne and Cambridge Platonism", *Proceedings of the Modern Languages Association* 81, 523–34.
MEINWOLD, C. (1992), "Goodbye to the Third Man", in R. Kraut (ed.), *The Cambridge Companion to Plato* (Cambridge), 365–96.
MEREDITH, A. (1980), "Porphyry and Julian against the Christians", *Aufstieg und Niedergang der Römischen Welt* 2.23.2, 1119–49.
—— (1990), "The Good and the Beautiful in Gregory of Nyssa", in H. Eisenberger (ed.), *Hermeneumata: Festschrift Horner* (Heidelberg), 133–45.
MERKELBACH, R. (1958), "Eros und Psyche", *Philologus* 102, 103–16.
MERLAN, P. (1944), "Plotinus and Magic", *Isis*, 341–8.
—— (1960), *From Platonism to Neoplatonism* (The Hague).
MIKALSON, J. (1975), "*HEMERA APOPHRAS*", *American Journal of Philology* 96, 19–27.
—— (1991) *Honor thy Gods. Religion Popular and Unpopular in Athenian Tragedy* (Chapel Hill).
MILLAR, F. (1997), "Porphyry: Ethnicity, Language and Alien Wisdom", in J. Barnes and M. Griffin (eds), *Philosophia Togata* II (Oxford), 243–64.
MITCHELL, S. (1999), "The Cult of Zeus Hypsistos between Pagans, Jews and Christians", in P. Athanassiadi and M. Frede (eds), *Pagan Monotheism in Late Antiquity* (Oxford), 81–148.
MORTLEY, R. (1972), "Apuleius and Platonic Theology", *American Journal of Theology* 93, 584–90.
MURRAY, G. (1935), *Five Stages of Greek Religion* (London).
MUSSIES, G. (1990), "Marnas, God of Gaza", *Aufstieg und Niedergang der Römischen Welt* 2.18.4 (1990), 2412–57.

NEUGEBAUER, O. and VAN OESEN, H.B. (1959), *Greek Horoscopes* (Philadelphia).
NOCK, A.D. (1933), *Conversion* (Oxford).
NORMAN, R. (1969), "Aristotle's Philosopher-God", *Phronesis* 14, 63-74.
O'BRIEN, D. (1981), "Plotinus on the Generation of Matter", in H.J. Blumenthal and R.A. Markus, *Neoplatonism and Early Christian Thought* (London), 108-23.
—— (1982), "Comment écrivait Plotin", in Brisson (ed.), *Vie de Plotin*, 329-67.
—— (1993), *Théodicée plotinienne, théodicée gnostique* (Leiden).
OIKONOMIDES, A.N. (1977), *Marinus of Neapolis. The Extant Works* (Chicago).
OLIVER, J.H. (1981), "Marcus Aurelius and the Philosophical Schools at Athens", *American Journal of Philology* 102, 213-25.
OLMSTEAD, A.T. (1942), "The Mid-Third Century of the Christian Era", *Classical Philology* 37, 241-62 and 398-420.
O'MEARA, D.J. (1989), *Pythagoras Revived: Mathematics and Philosophy in Late Antiquity* (Oxford).
—— (1993), *Plotinus. An Introduction to the Enneads* (Oxford).
O'MEARA, J.J. (1959), *Porphyry's Philosophy from Oracles in Augustine* (Paris).
OPPERMANN, H. (1929), *Plotins Leben: Untersuchungen zur Biographie Plotins, Orient und Antike* 7 (Heidelberg).
OWEN, G.E.L. (1966), "The Platonism of Aristotle", *Proceedings of the British Academy*, 125-50.
—— (1983), "Philosophical Invective", *Oxford Studies in Ancient Philosophy* 1, 1-25.
PARKE, H.W. (1977), *Festivals of the Athenians* (London).
—— (1985), *The Oracles of Apollo in Asia Minor* (London).
PARKE, H.W. and WORMELL, D. (1956), *The Delphic Oracle*, 2 vols (Oxford).
PATRIDES, C.A., ed. (1969), *The Cambridge Platonists* (London).
PÉPIN, J. (1967), "Porphyre, exégète d'Homère", in *Entretiens Hardt* 12: *Porphyre* (Geneva), 229-72.
—— (1992), "L'Episode du portrait de Plotin", in Brisson (ed.), *Vie de Plotin*, 301-34.
PICKARD-CAMBRIDGE, A.W. (1946), *The Theatre of Dionysus at Athens* (Oxford).

POTTER, D. (1990), *Prophecy and History in the Crisis of the Roman Empire* (Oxford).
PRAECHTER, K. (1916), "Zum Platoniker Gaios", *Hermes* 51, 510–29.
PUECH, H.-C. (1960), "Plotin et les Gnostiques", in *Entretiens Hardt* 5: *Les Sources de Plotin* (Geneva), 160–90.
—— (1978), *En Quête de la Gnose*, 1 (Paris).
RAINE, K. (1963), *Blake and Antiquity* (Princeton).
RAINE, K. and HARPER, G.M., eds (1969), *Thomas Taylor the Platonist: Selected Writings* (Princeton).
RANGOS, S. (1999), "Proclus on Poetic Mimesis", *Oxford Studies in Ancient Philosophy* 17, 249–71.
RAWSON, E. (1989), "Roman Rulers and the Philosophic Adviser", in M. Griffin and J. Barnes (eds), *Philosophia Togata* (Oxford), 233–58.
—— (1990), *Intellectual Life in the Late Roman Republic* (London).
RAYNOR, D.H. (1984), "Philostratus and Moiragenes: Two Views of Apollonius of Tyana", *Classical Quarterly* 34, 222–6.
REA, J., ed. (1972), *Oxyrhynchus Papyri* 40 (London).
RICH, A.N.M. (1954), "The Platonic Ideas as Thoughts of God", *Mnemosyne* 7, 123–33.
—— (1957), "Reincarnation in Plotinus", *Mnemosyne* 10, 232–8.
—— (1960), "Plotinus and the Theory of Artistic Imitation", *Mnemosyne* 13, 233–9.
RIEDWEG, C. (1987), *Mysterienterminologie bei Platon, Philon und Klemens von Alexandrie* (Berlin).
RIGINOS, A. (1976), *Platonica* (New York).
RIST, J.M. (1961), "Plotinus on Matter and Evil", *Phronesis* 6, 154–66.
—— (1962a), "*Theos* and the One in some Texts of Plotinus", *Mediaeval Studies* 24, 169–80.
—— (1962b), "The Neoplatonic One and Plato's *Parmenides*", *Transactions and Proceedings of the American Philological Association* 93, 389–401.
—— (1962c), "The Indefinite Dyad and Intelligible Matter in Plotinus", *Classical Quarterly* 12, 99–107.
—— (1963), "Plotinus and the Daimonion of Socrates", *Phoenix* 17, 13–24.
—— (1964a), "Mysticism and Transcendence in Later Neoplatonism", *Hermes* 92, 213–25.

—— (1964b), *Eros and Psyche: Studies in Plato, Plotinus and Origen* (Toronto).
—— (1967), *Plotinus: The Road to Reality* (Cambridge).
—— (1973), "The One of Plotinus and the God of Aristotle", *Review of Metaphysics*, 75–87.
—— (1988), "Pseudo-Ammonius and the Soul-Body Problem", *American Journal of Philology* 109 (1988), 402–15.
—— (1989), "Back to the Mysticism of Plotinus: Some More Specifics", *Journal of the History of Philosophy* 27, 183–97.
—— (1992), "Pseudo-Dionysius, Neoplatonism and the Weakness of the Soul", in H.J. Westra (ed.), *From Athens to Chartres. Studies in Honour of Edouard Jeauneau* (Leiden), 135–61.
RITTER, A.M. (1994), *Pseudo-Dionysius Areopagita. Über die Mystiche Theologie und Briefe* (Stuttgart).
RITVO, R.P. (1975), "A Vision B: The Plotinian Metaphysical Basis", *Review of English Studies* 31, 36–48.
RIVES, J.B. (1999), "The Decian Decree and the Religion of the Empire", *Journal of Roman Studies* 89 (1999), 235–54.
ROBIN, L. (1964), *La Théorie platonicienne de l'Amour* (Paris).
ROBINSON, H. (1991), "Form and the Integrity of the Intellect from Aristotle to Aquinas", *Oxford Studies in Ancient Philosophy*, supplement, 207–26.
ROHDE, E.R. (1871/2), "Die Quelle des Iamblichus in seine Biographie des Pythagoras", *Rheinisches Museum* 26, 554–76 and 27, 23–61.
ROREM, P. (1998), *John of Scythopolis and the Dionysian Corpus* (Oxford).
ROSENTHAL, F. (1975), *The Classical Heritage in Islam* (London).
ROSTOVTZEFF, M.I. (1957), *Social and Economic History of the Roman Empire*, 2 vols (Oxford).
RUSSELL, D.A. and WINTERBOTTOM, M. (1981), *Ancient Literary Criticism* (Oxford).
SAFFREY, H.-D. (1966), "Un Lien objectif entre le Pseudo-Denys et Proclus", *Studia Patristica* 9, 98–105.
—— (1971), "Abamon, pseudonyme de Jamblique", in R.B. Palmer and R.G. Hammerton-Kelly (eds) *Philomathes. Studies and Essays in the Humanities in Memory of Philip Merlan* (The Hague), 227–39.
—— (1975), "Allusions anti-chrétiens chez Proclus", *Revue des Sciences Philosophiques et Philologiques* 59, 553–63.

—— (1981), "Les Néoplatoniciens et les oracles chaldaiques", *Revue des Études Augustiniennes* 27, 209–25.
—— (1984), La Théurgie comme phenomène culturel chez les néoplatoniciens (IVe-Ve siècles)", *Koinonia* 8, 161–71.
—— (1987), "Comment Syrianus, le maître de l'école néoplatonicienne d'Athènes, considérait-il Aristote?", *Aristoteles Werk und Wirkung Paul Moraux gewidmet*, vol. 2 (Berlin), 205–14.
—— (1994), *Proclus: Hymnes et Prières* (Paris).
SALZMAN, M. (1993), "The Evidence for the Conversion of the Roman Empire to Christianity in the Theodosian Code", *Historia* 43, 362–78.
SAMUEL, A.E. (1972), *Greek and Roman Chronology. Calendars and Years in Classical Antiquity* (Munich).
SCHIBLI, H.S. (1993), "Hierocles of Alexandria and the Vehicle of the Soul", *Hermes* 121, 109–17.
SCHISSEL VON FLESCHENBURG, O. (1928), *Marinos von Neapolis und die neuplatonischen Tugendlehre* (Athens).
SCHMIDT, C. (1901), *Plotins Stellung zum Gnosticismus* (Leiden).
SCHROEDER, F.M. (1980), "Representation and Reflection in Plotinus", *Dionysius* 4, 37–60.
—— (1987), "Ammonios Saccas", *Aufstieg und Niedergang der Römischen Welt* 2.36.1, 493–526.
SCHROEDER, F.M. and TODD, R.D. (1990), *Two Greek Aristotelian Commentators on the Intellect* (Toronto).
SCHWYZER, H.-R. (1951), "Plotinos", in A. Pauly, G. Wissowa and W. Kroll (eds), *Realencyclopädie der classischen Altertumswissenchaft* 21.2, 471–592.
SCOTT, W.B. (1925–36), *Hermetica*, 4 vols (Oxford).
SCREECH, M.A. (1980), *Erasmus: Ecstasy and the Praise of Folly* (London).
SHARPLES, R. (1987), "Alexander of Aphrodisias: Scholasticism and Innovation", *Aufstieg und Niedergang der Römischen Welt* 2.36.2, 1176–1243.
SHAW, G. (1985), "Theurgy: Rituals of Unification in the Neoplatonism of Iamblichus", *Traditio* 41, 1–28.
—— (1988), "Theurgy as Demiurgy: Iamblichus' Solution to the Problem of Embodiment", *Dionysius* 12, 37–60.
—— (1995), *Theurgy and the Soul* (University Park, Pennsylvania).

SHEPPARD, A. (1980), *Studies on the 5th and 6th Books of Proclus' Commentary on the Republic* (Göttingen).
—— (1982), "Proclus' Attitude to Theurgy", *Classical Quarterly* 39, 212–25.
—— (1991), "*Phantasia* and Mental Images: Neoplatonist Interpretation of *De Anima* 3.3", *Oxford Studies in Ancient Philosophy*, supplement, 165–74.
SIORVANES, L. (1996), *Proclus. Neoplatonic Philosophy and Science* (London).
SIRONEN, E. (1994), "Life and Administration of Late Roman Attica in the Light of Public Inscriptions", in P. Castren (ed.), *Post-Herulian Athens* (Helsinki), 15–62.
SMITH, A. (1974), *Porphyry's Place in the Neoplatonic Tradition* (The Hague).
—— (1984), "Did Porphyry Reject the Transmigration of Human Souls into Animals?", *Rheinisches Museum* 127, 276–84.
SMITH, R. (1995), *Julian's Gods* (London).
SORABJI, R. (1983), *Time, Creation and the Continuum* (London).
—— (1987), *Philoponus and the Rejection of Aristotelian Science* (London).
STROUMSA, G. (1999), *Barbarian Philosophy* (Tübingen).
SUSANETTI, D. (1995), *Plotino sul bello (Enneade I,6)* (Padua).
SWAIN, S.C.R. (1996), *Hellenism and Empire* (Oxford).
—— (1997), "Biography and the Biographic in the Literature of the Roman Empire", in M.J. Edwards and S.C.R. Swain (eds), *Portraits. Biographical Representation in the Greek and Latin Literature of the Roman Empire* (Oxford), 1–38.
—— (1999), "Defending Hellenism: Philostratus, *In Honour of Apollonius*", in M.J. Edwards, M.D. Goodman and S.R.F. Price (eds), *Apologetics in the Roman Empire* (Oxford), 157–96.
TALBERT, C.H. (1978), "Biographies of Philosophers and Rulers as Instruments of Propaganda in Mediterranean Antiquity", *Aufstieg und Niedergang der Römischen Welt* 2.16.2, 1619–51.
TAORMINA, D. (1984), "Filosofia e magia in Plotino" in *Symbolon 1: Momenti e problema di storia del platonismo* (Catania/Rome), 53–83.
——(1989), *Plutarco di Atene* (Rome).
TARAN, L. (1969), *Asclepius' Commentary on Nicomachus' Introduction to Arithmetic* (Philadelphia).

—— (1984), "Amelius-Amerius: Porphyry *VP* 7.4 and Eunapius, *Vitae Sophistarum* 4.2", *American Journal of Philology* 105, 476–9.
TARRANT, H. (1993), *Thrasyllan Platonism* (Cambridge).
THEILER, W. (1933), *Porphyrius und Augustin* (Halle).
THOMSON, J. (1905), *Essays, Dialogues and Thoughts of Giacomo Leopardi*, ed. B. Dobell (London).
THOMPSON, D.J. (1990), "The Memphis Priesthood under Ptolemaic Rule", in J. North and M. Beard (eds) *Pagan Priests* (London), 97–116.
TOOHEY, P. (1990), "Some Ancient Histories of Literary Melancholia", *Illinois Classical Studies* 15, 143–61.
TRAVLOS, J. (1980), *Pictorial Dictionary of Ancient Athens* (New York).
TREGGIARI, S. (1991), *Roman Marriage* (Oxford).
TRIGG, J. (1991), "The Angel of Great Counsel: Christ and the Angelic Hierarchy in Origen's Theology", *Journal of Theological Studies* 42, 35–51.
TROMBLEY, F.R. (1993), *Hellenic Religion and Christianization, c. 370–529 A.D.*, Part 1 (Leiden).
TROUILLARD, J. (1982), *La Mystagogie de Proclus* (Paris).
TURCAN, R. (1975), *Mithras Platonicus* (Leiden).
—— (1989), *Les Cultes orientaux dans le monde romain* (Paris).
VADÉ, Y. (1977), "Sur la maternité du chêne et de la pierre", *Revue de l'Histoire des Religions* 191, 3–41.
VAN DER HORST, P. and MANSFELD, J. (1974), *An Alexandrian Platonist on Dualism* (Leiden).
VEYNE, P. (1990), *Bread and Circuses* (Harmondsworth).
VLASTOS, G. (1965), "Degrees of Reality in Plato", in R. Bambrough (ed.), *New Essays on Plato and Aristotle* (London), 1–19.
—— (1969), "Plato's Third Man Argument (*Parm.* 132a1–b2): Text and Logic", *Philosophical Quarterly* 19, 289–381.
VOGEL, C. DE (1953), "On the Neoplatonic Character of Platonism and the Platonic Character of Neoplatonism", *Mind* 62, 43–64.
WALSH, P.G. (1981), "Apuleius and Plutarch", in H.J. Blumenthal and R.A. Markus (eds), *Neoplatonism and Early Christian Thought* (London), 20–32.
WALZER, R. (1967), "Porphyry and the Arabic Tradition", *Entretiens Hardt* 12: *Porphyre* (Geneva), 275–99.
WATSON, G. (1988), *Phantasia in Classical Thought* (Galway).

WEIL, E. (1951), "La Place de la logique dans la pensée aristotélicienne", *Revue de Metaphysique et Morale* 56, 283–315.
WEST, M.L. (1964), *Hesiod: Theogony* (Oxford).
—— (1983), *The Orphic Poems* (Oxford).
WHITTAKER, J. (1967), "Moses Atticizing", *Phoenix* 21, 196–201.
—— (1969), "Neopythagoreanism and Negative Theology", *Symbolae Osloenses* 44, 109–25.
—— (1987), "Platonic Philosophy in the Early Centuries of the Empire", *Aufstieg und Niedergang der Römischen Welt* 2.36.1, 81–123.
WILSON, F.A.C. (1958), *Yeats and Tradition* (London).
WILSON, N.G. (1967), "A Chapter in the History of Scholia", *Classical Quarterly* 17, 144–57.
—— (1992), *From Byzantium to Italy* (London).
WITT, R.E. (1971), *Isis in the Greco-Roman World* (Cambridge).
WOLFSON, H.A. (1957), "Negative Attributes in the Church Fathers and the Gnostic Basilides", *Harvard Theological Review* 45, 145–75
WYCHERLEY, W.E. (1978), *The Stones of Athens* (Princeton).
YEATS, W.B. (1925/37), *A Vision* (London).
—— (1961), *Essays and Introductions* (London).
ZINTZEN, C. (1965), "Die Wertung von Mystik und Magie in der neuplatonische Philosophie", *Rheinisches Museum* 108, 71–100.
ZUCKER, F. (1950), "Plotin und Lykopolis", *Sitzungsberichte der deutschen Akademie der Wissenschaften zu Berlin, Klasse für Sprachen, Literatur und Kunst* (Berlin), 3–20.

INDEX OF PERSONS, WORKS AND PLACES NAMED IN PORPHYRY'S *PLOTINUS*

Figures indicate the chapter of the *Life of Plotinus* in which the name occurs.

Aculinus, Gnostic author: 16.
Adelphius, Gnostic author: 16.
Adrastus, philosopher read by Plotinus: 14.
Aeacus, fabled judge of dead: 22, 23.
Alcibiades, as character in Plato: 15.
Alexander of Aphrodisias, philosopher read by Plotinus: 14.
Alexander the Libyan, Gnostic author: 16.
Alexandria, chief city of Egypt: 7, 10, 20.
Allogenes, author of Gnostic text: 16.
Amelius (Gentilianus Amelius), associate of Plotinus.
　His antecedents: 7.
　His defence of Plotinus against charge of plagiarism: 17.
　His disputations: 16 (Gnostics); 18 (Porphyry).
　His influence on Plotinus: 5.
　His merits, assessed by Longinus: 19–20.
　His portrait of Plotinus: 1.
　His retirement to Apamea: 2, 3.
　His notes on seminars: 3, 19.
　His superstition: 10.
　His visit to the oracle: 22.
Amerius, as nickname for Amelius: 7.
Ammonius, Peripatetic teacher: 20.
Ammonius, teacher of Plotinus: 3, 20.
Amphiclea, associate of Plotinus: 9.
Andronicus of Rhodes, editor of Aristotle: 24.
Annius, Stoic philosopher: 20.
Antimachus, Hellenistic poet: 7.
Antioch, city of Syria: 3.
Antonius of Rhodes, tutor of Porphyry: 4.
Apamea, town in Syria: 2, 3.
　Numenius of: 17.
Apollo, god of poetry, prophecy and philosophy: 22, 23.
Apollodorus, editor of Epicharmus: 24.
Aquilinus. See Aculinus.
Ariston, husband of Amphiclea: 9.
Aristotle, eminent philosopher: 24.
　His *Metaphysics*: 14.

Aspasius, philosopher read by Plotinus: 14.
Athenaeus, Stoic philosopher: 20.
Athens, chief city of Greece and home of Platonic "succession": 15, 20, 24.
Basileus, as nickname of Porphyry: 17, 20, 21.
Campania, region of south Italy: 2, 12.
Carterius, painter of portrait: 1.
Castricius Firmus, associate of Plotinus: 2, 7.
Chione, widow and housemate of Plotinus: 11.
Christians: 16.
Claudius II, Roman Emperor 268–70: 2, 3.
Cleodamus, addressee of Longinus: 17.
Cronius, Pythagorean philosopher: 14, 20, 21.
Delphic Oracle: 22, 23.
Democritus, Platonist: 20.
Demostratus, Gnostic author: 16.
Diophanes, foolish pupil of Plotinus: 15.
Egyptian priest: 10.
Enneads, body of Plotinus' writings. Chronological order of: 4–6.
   Porphyry's arrangement of: 24–26.
Epicharmus, comic and didactic poet: 24.
Etruria, modern Tuscany and birthplace of Amelius: 7.
Eubulus, Platonic successor: 15, 20.
Euclides, Platonist: 20.
Eustochius, physician to Plotinus: 2, 7.
Gaius, philosopher read by Plotinus: 14.
Gallienus, Roman Emperor 253–68: 3, 4, 5, 6.
   His patronage of Plotinus: 12.
Gemina, name of two women associated with Plotinus: 9.
Gentilianus, forename of Amelius: 7. See Amelius.
Gnostics, sect attacked by Plotinus: 16.
Gordian III, Roman Emperor 238–244: 3.
Heliodorus, Peripatetic philosopher: 20.
Herennius, pupil of Ammonius: 3.
Hermaeus, Stoic philosopher: 20.
Hesiod, ancient poet: 22.
Homer, ancient poet: 22.
Hostilianus Hesychius, adopted son of Amelius: 3.
Iamblichus, father of Ariston: 9.
India: 3.
Isis, Egyptian goddess: 10.
Lilybaeum, Porphyry's abode in Sicily: 2, 11.
Longinus (Cassius Longinus), critic and philosopher. Plotinus' estimate of him: 14.
   His writings: 14 (*Basic Principles*, *Back to Basics*); 17 (*On Impulse*).
   On Plotinus: 19–20.
   On Plotinus, Amelius and Porphyry: 20, 21.
Lydus, Gnostic author: 16.
Lysimachus, Stoic teacher: 3, 20.

INDEX TO PORPHYRY

Malkus, as nickname of Porphyry: 17.
Marcellus, senatorial associate of Plotinus: 7.
Marcellus, addressee of Longinus' treatise: 20.
Maximus of Tyre, philosopher: 17.
Medius, Stoic philosopher: 20.
Megalos, as nickname of Maximus: 17.
Mesopotamia, modern Iraq: 3.
Messus, Gnostic author: 16.
Mikkalos, as nickname of Paulinus: 7.
Minos, fabled judge of the dead: 22, 23.
Minturnae, place of Plotinus' death: 2, 7.
Moderatus of Gades, Pythagorean philosopher: 20, 21.
Muses, goddesses of song: 22.
Musonius, Stoic teacher: 20.
Nicotheus, alchemist invoked by Gnostics: 16.
Numenius of Apamea, precursor of Plotinus: 3, 20, 21.
   Plotinus' use of him in seminars: 14.
   Plotinus accused of plagiarizing him: 17, 18.
Olympius, Alexandrian magician and rival of Plotinus: 10.
Origen, pupil of Ammonius. His works: 3, 20.
   Visits school in Rome: 14.
Orontius (Marcus Orontius), senatorial associate of Plotinus: 7.
Paulinus, associate of Plotinus: 7.

Peripatetics, school of Aristotle; 14, 20.
Persians: 3.
Philip, Roman Emperor 244–9: 3.
Philocomus, Gnostic author: 16.
Phoenicia, modern Lebanon: 19.
Phoebus, title of Apollo: 22.
Phoebion, Stoic philosopher: 20.
Plato, favourite philosopher of Plotinus.
   His dialogues: 7 (*Atlanticus* or *Critias*); 12 (*Laws*); 15, 23 (*Symposium*); 20 (*Republic*).
   His feast: 2.
   His immortality: 22.
Platonists, Platonic successors; 14, 17, 20.
Platonopolis, hypothetical city in Campania: 12.
Plotinus, hero of this narrative. His birth and early life: 3.
   His contemporaries: 15 (Eubulus); 20, 21 (Longinus' judgment).
   His daemonic/divine attributes: 2 (at death); 10 (Olympius); 22 (oracle); 23 (mystic experience).
   His death: 2 (described); 22, 23 (commemorated).
   His early associates: 3 (in Alexandria), 10 (Olympius), 14 (Origen), 16 (Gnostics).
   His household: 9, 11.
   His infirmities: 2 (disease); 8 (eyesight); 15 (irascibility).
   His insight: 11.
   His political associations: 3

(Gordian); 7 (senate); 12
(Gallienus).
His portrait: 1.
His predecessors: 14 (authors taught in school); 17, 18 (Numenius).
His sayings: 1 (on body); 2 (on death); 10 (on gods); 13 (on Porphyry's questions); 14 (on Longinus and Origen); 15 (on Porphyry's merits).
His school in Rome: 1 (accessibility); 7 (pupils); 13 (method of teaching).
His writings: 3, 20 (records of); 4, 5, 6 (chronological order); 8 (method of composition); 10 (on personal daemon); 15 (against mathematicians); 16 (against Gnostics); 24, 25, 26 (arrangement); 26 (*On Beauty*).
Polemon, associate of Plotinus: 11.
Porphyry, author and second hero of this narrative. His arrival in Rome: 4, 5.
His disputations: 13, 15, 19.
His edition of the *Enneads*: 7, 18, 24, 25, 26.
His name: 17, 21.
His poetry: 15.
His refutation of Gnostics: 16.
His studies: 4 (Antonius); 20, 21 (Longinus).
His union with God: 23.
His voyage to Sicily: 2, 6, 11, 19.
Potamon, ward of Plotinus: 9.
Probus, host to Porphyry in Sicily: 11.

Proclinus, Platonist: 20.
Ptolemaeus, Peripatetic philosopher: 20.
Puteoli, Italian town and residence of Eustochius: 2.
Pythagoras, legendary philosopher: 20, 21, 22.
Rhadamanthus, fabled judge of the dead: 22, 23.
Rhodes, Greek island and residence of Antonius: 4.
Rogatianus, senatorial associate of Plotinus: 7.
Rome, as residence of Plotinus: 2, 3, 5, 8, 9, 11, 20.
Sabinillus, senatorial associate of Plotinus: 7.
Salonina, wife of Gallienus: 12.
Scythopolis, home of Paulinus: 7.
Senate: 7.
Severus (Septimius Severus), Roman Emperor 197–212: 2.
Severus, philosopher read by Plotinus: 14.
Sicily, island visited by Porphyry: 2, 6, 11, 19.
Socrates, tutor of Plato: 2.
His feast: 2.
Stoic philosophers: 14, 17, 20.
Syria: 2.
Thaumasius, visitor to Plotinus' seminar: 13.
Themistocles, Stoic teacher: 20.
Theodosius, associate of Zethus and Ammonius: 7.
Theodotus, Platonic successor: 20.
Theophrastus, pupil of Aristotle: 24.

Thrasyllus, editor of Platonic
corpus: 20, 21.
Troad, western coast of modern
Turkey: 20.
Trypho, detractor of Plotinus: 17.
Tyre, Phoenician birthplace of
Porphyry: 7, 20, 21.

Longinus' residence there: 19.
Zethus, associate of Plotinus of
Arabian origin: 7.
Zoroaster, Persian sage
appropriated by Gnostics: 16.
Zostrianus, Gnostic author: 16.
Zoticus, associate of Plotinus: 7.

INDEX OF PERSONS, WORKS AND PLACES NAMED IN THE *PROCLUS* OF MARINUS

Figures indicate the chapter of the *Proclus* in which the name occurs.

Academy, school of Plato: 36.
Acropolis, citadel of Athens: 29.
Adrotta, Lydian city: 32.
Alexandria, chief city of Egypt: 8, 9, 10.
Andrians, Greek community: 15.
Apollo, god of poetry, prophecy and philosophy: 6.
April: 36.
Arabs: 19.
Archiadas: 12, 14, 17, 29.
Aristotle, eminent philosopher: *Suda*, 9, 12, 13, 14.
  His ethics, logic and physics: 13.
  His treatise *On the Soul*: 12.
Ascalon, city in Palestine: 19.
Asclepigeneia, daughter of Plutarch of Athens: 28, 29.
Asclepius, god of healing: 32.
  His "sons" (doctors): 3.
  Lion-headed: 19.
  As Saviour: 29.
  His temple: 29.
His affinity with Proclus: 30
Asia, Roman province in west of modern Turkey: 15, 23.
Athena, goddess: 29.
Athens, chief city of Greece: 10, 11, 14, 15, 29, 30, 33, 36.

Attic, pertaining to Athens: 10 (water), 28.
Attis, Phrygian god: 33.
Byzantium, modern Istanbul and birthplace of Proclus: 6, 9, 10.
Chaldaean Oracles, collection of philosophic verses: 13, 18, 26.
  Use in theurgy: 28.
  Proclus' estimate of them: 38.
Dionysus, Theatre of, in Athens: 29.
Dioscuri, tutelary demigods: 32.
Domninus, Platonic successor: 26.
Egypt and Egyptians: 8, 19.
Epidaurus, sacred site in Greece: 31.
Gaza, city in Palestine: 9, 19.
Greeks: 19.
Hegias, Athenian magistrate: 26.
Hecate, goddess of magic and nether world: 28.
Herculean courage of Proclus: 15.
Hermes, God of wisdom: 33.
  Hermaic chain: 28.
Hero, mathematician and teacher of Proclus: 9.
Iamblichus, philosopher and classic exponent of theurgy: 26, 27, 32.

Ibycus, ancient poet quoted by Plato: 1.
Isaurian (Leonas): 8.
Isidorus, successor of Marinus: *Suda*.
Isis, Egyptian goddess: 19.
Julian, anti-Christian Emperor 361–3: 36.
Lachares, Athenian philosopher and rhetorician: 11.
Leonas, sophist and friend of Proclus: 8, 9.
Lycabettus, mountain near Athens: 36.
Lycia, Asiatic province and adopted country of Proclus: 6, 8, 10, 36.
Lydia, Asiatic province visited by Proclus: 15, 29.
Machaon, son of Asclepius: 32.
Marcella, mother of Proclus: 6.
Marinus, successor and biographer of Proclus: *Suda*.
His encouragement of Proclus: 27.
His task as biographer: 1, 2, 38.
Marnas, obscure deity: 19.
Melampus, legenday prophet: 10.
Metroon, temple in Athens: 19.
Mother of the Gods: 33.
Her temple: 19.
Muses, goddesses of song: 6.
Neapolis, city in Palestine and birthplace of Marinus: *Suda*.
Nestorius, father of Plutarch: 12, 28.
Nicagoras, Athenian magistrate: 36.
Nicolaus, Athenian sophist: 10.
Nicomachus, Pythagorean philosopher: 28.
Olympiodorus, philosopher and teacher of Proclus: 9.
Orion, grammarian and teacher of Proclus: 8.
Orpheus, mythical poet: 27.
Verses ascribed to him: 18, 20, 26.
Pan, Greek god: 33.
Parthenon, temple of Athena in Athens: 30.
Patricius, father of Proclus: 6.
Pericles, Lydian philosopher: 29.
Philae, sacred site in Egypt: 19.
Philoxenus, father of Syrianus: 11.
Phrygia, region and province of central Turkey: 19.
Piraeus, harbour of Athens: 10.
Plato, favourite philosopher of Proclus: 4, 10, 11, 12, 13.
His dialogues: *Suda* (*Parmenides, Philebus*); 12 (*Phaedo*); 13 (*Timaeus*); 14 (*Laws*); 38 (*Theaetetus, Timaeus*).
His feast: 23.
Plotinus, founder of Neoplatonism: quoted, 25.
Plutarch of Athens, philosopher and mentor to Proclus: 12, 13, 17, 26, 28, 29.
Podalirius, son of Asclepius: 32.
Polles, legendary prophet: 10.
Porphyry, pupil of Plotinus: 26.
Proclus, hero of narrative. His ancestry: 6 (parents); 28 (Nicomachus).

His benevolence: 14 (bequests); 14, 17, 29 (Archiadas).
His birth: 6 (Byzantium); 35 (horoscope).
His death: 25 (lifespan); 35 (horoscope); 36 (burial and epitaph); 37 (eclipse).
His diet: 12, 19, 21.
His dreams and visions: 7 (Telesphorus); 25 (Plutarch); 28 (poetry, Nicomachus); 30 (Athena), 31 (Asclepius).
His education: 6, 8 (Rome), 9 (Alexandria), 10 (Athens), 11 (Syrianus), 12 (Plutarch).
His illnesses: 7; 26; 31 (arthritis).
His irascibility: 16, 20.
His miracles: 23 (halo); 29 (healing).
His piety: 15 (Lydia); 19 (exotic); 29 (Asclepius); 30 (Athena); 33 (Mother of Gods); 36 (Athenian heroes).
His predecessors: 10 (Plato); 14 (Aristotle); 25 (Porphyry, Iamblichus); 28 (Syrianus).
His theurgic interests: 18, 20, 21, 26, 27, 28.
His travels: 8 (Lycia, Alexandria, Rome); 9 (Byzantium, Alexandria); 10 (Athens); 15 (Lydia); 32 (Adrotta).
His virtues: 1; 3 (body); 4 (soul); 5 (mind); 15 (political); 18 (purificatory); 19 (piety); 21 (concentration and temperance); 22 (mystagogic); 24 (justice); 25 (impassibility); 34 (summary).
His works: 13, 38 (*Timaeus* commentary); 14 (commentaries on *Laws* and *Republic*); 23 (originality); 27 (on Orphics); 28 (lectures, verses); 38 (*Theaetetus* commentary).
Pythagorean sect and teachings: 15, 17, 28.
Romans and their customs: 8, 19, 36.
Rufinus, political figure: 23.
Socrates, teacher of Plato: 10. His feast: 23.
Solon, Athenian hero and ancestor of Proclus: 26.
Sophocles, Athenian dramatist: 29.
Syria: 26.
Syrianus, philosopher and tutor to Proclus: 11, 12, 13, 26, 27, 29. His epitaph: 36.
Telesphorus, emissary of Asclepius: 7.
Theagenes, Athenian plutocrat: 29.
Theandrites, obscure deity: 19.
Theodorus: magistrate of Byzantium: 9.
Ulpian of Gaza, philosopher: 9.
Xanthus, city in Lycia: 6, 14.

MAPS

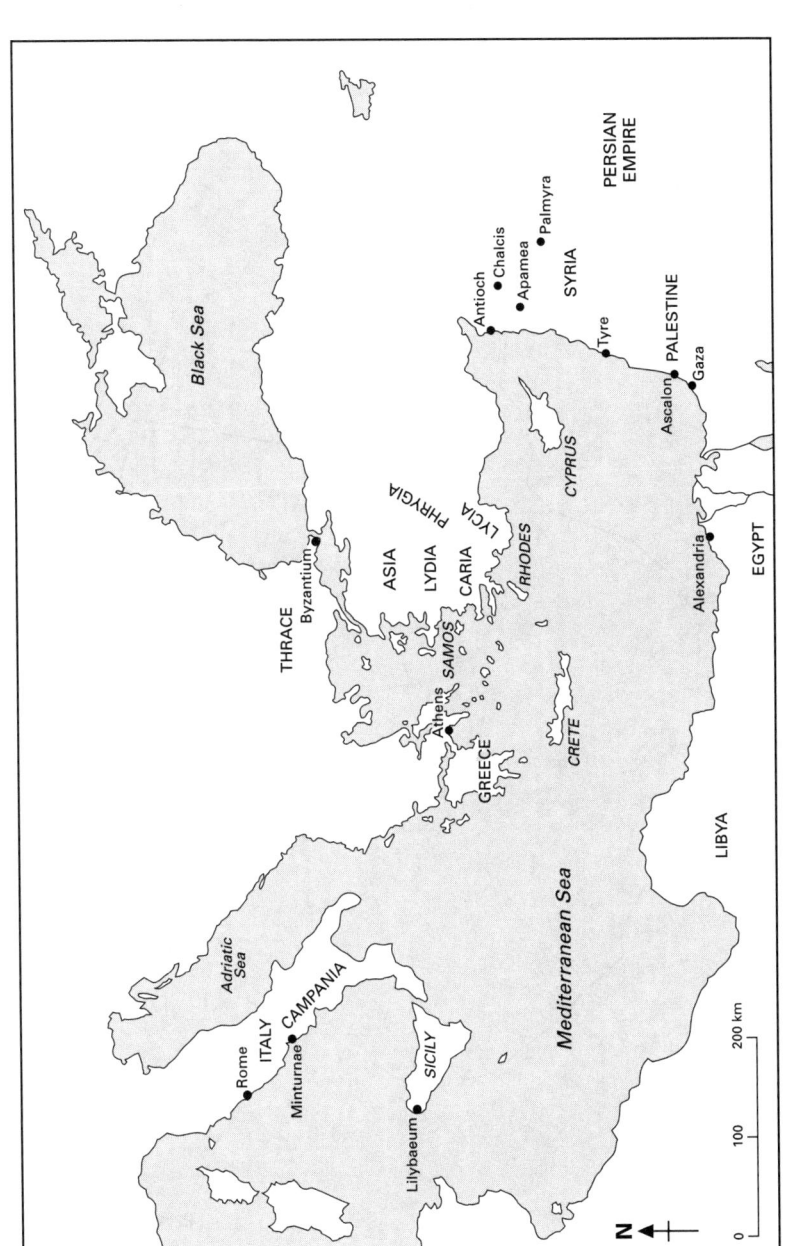

The World of the Neoplatonists

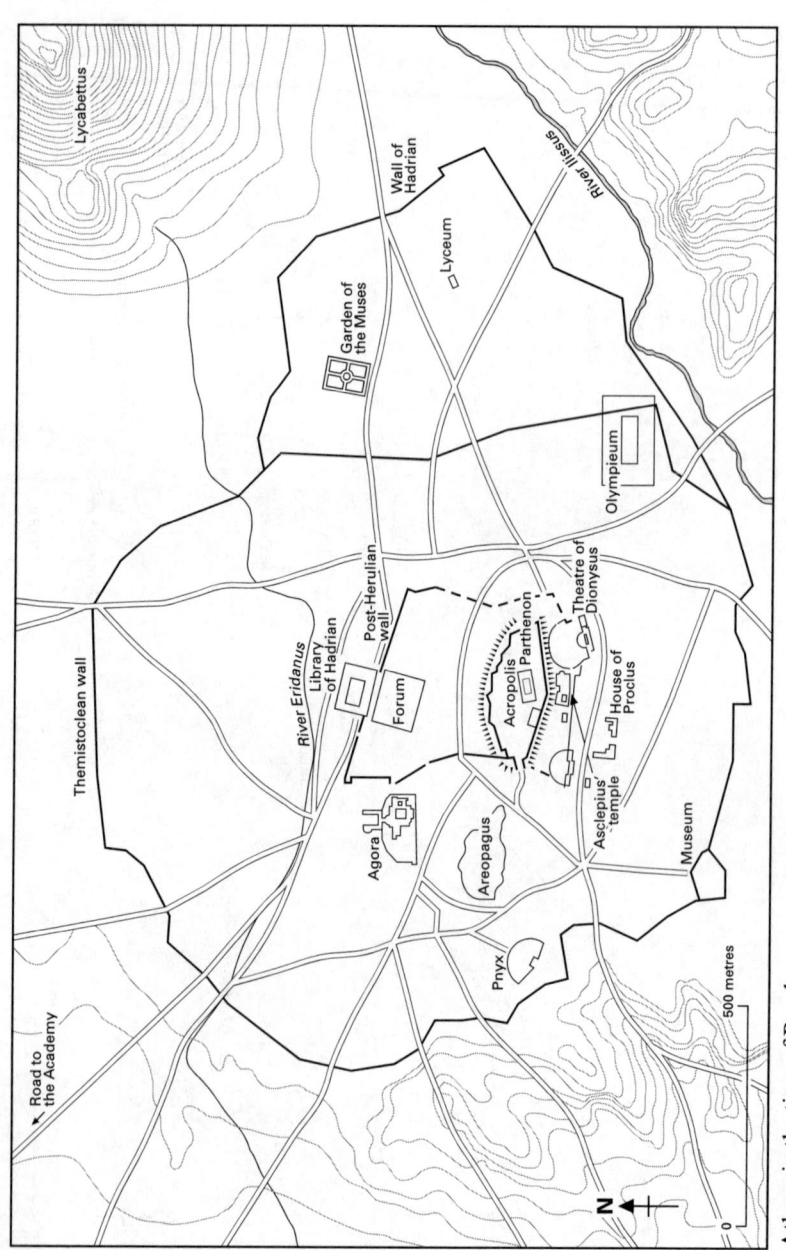

Athens in the time of Proclus